STARTING O

HUMAN HORIZONS SERIES

STARTING OFF

Establishing Play and Communication in the Handicapped Child

by

**CHRIS KIERNAN, RITA JORDAN
and CHRIS SAUNDERS**

**A CONDOR BOOK
SOUVENIR PRESS (E & A) LTD**

First published 1978 by Souvenir Press (Educational & Academic) Ltd,
43 Great Russell Street, London WC1B 3PA
and simultaneously in Canada

Reprinted 1980

ISBN 0 285 64851 9 casebound
ISBN 0 285 64852 7 paperback

Printed in Great Britain by
Clarke, Doble & Brendon Ltd,
Plymouth and London

Contents

	List of Tables	7
	List of Illustrations	9
	Acknowledgements	11
1	So he is Handicapped	13
2	How to Change Behaviour	23
3	An Example: 'He won't pay Attention'	47
4	Organising a Teaching Programme	52
5	Developing Rewards and Interests	68
6	Developing Choice and Self-Control	91
7	Finding Out about the World	98
8	Developing Ideas about Objects and People	114
9	Ways of Communicating	134
10	Teaching the Child to Communicate	158
11	Learning to Feed	186
12	Dressing, Toileting and Washing	219
13	Moving About	244
14	Behaviour Problems	264
15	Getting More Help	292
	Bibliography	318
	Index	319

List of Tables

Chapter 5

   Table 1   Responsiveness to material rewards   73
   Table 2   Responsiveness to physical social rewards   74
   Table 3   Responsiveness to verbal rewards and punishers   75

Chapter 6

   Table 4   Choosing and self-control   91

Chapter 7

   Table 5   The ability to look at an object   101
   Table 6   Visual exploration   103
   Table 7   The ability to follow a slowly moving object with the eyes   105
   Table 8   Visually directed grasping   107
   Table 9   Response to sound   111

Chapter 8

   Table 10   Object permanence   116
   Table 11   Exploratory play behaviour   126

Chapter 10

   Table 12   Needs and interests   160
   Table 13   Understanding   160
   Table 14   Basics of non verbal communication   162
   Table 15   Communication by manipulation   163
   Table 16   Communication by gesture   164
   Table 17   Motor imitation   165
   Table 18   Development of sounds   168
   Table 19   Verbal imitation   170
   Table 20   Communication by sounds and words   170

Chapter 11

    Table 21   Self feeding   188
    Table 22   Types of food   188
    Table 23   Problem behaviour   188

Chapter 12

    Table 24   Washing skills   239

Chapter 13

    Table 25   Posture   253
    Table 26   Mobility   255
    Table 27   Fine motor movements   259

List of Illustrations

1   Postures involved in the British Sign Language   142

2   Postures involved in the Paget-Gorman Sign System   144

3   Rebus symbols   151

4   Bliss symbols   152

5   Postures from the Imitation Test   167

6   Illustration of changes in behaviour in a teaching programme   198

7   A graph for plotting behaviour problems   268

The photographs between pages 160 and 161 show examples of signing in the British Sign Language.

A*

ACKNOWLEDGEMENTS

This book represents the joint effort of many people. Several of the programmes described were planned or run by colleagues, in particular Barbara Riddick, Shirley Harries and Malcolm Jones. Jack Tizard provided an unstinting commitment and unfailing encouragement throughout the projects.

We are especially grateful to Linda Jones who struggled with the many drafts of the manuscript and whose personal feelings about the importance of the book helped to keep us going. Writing is especially traumatic for the families of the authors. Our families were encouraging, tolerant and endlessly patient.

We would like to express our grateful thanks to the DHSS who funded most of the projects from which the material of this book is formed. We owe warm thanks also to the schools, hospitals and other agencies who have welcomed us and let us work with them. Much of our motivation has come from parents, teachers and nurses who have given us guidance, encouragement and friendship and who have trusted us to try to produce worthwhile results to our research.

"We gratefully acknowledge permission to reproduce Rebus and Blissymbolic material from the American Guidance Service and Copyright holders. We would also like to thank Andy Blanchard who drew the hands."

Finally we would like to thank the mentally handicapped children with whom we have worked. We believe that the purpose of research in this field is to learn how the mentally handicapped view the world, how they learn and how they develop, and then to pass that knowledge and skill on to others. We have learned from the mentally handicapped children with whom we worked.

Through this book we hope that we can give these children a voice which will allow them to help their handicapped companions.

1: So he is Handicapped

This is a book about the beginnings of development. It is concerned with children who are handicapped and who are either young or severely handicapped. We will be concerned with the origins of development of play, of communication, of self-help skills and of movement.

More precisely the book is directed at parents, teachers, nurses and social services personnel who are living and working with the following groups:

(1) Young mentally handicapped children who may also be physically handicapped. These are children who will need help in starting off their development in many areas.

(2) Children in ESN(S) schools, especially those children who are in Special Care or Nursery units and who again need help with fundamental skills.

(3) Adolescents and adults who are at home or in special care units in social services settings or subnormality hospitals. Again these people need help with fundamentals. In this book we will talk mainly about children, but the approach and content should be relevant to these groups also.

(4) Any child or adult who has a severe handicap in one of the areas covered by this book. A child may be completely able in one area, say play, and yet have terrible problems with communication. Again we have a problem about starting off, in this case only in one area.

Children and adults with very severe handicaps were for many years neglected, and it is only during the last decade that authorities have paid serious attention to them. Quite recently, parents of a severely handicapped child would be told that nothing could be done educationally for him until he was 'ready' for education. How the child was to be made 'ready' was left to the parents and to chance. Quite often the child failed to reach the acceptable levels and he then would be deemed 'ineducable'.

But the position of the young and severely mentally handicapped child has changed quite dramatically within the last decade. Advances in the understanding of early development and education have moved quickly, so that we now have pretty clear ideas about how to change the behaviour of even the most severely handicapped child. And services have also developed apace.

Possibly the greatest single advance has been the transfer of responsibility for the education of the mentally handicapped from medical to educational control. This has brought widespread changes in the approach to the handicapped child. He is now seen as educable and as having a right to education, regardless of his degree of disability. Parallel changes in control of residential facilities are taking longer to make their impact, but again new possibilities are emerging which offer a brighter future for the mentally handicapped than ever before. The new short- and long-term residential facilities which are being opened and run by social services departments have the aim of fostering the development of the individual as an independent human being, again no matter what his degree of handicap. They are also in settings which make the achievement of these aims possible.

The idea behind this book is to describe to parents, teachers, care staff in residential and hospital settings and field social workers some of the principles and programmes to help the severely handicapped child which have been developed in service and research settings. We hope that the book will allow people who are working with the handicapped to be more effective in helping them to lead fuller and more rewarding lives.

The young or severely handicapped child presents a multitude of problems to the parents, teachers and others working with him. He may have physical as well as mental handicaps. He may be blind, or we may suspect that he does not see although we cannot really test him properly. He may be unable to walk or even move effectively. He may have problems in sleeping, be apparently unable to learn to feed himself, he may be doubly incontinent. His play may be rudimentary. When given a toy he may simply mouth it or bang it until it breaks. He may not look at you when you speak. He may be impossible to control when he is out, rushing across roads ahead of a mother petrified that his next dash will be his last. He may scream in shops. He may have no speech and no way in which he can tell you what he wants, to the extent that his parents despair of understanding him. He may break his sister's toys quite senselessly; then, when smacked, he may cry but break some more the next day. Or worse still, when smacked he may look completely puzzled at what is happening to him.

The numbers of such children and adults are not large. Severely mentally handicapped people represent a maximum of four per thousand in the population, the very severely handicapped only around one per thousand.

Before the advances of the last decade little was done for the young or severely handicapped child. As late as 1950 eminent doctors were writing that the mentally handicapped were degenerates who would pollute society and needed to be put away. And even in the 1970s some psychiatrists are still telling parents that their mentally handicapped children will never learn anything and should be put in an institution before they damage the rest of the family.

Until recently the best that the child could hope for was care—someone who would look after him and love him in an institution where his oddities could be coped with and contained. Many people working in these institutions (subnormality hospitals) offered this love and care with astonishing generosity; but like staff in the old Junior Training Centres, which became the schools for the 'severely educationally subnormal' in 1971, they were encouraged to see containment, care and occupation as the only possible goals.

Similarly very little was done for the parents and siblings of the handicapped child. They were given little or no advice on home management, and were faced with the choice of putting up with it or getting rid of him.

There are still people who feel that care and containment are the only realistic solutions. Education is seen as being a waste of time. These people will ask—'Well, what can you teach a severely mentally handicapped child to do?' We may answer, 'We can probably teach him to feed himself if his food is put on his tray in front of him, and we can teach him to tell us when he needs to go to the toilet and we can teach him to play with some toys.' 'How long will that take?' 'Possibly six months, more likely a year.' 'And how much manpower will that take?' 'Oh, probably one person working a couple of hours a day for the year.' 'Well, is it really worth it, wouldn't it be better to invest that time and manpower in more capable children?'

It is true that the development involved may not be great in relation to the effort. It is also true that consistent effort over a long time may still never enable the child to reach the point where he can live an independent life. It is even true that teaching the child to play and explore his environment may actually cause more trouble than leaving him alone. The answer to the question 'Is it really worth it?' ultimately depends on one's most basic attitudes to the value of human life.

Several years ago one of us was discussing a child with her parents. We were talking about her behaviour at home, and it emerged that she had a habit of going into her parents' bedroom, opening the chest of drawers and taking all the contents out one by one, glancing at them, and dropping them on the floor. We asked whether this wasn't a problem that they could well do without. Their answer was that up to the age of three their child had not played at all. She had rocked, fed and slept but had shown no interest in toys. Gradually, with a great effort, they had 'brought her out of herself'. She had begun to play and the drawer emptying was one of her still rare games. The last thing in the world they wanted to do was to stop her.*

Like these parents, we feel that however small the gain it is worth trying to teach the child or for that matter the severely handicapped adult. Our basic position emphasises caring, and caring for us includes encouraging the individual to learn. The question of priorities, whether it is more important for one child to be taught to tell you when he wants to go to the toilet than for another to be got through his French 'O' Level, is a decision that society and the individuals in society must make. What can easily be demonstrated is that the more independence we give the severely handicapped through teaching, the less of

---

* Nowadays we would hope that those parents would have early access to constructive advice or at least that their child could be given educational help from the age of two or younger.

a financial burden they will be. It costs far less per annum to maintain a capable mentally handicapped person in a community hostel than it does to provide a subnormality hospital placement for a less capable person. Certainly it is much easier and more pleasant to live and work with a person whose self-help skills are good, and who has some skills in communication, than it is to live with a doubly incontinent child who is totally unresponsive.

We are not minimising the need to offer unconditional love to the child. That must be central to all programmes. The fundamental point in our view is that to be educated according to whatever capabilities he may have is a child's right as a human being. Human beings are 'learning organisms'. One of *the* most important things about the human species has been its desire to learn, to master things, to find out how things work, to understand. The child who learns how to play with a toy, how to make a tune, how to feed himself, is gaining mastery, is gaining in dignity as a human being. We surely cannot deny him this right even though we may feel that what he is learning will never change the world.

We would question the extreme pessimists' belief that the severely handicapped child has an inalterably limited future. Clearly there will be limits to what he can achieve. A severely mentally handicapped child who is blind and physically handicapped may indeed never see and never walk. But such has been the neglect of this field that we can as yet have little confidence in predicting what the limits of any child may be.

New and better methods of helping and dealing with problems are emerging every year. And once the child is in a good caring and educational environment he also plays a part in what happens. He partly determines his future. We should not offer false optimism, but it is cruel to offer false pessimism.

We can illustrate this point with an example from a study in which mentally handicapped adults are being taught to use the sign language of the deaf. One of the students is a man of over 50, whom we will call Mr Jones. Mr Jones had no speech, he had never learned to talk and until he joined the programme, had no way of communicating. In the first few sign language classes he was socially withdrawn and appeared disinterested in what went on around him. The teachers on the project persisted with him. He learned a number of signs 'under protest'. Then one day he was taught the sign for 'train'. The following day the teacher and psychologist running the group were delighted when he suddenly produced a picture of a train in a newspaper, and made the sign for train. He had remembered the sign, had found the newspaper and brought it to show them. After over 50 years, and six months' hard work, was it worthwhile?

Following the train incident Mr Jones took to bringing other things referred to in the sessions. He was forming relationships based on his new communication system. Mr Jones is being helped by one of the newer developments in teaching the mentally handicapped. How far he gets will depend on how much teaching and encouragement he gets. He may never be able to live independently—but he is off the ground and flying.

THE NATURE OF HANDICAP AND THE APPROACH TO TEACHING THE HANDICAPPED

The normal child learns a great deal for himself about his world. He plays continuously, he responds readily to his mother and father and to the rest of the family; he learns to imitate what they do, to talk, to get on with other children, to ask questions to extend his knowledge, to respond to the challenge of new situations, because they are there and because he gets praise for this kind of behaviour.

On the other hand the mentally handicapped child characteristically fails to develop in play. He may not play at all, or his play may be stereotyped and not change from year to year. He may be socially unresponsive and appear not to learn through imitation or because he is praised. Or, more puzzling, he may be responsive socially but still not appear to understand and completely defeat our teaching efforts by simply smiling every time we speak to him.

These pictures give us the clue to what is the most obvious and fundamental problem of mental handicap. The mentally handicapped child does not learn spontaneously, he does not teach himself. Because of this he does not learn the basics of dealing with the physical world or the basics of social interaction.

The solution looks equally obvious. We must find out what

he is failing to learn and teach him. Then he will have the grounding which other children have and he will be able to go on from there.

Unfortunately although the solution is clear enough we lack many of the essential tools for putting it into practice. First of all we do not know enough about how the very young normal child does learn. We know that he learns words, learns to reach and grasp objects and learns to walk. But we don't know much about the process behind these first words and first actions. Second, the severely mentally handicapped child has often suffered brain damage. Consequently, even if we did know more about the detail of normal development, it would not necessarily help us to teach the mentally handicapped child. What we need to know is how to reach the goals of normal development even if the normal route is not open to us.

We do know that the mentally handicapped child lacks some of the basic strategies for learning which the normal child uses. We know that he does not play in the same way and that his social responsiveness is different. So one thing we should aim to do is to teach him these basic strategies. In addition to teaching him how to play, we need to ensure that he is socially responsive, that he can and does imitate, that he has some means of communication, so that later on he can learn to ask questions and to act on the answers. If, in the case of a child who is physically handicapped, his handicap is going to limit his learning, we need to analyse in advance how this is likely to happen, and to provide the child with experience which will offset his disability as far as possible.

For instance, we know from experimental studies that children handicapped with cerebral palsy fail to develop an adequate understanding of space. They are not as good as the normal child in judging how far away something is or what is in front of what. This almost certainly happens because, being physically handicapped, they are unable to move around and are consequently unable to learn about spatial cues. The remedy here is obvious. Their education should include being moved around, and learning to move themselves around in a chair or buggy, so that they gain access to the cues.

Our basic approach therefore is to discover what the child lacks, and to teach so as to fill in the gaps. We must concentrate, if possible, on teaching the child general strategies which will allow him then to learn for himself in a good educational environment.

How do we teach him? Very often the mentally handicapped child seems at first sight unteachable, his own worst enemy, happily flinging carefully chosen educational toys against the wall. The remedy which has come to be accepted by more and more educators over the past decade is to begin to teach the child in highly structured teaching situations. These settings allow the child to see exactly what we want him to learn, and allow us to improve the conditions of learning in such a way that the likelihood of success is maximised.

The combination of specifying what the child needs to learn and being structured in our teaching can and does lead to success. Well worked out teaching programmes do lead to faster development. But they need to be related very carefully to the individual child. We cannot write prescriptions for what to teach. Teaching must take into account the needs and idiosyncrasies of both child and teacher. Teaching must be responsive to changing needs of the child and to the needs of the day. What can be described are principles on which programmes can be developed. In this book we will describe these principles, but we cannot write recipes for any child, let alone for the highly individualistic children we find amongst the mentally handicapped. Only the people who know the child best can hope to plan programmes in detail.

This leads to our next point. The approach taken here is educational. It sees mental handicap as an educational problem which can be helped only by educational means. It reflects the increasing realisation over the past couple of decades that, although medical and other authorities have a contribution to make, the fundamental responsibility for changing the behaviour of the mentally handicapped lies with the people who are with them all the time, and who in the broad as well as the narrow sense offer them education. It is the parents, teachers, care staff and nurses who are really responsible for helping the handicapped and who in turn need help.

This approach has a number of consequences. For the parents who suspect that their pre-school child may have a serious problem we would suggest that they get help as fast as possible. It is better to be safe than sorry. The type of help needed depends at first on what the problem is, but if it appears to be a general delay in development the child needs early education. Most education authorities now take children into their schools who are as young as two years old and some offer educational advice for even younger children. These early years can be critical. If the child cannot get a place in a school but is offered an alternative not run by the educational authority, we would suggest that parents should enquire very closely into what is offered. Is the establishment a DES recognised school or a day centre run by or recognised by Social Services? Is your child being taught by a DES recognised teacher or a worker with a recognised Social Services qualification in Day Care or Residential work with the handicapped? If the answers are no then be very careful. We have come across many cases where children have been held back in their development because they have been in inadequate settings.

This is not to say that people without specific relevant training do not have a massive contribution to make to the education of the child. Parents and other members of the family, care staff and subnormality hospital nurses need to build the child's emotional and social security, for instance, and this requires skilled judgement and patient guidance. But teachers are paid to teach, and they represent an indispensable element in the development of the mentally handicapped child.

What is the contribution of other agencies and therapists? Physiotherapists and speech therapists can offer specialised advice on therapy, on problems of movement and speech development. They tend to see children only periodically and so they really work as consultants helping direct care staff and teachers. Psychologists and psychiatrists or other doctors are also of value in helping with particular problems. These may range from physical problems which can be cured by operation, to advice with behaviour problems. Only a very small number of mentally handicapped children, however, need a lot of nursing and medical care because they are physically ill—the vast majority are no more ill than the child in the normal school. Even children who are on drugs can, in general, function perfectly well in a normal day-to-day school atmosphere. We need to get away from the old-fashioned idea that

the mentally handicapped are in some way sick in their minds
and so need doctors and nurses. Mental handicap is in the main
an educational not a medical problem.

WHAT THIS BOOK IS ABOUT

In this book we will be describing ways of assessing and
teaching basic skills which the young or severely mentally
handicapped child or adult may lack. We will begin by
describing the methods which we and others have found most
effective in teaching these groups. We will describe how to work
out priorities in teaching, and how to put learning programmes
together. We will then go on to describe several types of
programmes, in such a way that we hope parents, teachers and
other people working with the handicapped can adapt them for
their own use.

The examples which we will describe have been drawn from
our own direct experience, or from people we have worked with
in schools or hospitals. One or two isolated examples are drawn
from published literature.

In this chapter we have described our basic approach. It is
one which fully recognises the problems which the handicapped
child has and brings to his family; yet insists that he *can* be
helped to learn and to lead a full life. A few years ago a parent
of a mentally handicapped child spoke on a radio programme.
She was demanding education for her child. He was very
handicapped, and she had been told that he would never do
anything economically worthwhile. 'I don't mind that,' she
said. 'I don't mind if he only ever learns to pick daisies. But if
that is it, I want him to be the best damned daisy picker in the
world.' It is to that parent, and to all parents, teachers, nurses,
and social services workers who want to see their charges learn,
that this book is addressed and dedicated.

2 : How to Change Behaviour

In this chapter we will describe some methods which have been found effective in changing the ways in which mentally handicapped children behave. The methods are basic to nearly all learning, but they have to be used in their most explicit form when teaching people who are mentally handicapped.

WHAT THE CHILD DOES IS WHAT IS IMPORTANT

In this and later chapters we will talk mainly in terms of what the child *does*. This we will refer to as his behaviour. Behaviour can be anything from breathing to talking. Use of the term behaviour does not mean, however, that we are not concerned with what the child feels, thinks or needs: indeed his feelings, needs and thought processes are a central theme to the book. The point is that we *see* behaviour.

We do not *see* the child feeling hungry, for instance. What we see is the child with a distressed expression on his face, wandering around the kitchen and looking in cupboards. When he finds something which we know he likes—that is, he has chosen it from among several foods offered him in the past, he eats it very quickly. We may also know that he has just come back from a shopping trip with his mum and that he has not had any food for six hours, whereas he usually eats every two hours.

Because we see the child behaving and because we know something about his 'history'—he eats some foods for preference, he has not eaten at his usual times—we *infer* that he feels hungry. We see him behaving in certain ways, and then deduce the explanation.

Similarly if we want to know whether a child understands something we infer it from something he does. This usually involves devising a suitable test. If for instance we wanted to know whether a child understood what the number three meant, we might ask him to count to three, show us three fingers, get us three counters, or, at a more sophisticated level, tell us how much six divided by two was.

The point is that we can observe or test a person's behaviour in such a way as to answer the questions 'what can he do?' or 'what does he understand?'. We build up a picture of his abilities or ideas from looking at him in a number of settings, we then inferring what he knows from what he does.

Usually if we want to know what a child knows, we ask him. His reply—his verbal behaviour—may tell us what he knows (although quite often we will ask him to show us as well). But the mentally handicapped child often cannot tell us what he knows. We have to find out what he knows by observing him carefully and in a variety of contexts.

Observation sounds very simple. Parents and other people will often say 'Oh, I don't need to observe my children, after all I know them very well'. All we can say is that when we have asked parents, teachers or nurses to observe a particular behaviour, the outcome has usually been different from what they anticipated. For instance, a teacher in an in-service training course wanted to get rid of a very upsetting and dangerous piece of behaviour in one of her charges. The child, we will call him Philip, was hitting himself in the face with his fist. We asked when this happened. The teacher, who was one of the most creative and sensitive teachers we have met, said that it occurred in all sorts of contexts. For instance she said that Phil would hit himself when frustrated, when he was ignored, when he felt upset because of disturbance at home, when he was hungry, when the teacher was out of the room, or when she was attending to another child. We asked the teacher to keep a detailed record, for a week, of exactly when Phil hit himself, what he and the teacher were doing at the time and what happened when he hit himself. The outcome was very interesting and surprised both the teacher and ourselves. Phil hit himself only when the teacher was near him and playing with another child. The teacher ran a successful programme to get rid of the behaviour. The crucial point here is that this was an excellent teacher who, simply because she was normally busy with a number of tasks around the classroom, had not closely observed Phil and so had got the impression that his behaviour was much more complex than it actually was.

We have made two points then. The first is that we can deduce how the child feels or thinks from this behaviour. The beauty of this approach to the mentally handicapped child is that he does not need to tell us in words, he can tell us by what he does.

The second point is that in order to do this effectively, we must observe the child carefully and closely, testing out our ideas about what he feels or thinks by putting him in new situations and seeing the results. Mentally handicapped children are sometimes thought to be simple souls, easy to understand. This is not so. The mentally handicapped child is a fascinating puzzle whose behaviour can be very complex. But, like most puzzles, observing and trying out different solutions can lead to understanding in the end.

HOW DO WE CHANGE BEHAVIOUR?

Behaviour is changed by changing what happens when we do something. If I turn on a new TV programme and it makes me laugh, I will be more likely to watch again next week. If I turn the tap with the red top and get scalding hot water all over me, I will be less likely to do it again. Similarly with a mentally handicapped child: if he is rewarded for doing something he will be more likely to do it again. If we give him a cuddle and a small drink of tea every time he puts a piece in a posting box, we will find that he will put the pieces in more readily next time we give him the box. If we punish him by shouting at him every time he puts the pieces in, we would expect him to stop.

One way to look at consequences is in terms of rewards and punishments—or, more precisely, punishers. Rewards and punishers tell us and the mentally handicapped child about the world. They tell him what he can do for our approval and also what will gain our disapproval. For the child who does not understand speech very well, rewards such as a cuddle and a drink are more than just pleasant events, they say 'that's right, you've done it right', in what may be the only way he can understand. Rewards are a crucial way of talking to a child who cannot understand speech.

This then is the central idea. What we do is affected by the consequences of our behaviour. We repeat behaviour that leads to reward, we tend not to repeat behaviour that leads to punishment. A great deal of this book will be concerned with how we apply this simple idea to the handicapped. For example, how do we decide what is a reward and what is a punisher? How do we deal with a child who appears not to be rewarded by anything? How do we arrange rewards in a programme to change behaviour?

At this point we must go on to put rewards and punishments into the context of teaching and the development of a teaching programme. We turn first to how we decide on priorities in a programme. Next, having decided priorities, to how we plan teaching, and how we teach and record what we have done. We will then give an example which we hope will illustrate the points which we have made in the chapter.

DECIDING PRIORITIES

One of the most frequent questions which parents and teachers ask is, where do we start? There is no single answer to this question. What we can do is to suggest a way in which *you* can decide where to start.

We can do this in terms of four questions:

1. Does the child have behaviour which is dangerous, or which is a barrier to development?
First priority can be given to behaviour which is dangerous to the child or to other people. This may range from head-banging, or scratching at other children's eyes, to climbing out of bedroom windows or running across busy roads.

Close on the heels of dangerous behaviour is behaviour which represents a barrier to development. For instance, one child threw away everything which was given to her, except food, and avoided all social contacts. This meant that, in the classroom or at home, she was learning nothing because she would not play or work with anything or anyone. Her throwing and avoidance were effective barriers to her development. Some kind of attack on these problems was therefore first priority.

Happily, most children do not show this extreme of behaviour. There are usually some problems and some strengths.

We will deal with the ways which we can get round problem behaviours in Chapter 14. At present it is enough to say that we can really do any of three things. We can try to attack the behaviour directly, that is we can punish the behaviour. This is usually *not* the method of choice except in extreme circumstances, for example with a very dangerous behaviour, and even if punishment is used it should always be used in conjunction with reward for alternative behaviour. Thus a child would be heavily rewarded, for instance, for walking sensibly along the pavement with his mother even if we decided that we had to punish running into the road. This gives us then our second strategy: replace the unacceptable behaviour with an acceptable behaviour. The third strategy is to cope with the behaviour, to prevent it happening. This is sometimes the only solution. Punishment tends to be an ineffective way of changing behaviour, and building up alternatives takes time.

An example of a need for a third strategy was Janet. Janet has a strong tendency to wander out of her own classroom and into other classrooms. She used to be quite nicely rewarded for this because the children in the other classes liked the break in lessons, and vied with each other for the privilege of taking her back. So she always had a fuss made of her. The teacher in Janet's class could not keep an eye on her all the time whilst teaching the other children. The long-term solution was to develop Janet's behaviour so that she found her own classroom more interesting than the others, but this was to be a long job. So a simple coping solution was used in the shape of a small bolt high on the door. No one liked it particularly, but it did give the teacher the chance of building up Janet's skills and those of the other children without the interference of Janet's wandering.

We should not be afraid of coping solutions provided that they really do allow us to build up alternatives to the dangerous behaviours or the barriers to development. If they simply contain the child and are not backed up by positive aspects of the programme designed to develop behaviour, then they are not acceptable in a good programme.

Assessing problem behaviour. Dangerous behaviours or barriers to development can be tackled most effectively if we understand them. This means observation and assessment. We have found that the easiest way to find out how some problems are caused is to observe in terms of an ABC assessment. A, B and C are the Antecedents, or things which happen *before* the behaviour happens; Behaviour, or exactly what the child does; and Consequences, or what happens, what you or other adults do, immediately following the behaviour. So, in the example of Phil, A was the teacher attending to another child whilst Phil was near, B was head hitting, and C was the teacher attending to Phil as soon as he banged his head. Phil's behaviour was an attempt to deflect attention from another child—and it was very successful.

We will say more of how to assess problem behaviour and how to deal with it in Chapter 12. For the moment let us simply repeat that in deciding priorities, a first priority needs to be given to dealing with behaviour which is dangerous to the child or other people, or behaviour which represents a barrier to development.

2. Does the child show likes and dislikes, needs and preferences?

The answer to this question is again a key one. If he does not show likes and dislikes and cannot express his needs or preferences, we will have very great difficulty in finding rewards which we can use to change his behaviour. We have usually found it possible to hit on something which a child likes if we look hard enough, but even then one reward is of very limited value. If the child has very few or no events he likes or dislikes then we must include in his programme a strong element of work on developing likes, and teaching him to express his needs and preferences. Chapter 5 deals with this area in some detail.

Assessment of likes and dislikes involves a whole variety of techniques, including interviewing parents and careful observation. These are described in Chapter 5.

3. Does the child have a means whereby he can relate to adults or other children, and communicate with them?

If the answer here is 'no', then this area again must be given high priority. Human beings are by nature social animals. The child's survival and development depend critically on his being found some way to relate to other human beings, even if it is at a very rudimentary level, such as responding to being touched or cuddled, or looking at you when you speak to him.

Beyond the level of simple social responsiveness, but closely meshed with it, is the ability to communicate. Needs and preferences can be meaningful in a social context only if the child has some way of telling his mother or teacher what his needs are.

Again we would feel that if the child has no social contact with adults, this problem must be a priority in putting together a programme. And parallel to this we must give highest priority to establishing a means of communication which the child can build on as he develops new needs, preferences and ideas.

Techniques of teaching communication have advanced rapidly in the last decade. We will deal with these developments in Chapter 9 and discuss the assessment of communication and development of programmes in Chapter 10.

4. Does the child play with objects in his environment in such a way that he can find out how they work, and benefit from experience with them?

This question concerns the child's sensori-motor coordination; his ability to reach, grasp and examine objects; and his play with them.

Normal play involves reaching and grasping, and then manipulating objects. If the child does not show this basic sensori-motor coordination, we need to focus on this response alone. The attainment of reach and grasp is critical for the development of a great deal of other behaviour, ranging from self-help skills to development of ideas about the world and people.

Even if the handicapped child has reached this stage he may still not play very effectively. His play may consist of repetitive banging of objects or mouthing of everything he grasps. If this is happening he is not going to progress very much in finding out about his world through play. Again we need to treat this as a priority area and try to develop his play behaviour, or at least get round the problem by direct teaching.

These considerations apply especially when the child has

physical problems. Here we must attack the problem directly, through helping him to control his head, to move his arms and hands, or, if he cannot walk or crawl, to manipulate a trolley or wheelchair. We must devise means whereby we bring the missing experiences to him if he cannot go out to meet them himself.

Chapter 7 deals with sensori-motor development and Chapter 8 with development of ideas. Chapter 13 deals with basic mobility.

5. Can the child feed himself, wash, dress and take himself to the toilet?

In other words, does he have basic self-help skills? We have left this priority until last because it is of a slightly different type. Self-help skills are important in three ways. They can be used to help to develop sensori-motor skills. The action of taking the spoon to the mouth, for instance, can be presumed to help in the development of hand control. This point will be taken up in Chapter 11. The second value of self-help skills is clearly social. The child who can feed himself, use the toilet appropriately and wash and dress himself is clearly more 'socially acceptable' to other people than one who cannot, and he can also gain self-respect in his independence. Finally, self-help skills can operate as a basis for the development of communication. Self-help skills have concrete, easily under- stood goals which, at least in the case of feeding and toileting, reflect basic needs. These situations can be used as starting points for the child learning to express himself.

On the other hand we would not give self-help skills precedence over other areas. Though clearly there can be circumstances under which self-help skills may be critical to the child's survival in the environment—if the child is doubly incontinent his parents may feel that the strain of keeping him at home is too great, for instance—in general, we would place priority on the other areas we have listed. A programme which was based primarily on self-help skills would seem to be very limited indeed. One of the strongest arguments for teaching the child self-help skills is simply that once the child has acquired these skills, the parent, teacher and other care workers can spend their time on other matters.

WHAT HAPPENS IF THE CHILD HAS PROBLEMS IN *ALL* AREAS?

If this is the case, and in our experience it is not unlikely, then the particular needs of the child, his parents and the other people involved in the situation have to be considered on their merits. In many cases programmes which kill two birds with one stone can be devised: a programme involving asking the child to give the parent one of two objects, which the parent names, would for instance combine sensori-motor coordination and communication in one programme. And it is not impossible to put together a programme which can take into account *all* areas of development.

From general aims to specific teaching

A. Deciding what you are going to teach: objectives and targets
Suppose that the development of communication skills is decided on as the general aim in treating a non-verbal mentally handicapped child. We will then need to use assessment techniques (which we will describe) to narrow our general aims to specific ones, by isolating particular aspects of behaviour which may be causing trouble in development. Our assessment may tell us, for instance, that the child can express needs by crying or shouting, but that he does not push or pull adults towards things which he wants. This will direct us to a possible area of teaching—to try to teach the child to communicate by manipulation of adults. Whether we select this means of communication rather than speech or signing will depend on our assessment of the child's abilities in other areas: can he make speech sounds, for instance? In making this decision we need to get as much advice as we can from relevant professionals, and also to bear in mind that the most important information may come from the person who knows the child best.

The first questions will be whether the child has any idea at all about communicating with other people; and what would be the most effective thing for him to learn in his environment. If the child can move about and is known to have preferences for specific things or activities in his environment, we could start by teaching him to lead us towards the things that he wants. This way he will get the idea that he can tell us about a variety of different needs.

We will call this general statement of what we want to do in the end, the aim or objective. In this case your objective would be to reach the point where, instead of standing helpless while the child cries or fumes about something, you are able to hold your hand out to be led and say 'show me'.

This aim or objective is too broad to start teaching from, however, because it covers too many possible situations. The next step is to decide on a specific target behaviour, on *one* piece of behaviour which we are going to teach first. This might be to teach the child to take us by the hand to a cupboard to open it when he wants a favourite toy. The whole trick in teaching the mentally handicapped child lies in setting up very simple situations in which the child and the parent or teacher can have rapid success. This way the child is encouraged to cooperate because the experience is pleasurable. And the simpler the situation the more likely the child is to be able to understand what is required of him.

There are several rules we can follow in deciding on targets. We can give the first two rules now:

Rule 1. Pick a target behaviour which fits in with the child's general needs in development.
Rule 2. Pick a behaviour which you are going to be able to teach the child fairly easily, say, within a period of two weeks.

We will give other rules or guidelines as we go on.

B. Deciding how to teach the behaviour
We have already said something about rewards and punishers. Rewards are events the child enjoys, punishers events which he dislikes. We teach by rewarding behaviour we want and, sometimes, by punishing what we don't want. What we will do now is to say more about how to use rewards and punishers. We will describe several teaching situations.

Reward teaching
As soon as the child does what we want, we reward him. Suppose we are trying to get him to imitate a sound. We say

'ba-ba-ba-ba', then he says 'ba' and we *immediately* reward him by saying 'yes' or 'good' and smiling, cuddling him and giving him a kiss. We then pull back and get his attention. Then we say 'ba-ba' and he repeats 'ba' and again we reward him. Next time we may say 'ba' and he immediately repeats 'ba', and we reward him.

Reward teaching should be the way in which we teach virtually all new behaviour. It is also crucial in getting rid of unacceptable behaviour. So it is very important we get it right.

In order to work well we need to be sure of four things in reward teaching.

1. Reward must be immediate

We said before that rewards tell the child what we want him to do. In order to communicate properly the reward *must follow directly on the response we want*, not several seconds later when the child may be doing something else. Suppose we want to reward him for stacking blocks. He picks up a block, puts it on top of another one, then bangs his hand down on the table and pushes the pile of blocks, dropping one on the floor. All this can happen in the space of two or three seconds. Try it yourself. If we are on time with our reward we will reward him for putting one block on top of another. One second late and we will reward him for banging his hand on the table. Two or three seconds late and we will reward pushing the other blocks over on the floor.

This begins to sound very difficult. In fact it just takes practice and careful arrangement of the teaching situation. We also have to select our rewards carefully. One advantage of verbal rewards such as 'good' or 'yes' is that we can say them quickly, at the exact point when the child has succeeded.

2. Rewards should be given every time at first, but can be phased out as the child learns

At the beginning of a new piece of teaching we need to reward the child a great deal. So, at the beginning of teaching it is a good idea to use more than one reward at a time. Verbal rewards and smiling are easy to give and can be given very frequently. Kissing and cuddling may be more awkward to give every time. So we can give a kiss every other time, perhaps, and

B

a cuddle roughly every third time. We might also give the child a half chocolate drop, say about every sixth time, and swing him round at the end of a successful teaching session.

The schedule of rewards might then look like this:

Trial 1.   Yes, smile, cuddle, kiss, sweet (to get him started).
Trial 2.   Yes, smile, cuddle.
Trial 3.   Yes, smile, kiss.
Trial 4.   Yes, smile, kiss.
Trial 5.   Yes, smile, cuddle.
Trial 6.   Yes, smile, kiss, sweet.
Trial 7.   Yes, smile.
Trial 8.   Yes, smile, cuddle.
Trial 9.   Yes, smile, kiss.
Trial 10. Yes, smile.
Trial 11. Yes, smile, kiss.
Trial 12. Yes, smile, swing round (end of session).

The second point can be made by looking at the schedule. We do not need to reward every time the child responds. In fact, as the child learns, we can phase out rewards until in the end the child may be rewarded only at the end of the session.

Suppose we want our child to stack all the blocks into stacks of four. We would get him to build a stack in each trial, maybe using the schedule given above. We could then phase out the rewards. We might reduce the frequency of cuddles, then of kissing, then give the sweet only at the end, and drop the swing round. Finally we might reduce the frequency of 'yes', first to saying it every other time, then every fourth, then only at the end. So our final teaching situation would involve 12 independent trials with no reward until the end, and then 'yes', a smile and a half chocolate drop.

3. The child must be aware of the reward

The effect of the reward will be minimal if the child is not listening or looking when you reward him. Auditory rewards like 'good', or the playing of some music, must be loud enough to be clearly heard. And if the child is not looking, the visual reward will either be lost, if it is a smile or a visual display—such as Christmas lights flashing—or delayed if it is the offer of a sweet or a piece of Marmite toast. It may thus be better actually to put a chocolate drop into the child's mouth when rewarding him, rather than putting it down on the table in front of him.

Once the child has learned about rewards, he will usually look. But we will give an example later where the child had to be taught to attend to rewards.

4. Rewards should be generous rather than mean

The fastest learning will happen if the rewards used are highly valued by the child, and big rather than small. Children seldom respond to a grudging 'good boy' said with a straight face, for instance, and the definite implication that he ought to want to do the task without a reward! An enthusiastic response will be much more likely to catch his attention and turn him on to the task.

There are on the other hand problems in using very big rewards if we are using sweets, food or the opportunity to play with toys. The child can get satiated too quickly. So we need to strike a balance between giving good rewards and getting enough trials in a session. Since we should aim to get between 10 and 30 trials in a session, and we may find that we have to begin with fewer because the child ceases to respond to the reward, we should try to reduce the amount of reward per trial as quickly as possible without causing the child to get discouraged or frustrated.

In practice we have found that good rewards can be given in quite small measures and still be effective. Quarter chocolate drops, a 20-second burst of singing, half a minute of play with a favourite toy, half a crisp, a half centimetre of orange juice in the bottom of a cup are all rewards which we have found successful.

One further point must be made about material rewards. Studies on the effect of sweet and drink rewards show that children in programmes using these as rewards do not suffer from extra tooth decay. They have teeth as good as and often better than children who are not in such programmes. The point probably is that the best programmes include care of teeth as part of their overall teaching.

We can now summarise our four guidelines for making rewards effective:

(1) Rewards must be immediate.
(2) Rewards should be given every time at first but can be phased out as the child learns.
(3) The child must be aware of the reward. He must be looking at or listening to visual or auditory rewards when they are given.
(4) Rewards should be generous rather than mean.

Withdrawal of reward as a teaching method, time-out from reward

Quite often we can see that problem behaviours persist simply because they get attention. One way to get rid of these is therefore to stop attending to them. The reward of attention is withdrawn. The usual pattern following withdrawing reward is that the frequency of the behaviour first goes up—the child is frustrated—and then the behaviour falls off and eventually disappears.

When we withdraw attention from the child for behaving in a particular way, we do not stop attending to him completely! We withdraw attention for a few seconds or for the duration of the unacceptable behaviour, and then attend again when he is behaving well. So instead of talking about withdrawal of reward, we prefer to talk about time-out from reward.

In fact in using time-out in this way, we need to make sure that the overall amount of reward the child gets in the session is not lowered by the procedure. Suppose we are trying to get rid of a child's silly noises in a language teaching session. We might be rewarding good naming of pictures with social rewards and the occasional half crisp. We decide to try to get rid of the noises by time-out. Here time-out might involve ignoring the child when he makes the noises, and also delaying the next chance for him to earn reward by delaying the presentation of the picture by 5 seconds. This procedure might have the effect of reducing the amount of reward in any five minutes of the session by half. This could be dangerous: the whole experience could be so much less pleasant for the child, that he might get turned off the whole session. What we would do as a precaution would be actually to increase the reward given for good behaviour. This would emphasise the difference between the acceptable and unacceptable behaviour.

We *always* have to make sure that the overall amount of reward does not sink too low. As a general guideline we would say that 80 per cent of all experience the child has should be positive, and a maximum of 20 per cent negative. It would be interesting in this connection to make a systematic study of how much of the interaction of a child with his parents, brothers and sisters or teachers is positive and how much ignoring or even punishing. We would expect to find a direct ratio between the overall balance of the relationship and rate of learning.

Quite often it is necessary actually to teach a child a new response in order to make time-out work in getting rid of an unacceptable bit of behaviour. Eva was a child without speech who was nonetheless fond of adults. She had a rather unacceptable way of getting attention. She would walk up behind you and hit you in the back with the heel of her hand. She clearly did not realise she was hurting—it was just a *very* effective way of getting you to turn round. Ignoring Eva would have been difficult, and, since she did not know another way to get attention, it would have been cruel just to get rid of this response. In any case we know that if we try to time-out a response without replacing it with another one which attains the same goal, we are likely to fail: the child will just get more persistent and desperate.

So what we did with Eva was to teach her to approach adults from the front, where we could take her hand as she raised it. This involved rewarding Eva very generously for approach from the front. Simultaneously she was ignored when she hit us on the back. So the unacceptable behaviour was pushed out—competed out—by a socially desirable response.

In using time-out we must make sure that rewards do not drop off. Sometimes we may have to increase reward for other alternative or competing behaviour, and sometimes we may have to teach new responses to meet the same needs as the unacceptable ones.

Time-out is like reward in one very important respect. Just as reward tells the child we approve, time-out tells the child that we don't approve. In order to tell the child as clearly as possible what it is we want him to stop, we must withdraw attention or other reward immediately the behaviour occurs. We must also be quite consistent in timing him out. It will not

help the child if you 'give him another chance because
he forgot'. Consistency is the key to teaching him to remember.

Reward learning and time-out are the two key methods for
trying to change a child's behaviour. Reward training will
build up new behaviour, time-out should be used to get rid of
unacceptable behaviour. But we must remember that the most
effective way to make time-out work is to replace an unacceptable response with an acceptable one which leads to the
same goal.

The use of punishment

What about the use of punishment, such as smacking, to reduce
the frequency of unacceptable behaviour? In general punishers
work only if they are used in the same way as time-out. In other
words, punishment works only if it is paired with an increase
in reward for an alternative response, or if we teach the child
some new response to replace the one which we are punishing.
Reward tells the child what you want him to do. Punishment
tells the child what you do not want him to do, but it usually
cannot tell him what he should be doing.

Take for instance a child who runs from one bedroom to
another, shouting and throwing things, when you try to put him
to bed. You go up to his room and smack him. This tells him
what you don't want him to do. But it does not tell him what
you want him to do. So when he is playing quietly and in bed,
you must be sure to go up and talk to him or cuddle him. This
tells him what you would like him to do.

At a simpler level, it is much better to help the child to use
his spoon and to praise him for using it when eating, rather than
to smack him for using his fingers.

If we use punishment alone, the best we can hope for is that
the child will learn what we want by chance. What more
usually happens is that child and adult just get to dislike each
other.

Punishment in short can be effective only if parents, teachers
or care staff are prepared to follow the same set of rules as lead
to good reward teaching: the punishment must be given
immediately, given every time, especially at first, and it should
be substantial, a 'generous' punishment. This makes the use of

punishment unacceptable to most people. They just cannot bring themselves to be ready to shout 'no' *every* time the child does something wrong. In addition, such a policy of extreme punishment, although specifically effective, is likely to frighten the child. And a frightened child will learn less well than a relaxed happy one.

There are two situations in which the use of punishment may be necessary:

(1) When the behaviour involved is dangerous to the child or other people, or represents a clear barrier to development. Here punishment, which may be relatively mild, coupled with heavy reward for alternative behaviour may be necessary.

(2) When the behaviour can be 'punished' in a way which is humane, and does not distort relationships between the child and the adult; and when the punishment is found to be very effective.

The best example here is a technique which has been developed for preventing children making themselves sick. This is a fairly rare phenomenon, but a child sometimes learns how to prevent food going down into his stomach, or learns how to put his fingers down his throat to make himself sick. If this happens frequently, in some cases after every meal, it is not only very unpleasant, but also a danger to the child's health.

This vomiting habit represented a big problem for some children, until it occurred to someone to analyse it as follows. If the child brings back food, we can presume that he finds the taste of the regurgitated food in the mouth pleasant. So why not make it unpleasant? The system used was to squirt a small amount of unsweetened lemon juice into the child's mouth as soon as he regurgitated. This punished the response immediately. In the original reported case and several recorded since the effect was rapid and clear cut. The vomiting stopped.

Nagging

So far we have been talking about punishment training: where unacceptable behaviour is followed by a punisher. But we can use mild punishment in another way. We can keep on at the child until he does what we want him to do.

We can nag him. Here, if he learns at all, he learns because we *withdraw punishment* when he makes an unacceptable response. This is the opposite situation to time-out.

Nagging is a poor way to teach. It has several disadvantages. One is that our nagging may upset the child and make him less able to learn. But the major problem is that the child has no reason to want to complete a task: there is no reward at the end. In fact he will probably just be given another task which he is nagged through. Further, unless the child is already thoroughly familiar with the task, nagging does not tell him what to do. It only tells him what you don't like him doing.

If you find that you are reduced to nagging to deal with a child, then you need to look carefully at his rewards. Do they fulfil the four conditions we have set out on page 36? Are you using them correctly?

CONCLUSION

Reward learning then is our one sure way of teaching new behaviour. Time-out and punishment are our two ways of getting rid of behaviour; but both rely for their effect on the reward learning to teach the child alternative ways of achieving his goals. Punishment on its own is not effective and nor is nagging. Both lead fairly inevitably to the child and adult disliking each other.

During the next chapters we shall give a number of examples of the use of reward learning and time-out, and some examples of punishment training. We shall also mention one or two other techniques in Chapter 14 on Behaviour Problems.

Now we should return to the build-up of our teaching situation.

We had decided that we were going to teach the child to take us by the hand to the cupboard when he wanted a favourite toy. We can now consider how we are to teach this.

We can see immediately that we have selected a behaviour which can be rewarded very easily. In fact reward is built into the situation. We have also picked a behaviour where we can control the reward very easily.

We can therefore use a reward teaching technique, the reward being that the child is given the toy to play with.

In fact we will probably find that the child, once given the toy, wants to play with it all the time, so that he objects to having it removed from him. So it might be a good idea to add another reward, to offset loss of play time when you want to go on to another activity. Unacceptable behaviour, at this point, like whining or shouting, might well need time-out, the child being ignored until he quiets.

We can now write a further rule about target behaviours.

Rule 3. Pick a behaviour which you can teach the child by reward teaching, with time-out from reward as the way of getting rid of unacceptable responses.

C. Breaking things down into steps

We have emphasised the importance of picking a target behaviour which is easy for the child. One way to make things easier still, is to break down the behaviour into steps, and then to either show the child how to do each step, or to prompt him to follow the steps.

Let us use our example to make these points a bit clearer. If we just take the child's toy from him and put it in the cupboard, he may cry, walk away or just stand. It is very unlikely that he will come to us straight away, since this is the very behaviour we are trying to teach!

What we can do is to break the behaviour down into steps. Roughly, these might be:

(1) Coming to the adult.
(2) Getting hold of the adult's hand.
(3) Taking the adult to the cupboard—this can be broken down further in terms of distance.
(4) Putting the adult's hand on the handle.

If we can break the behaviour down into these steps we can teach one at a time. This gives us our fourth rule:

Rule 4. Pick a behaviour which you can break down into small steps—the steps to be taught one at a time.

Where do we begin then? The answer is that we usually begin at the end! We teach the last response first. This makes sense if we look at it from the child's point of view. If we teach him to put the adult's hand on the handle first, then he can get rewarded straight away and learn very quickly how he can get the reward.

Once the child has learned to put the adult's hand on the handle, we then stand a foot away from the cupboard, holding his hand. It will probably take no time at all for him to learn to pull the adult to the handle. The distance can then be increased to, say, ten feet. The next step would then probably follow without specific teaching. The toy is put in the cupboard, the child goes and gets the adult to open the cupboard.

This way of working through the chain leading to the final response is called backward chaining. We shall see it used very frequently.

We can also work the other way—beginning with the first step and working through. This procedure is called forward chaining. To work, this technique depends on the extensive use of prompting—a technique which we turn to now.

In our example we have a problem about how the child can know what he should do at the beginning of teaching; and possibly what we should do in steps 1 and 2. How are we going to teach him to take hold of the adult's hand? The answer is that we show him. In this case, the child may be guided by another adult or another child, who takes the child's hand and puts it in the adult's hand. The child is prompted to make the correct response. As the child gets more confident of his performance the prompts are faded until they are completely withdrawn.

A prompt may be necessary also at Step 2. Another child or adult may have to take the child to the adult and put his hand in the adult's hand, to start him leading the adult. Or the child may need prompts for Step 1, approaching the adult.

Just as we would build up behaviour from Step 4 backwards, so we would fade prompts starting with the last prompt. Suppose the child needs prompting to make Step 1, approaching the adult. We would begin by prompting him fully, taking him, say, 10 metres to the adult who was going to open the door. We would then take him only nine metres, and leave him to go the rest of the distance, then eight and so on until the child needed no help in going from 10 metres.

This example uses prompts to initiate some steps in a

backward chaining teaching procedure. In forward chaining, on the other hand, we must prompt the child right through all the steps at first, and then fade prompts from the last one backwards.

Not all children need prompting in this way. Some children will imitate at once when you show them how to do something. And since this is a very useful skill, which we can usually teach, we shall describe teaching imitation in Chapter 10.

Some responses are very hard to prompt. Speech for instance is very hard to prompt. It is possible to hold the child's lips together whilst he blows and then release his lips to give a 'p' or 'b' sound, but we cannot physically prompt most speech. On the other hand speech can be imitated once the child has this skill.

In general we would suggest that, for effective teaching, you pick a behaviour which you can prompt. This gives us another rule:

Rule 5. Pick a behaviour in which you can prompt the child through the various steps.

D. Arrange the conditions of learning to make things easier for the child to learn and you to teach

We can arrange conditions in such a way that the likelihood of the child learning is made as high as possible. We do this by getting rid of anything which is likely to distract the child, or to confuse him about what you want him to do. So if you are trying to get him to learn how to do a form-board puzzle, have only the puzzle, the child, yourself and whatever you are using as a reward on the table or in the teaching area. Try to find a quiet place, well away from windows through which he can see exciting things happening outside.

Once the child has got the idea, learned the behaviour, *then* is the time to bring him back into the hurly-burly of a classroom or a living-room.

This gives us a further rule:

Rule 6. Pick a behaviour which you can teach in a setting which is quiet and distraction free, so that the child has the best chance of learning.

E. Recording

At this point people usually stop reading. Recording what the child is doing is often seen as unimportant—we can surely remember what he is learning. The fact of the matter is that we do not remember. And because of this we lose a lot. The advantages of even simple recording are as follows.

First, we have a way of knowing how we are progressing. Progress may be slow and hard to detect. Simple records made once a week, say a count of the number of pictures the child correctly identifies by name, can give us a very good idea of progress.

Second, these records can be used as a basis for discussion with others involved in the care of the child. The parent for instance who can give a record of the number of times a child speaks, and what words he says, will be well away in a discussion with a psychologist or speech therapist when it comes to discussing the child's communicative abilities.

Finally these records can help to identify particular problems. For example, one child we worked with was said to be blind. We set up a programme to teach him to name objects. Although he was severely physically handicapped, we soon found that he was certainly not blind, because of the way in which he learned the names of objects.

We had a list of about 30 things he would readily identify. This list was used each day to structure his session, and a tick or cross was added according to whether he got an item wrong or right. Wrong responses were corrected, 'No, not teddy, it's a car. What is it, Jack? It's a car', and Jack would repeat 'car'. But we found that he found some names were very difficult to learn. We looked carefully at the records, and found that he was behaving quite consistently—we could see exactly what he was doing.

Jack would make systematic errors. He confused a small shiny black purse with an LP record, which was also black and shiny. He confused a yellow teddy with a yellow car. Jack's records showed quite clearly that he was responding to objects in terms of their colour only and ignoring their shape and size.

He clearly could not be blind. And this emerged only because we had simple but extensive records. Once we had worked out what was happening, Jack's programme was shifted to help him learn to use size and shape cues in identifying objects.

Usually we can make our record very simple. We can count the number of spoonsful of food a child gives himself, the number of successful imitations he makes, the different kinds of play he uses with the same toys. At worst we can put in a couple of minutes of 'testing' at the end of the session, or in a once weekly test.

But we should plan some system of recording at the beginning of teaching. This gives us our seventh rule:

Rule 7. Plan a method of recording your teaching at the time when you set up your target.

In our example we could record how many prompts it took before the child put the adult's hand on the handle of the cupboard. Then how far the adult could move away from the cupboard. Then how many prompts were needed for Step 2 and Step 1.

SUMMARY

Let us summarise what we have said in this chapter. In teaching we should look at what the child does. This will tell us what he is thinking and feeling. The way in which we can change what the child does is to change the consequences of what he does. In deciding our priorities in teaching the mentally handicapped child, we need to consider several questions:

(1) Does the child have behaviour which is dangerous or which is a barrier to development?
(2) Does the child show likes and dislikes, needs and preferences?
(3) Does the child have a means whereby he can relate to adults or other children, and communicate with them?
(4) Does the child play with objects in his environment in such a way that he can find out how they work, and benefit from experience with them?
(5) Can the child feed himself, wash, dress and take himself to the toilet?

Thinking within the framework of these five questions should lead to the formulation of an overall strategy for teaching—a general programme. The succeeding chapters will give you ways in which you can assess what the child can do and allow a clearer picture of his strengths and weaknesses to emerge.

Moving from the general to the specific involves deciding general objectives and then specific targets for teaching. A target behaviour is something you want to teach in a particular situation. We have suggested seven rules for choosing targets. These are:

Rule 1. Pick a target behaviour which fits in with the child's general needs in development.

Rule 2. Pick a behaviour which you are going to be able to teach a child fairly easily, say within a period of two weeks.

Rule 3. Pick a behaviour which you can teach the child by reward teaching, with time-out from reward as a way of getting rid of unacceptable responses.

Rule 4. Pick a behaviour which you can break down into small steps—the steps to be taught one at a time.

Rule 5. Pick a behaviour in which you can prompt the child through the various steps.

Rule 6. Pick a behaviour which you can teach in a setting which is quiet and distraction free, so that the child has the best chance of learning.

Rule 7. Plan a method of recording your teaching at the time when you set up your target.

3: An Example: 'He won't pay attention'

In this chapter we shall run through an example, one which is especially important and which brings up all the points which we have raised so far.

One of the most frequent things people say about mentally handicapped children is that they can't or don't attend or concentrate. This complaint is often offered as an 'explanation' for why the child doesn't learn or is not learning fast enough. And it classically illustrates the need to say exactly what it is that the child is doing in the problem situation. Only that way will we be able to do something about changing his behaviour.

We have identified at least five meanings to the statement 'he doesn't concentrate' or 'he doesn't attend'.

1. Looking or orientation
'He doesn't attend' may mean 'When I call him he doesn't stop what he is doing, turn and look at me'. In this case the child may simply not have learned that people want him to look at them when they call his name, or he may not know his name.

2. Sitting down with an adult
'He doesn't attend or concentrate' may mean 'He won't sit down when I ask him to, and do what I want him to do'. In this case the child may not have learned that you want him to sit in one place and play a certain game, for instance. The invitation to sit may be seen as an invitation to sit only for a minute, then to rush off so you can amuse him by chasing him or shouting at him. Or he may not have learned that two quiet minutes with you are usually followed by reward. Or you may be using a task he finds too boring, in spite of the reward.

Very often children who are 'suffering' from this kind of inattentiveness are quite capable of spending an hour absorbed in an activity of their own choosing. Such children are often quite wrongly called 'hyperactive', when in fact their problems can be explained more rationally as a function of how they see the teaching experience.

3. Looking at what he is doing

'He doesn't attend or concentrate' may mean 'When he is doing something with his hands he doesn't look at what he is doing'. The child may sit and do a task very readily, but he doesn't use visual cues in guiding what he is doing. This may be because he does not know how to put the information he receives through his eyes, and information he receives from his hands, together. In which case he can be taught. Or he may not be motivated to do the task carefully—by looking at what he is doing—because the pay-off for good performance is not good enough. In which case the reward needs to be improved. We will say more about these problems in Chapters 5 and 7.

4. Staying with one task until it is finished

The child may not have learned to play with one toy for a sustained period before sampling another one. He may not have learned very good 'choosing skills'. He may not have learned that he is supposed to complete one task before moving on to another. This will be discussed further in Chapter 6. Or he may exhaust the possibilities of a toy, as he sees them, within a few seconds because he does not know how to exploit the equipment (see Chapter 7 for more about this).

5. Responding selectively to one aspect of the environment

As in the case of Jack described above, 'he doesn't attend or concentrate' may mean 'He doesn't respond to shape and size but only to colour'. Or the child may 'attend' only to what you say and not to your facial expression. Or he may be interested in how things smell rather than how they look or feel. The possible reasons here are many and various. In Jack's case he had had no experience of looking and handling at the same time. This probably accounted at least partly for his failure to develop pattern vision. In another case the child may have brain damage in one specific area. In another it may be a personal preference which is either odd or very exaggerated.

We have described five clearly different meanings of the statement 'he doesn't attend' or 'he doesn't concentrate'. We have also found that we could have any one of 12 explanations for the complaint 'lack of concentration'. And we are confident that we could push the number of possible explanations up to about 30.

Our point is that it is not enough just to say that the child 'doesn't attend'. We need to say exactly what the child is doing or not doing. When we know this, we can decide how to set about changing it.

SITTING DOWN AND WORKING WITH AN ADULT

Let us return to our example of the child whose major problem was that he would not sit down and work with an adult. He would look when called and was capable of completing several small tasks on his own: such as putting small pegs in a box or putting a couple of shapes in a posting box. He appeared to attend appropriately to visual and other cues. But he would not sit for more than 10 to 20 seconds at a time.

Now there are a limited number of teaching tasks which can be completed in a matter of seconds, so his failure to sit became an obstacle to further learning. We might of course have followed the despairing advice of an eminent psychologist who once told a teacher that the only way to deal with a child like this was to chase him round as he flitted from place to place, clutching your teaching equipment and getting in 10 seconds teaching here and 10 seconds there!

What we did was to decide to select the following target: to have the child sitting and working with the teacher for 10 minutes. This was in line with our Rule 1, a target fitting in with the child's needs in development. It was also in line with Rule 2, pick something you are going to be able to do.

The target also conforms to Rule 3. We could teach it by reward training. The child was responsive to social rewards, but much more so to small bits of crisp and sweets. We decided to use reward for sitting with the teacher, and additional rewards for completing tasks.

We timed how long he would sit before the programme started, and found that the average period was about 20 seconds. So we decided to begin by rewarding him once every 20 seconds, with the interval between rewards getting longer as he sat longer. Just sitting was potentially boring, and in any case we hoped to get him working on a variety of new tasks with the teacher as a second target in the programme, so we also gave him several tasks to do, each of which he could do reasonably well. Whenever he completed a task, about once every 30–40 seconds, he got an additional reward.

A certain amount of prompting was used (Rule 5). When he looked as if he was going to get up, the teacher tightened her arm around him slightly, but if he struggled, showing he really wanted to go, he was allowed to. But, as we shall see, when he got up he lost the opportunity of a reward. We also prompted tasks which he seemed to have difficulty with.

Another use of prompting came about quite unexpectedly. Although he would normally respond to his name, the teacher found that he did not respond at all well in this situation. She therefore used a standard looking programme. The child's name was called, if he did not look at her she repeated his name and then prompted him by putting her hand round his chin and turning his face to her. As soon as he was looking at her she smiled and rewarded him. If the child looked the first time his name was called, he was rewarded. This very simple programme brought the child to the point at which he was looking following the first call on eight out of 10 occasions after four daily teaching sessions.

In this programme Rule 6, concerning the general setting, was very important. We had to move the child out of the main part of the classroom into a quiet area with a door which he could not open. This we did to enable us to control his behaviour when he got up. In the classroom he could just have gone too far away. In the quiet room the only interesting things were on his table, so going away meant that he not only lost social and material reward, but there was nothing to do either. He was allowed to stay away only for around half a minute, and then led back to the table and sat down.

Then, still as part of the programme, the child was phased back into the classroom. First the door to the classroom was left a little open; and, once he was sitting for the 10 minutes, sessions were run in the classroom.

The behaviour was recorded in terms of the number of times the child got down in the 10-minute session. This total dropped from 12 occasions in the first session to none in the fifteenth. There was a rise after three sessions, when he took to getting down and then coming back on his own. After that there was a steady decline. The actual amount of time working went up from about two and a half minutes to 10.

Within the session rewards were faded out until the reward for sitting was eliminated. Rewards for tasks were retained, but the tasks were changed once he had learned to sit for ten minutes. New tasks were introduced which took longer than the originals. At this stage the session was moved into the classroom. And finally the length of the session was gradually increased to 20 minutes.

CONCLUSION

This programme, aimed at one of the problems covered by the phrase 'he won't pay attention', was a fairly routine example of what can be done by thinking out and carefully planning an intervention with a handicapped child. In the next chapters we will describe many such programmes. First of all, however, we turn to the question of how we might arrange or rearrange the living and teaching environment to accommodate requirements of our new programmes.

4: Organising a Teaching Programme

Any scheme of work will need to take into account particular factors. The first of these will of course be the individual learning needs of the child. But there will also be enormous variations in the time available for the programme. And parents or teachers will vary in the degree to which they prefer flexible or rigid schemes of work.

Highly programmed schemes dictate exactly what must be done from day to day. The danger here is that they may not adequately consider the needs of the other members of the family or class; or that, if they do not show the expected results at exactly the expected time, enthusiasm will wane and the parents or teachers will feel 'failures' for not keeping up with the programme.

Every teacher or parent should select a way of working with the handicapped child which fits into their own pattern of living or working. There are, however, general guidelines which can be followed in organising a programme, some of which we have already described.

The first principle involves choosing the right time for teaching a particular skill. Recognising the 'right time' largely depends on observing whether the child has all the preliminary skills he will need for the new activity. For instance, when you see that he can hold his head up, he can get his hand to his mouth, he can chew and swallow, he can reach and grasp objects and bring them to his mouth, you may decide that it is time to teach him to feed himself.

Then you need to work out in detail exactly what you are going to teach, and in what order. Ways of doing this are explained in later chapters. Here we will assume that you have broken down your teaching into suitable steps, so you have to decide on when and how often you are going to teach a particular step. If the task is feeding, it might seem obvious that you would want to teach three times a day—at the child's mealtimes; but that is not always best. As a general rule the more frequently the teaching situation occurs the better, so three times a day may not be enough and you may decide to give him smaller meals at more frequent intervals for a while, so that he gets more practice. Alternatively, he may have some meals in different situations (home and school or school and hospital ward), or he may not have time to feed himself in the mornings (when you may be more concerned that he manages to get some breakfast down before going to school). In this case you may want to limit your teaching to one or two meals a day. The learning may take longer, but it may fit in better with your routine.

It is possible also that your child is not a good eater anyway— maybe he doesn't seem to like food much or at least only certain foods, and you are worried that if you try to get him to learn something new at mealtimes, you may put him off his food even more. If that is the case, you could add something extra to the situation that he likes better than food—for instance social reward. Or you could teach him to feed himself at a totally different time of day, and in a different situation, from his mealtime one, and start with foods he really likes (or at least prefers to his dinner). In that way, if you do have problems with teaching the new skill, you may prevent them from generalising to the mealtimes. Once he has learnt the skill in these 'special' circumstances, you will of course have to teach him to use it with his meals; but both he and you will be more skilled by then.

In deciding when to teach, you will need as well to take into account what is happening for your child in situations when you are not dealing with him. Taking feeding again as the example, you will need to know whether he is being fed, or being taught to feed himself, by others (at home, or at school for instance). If he is being taught the same skill by someone else it is obviously best if you can work out a common programme between you so that the child does not become confused by a variety of methods. If, however, this is not possible, or you cannot accept the method used by the other person, then you should at least be aware of the problems that could arise and try to avoid confusion by making your situation very different from the other one. Children, including slow-learning children, do learn to behave differently according to the situation; but it obviously takes longer to learn two new ways of behaving than one.

Once your child has learnt the target skill in one setting, the next step is to make sure he can apply it to other situations. We call this process *generalisation*. Sometimes this happens spontaneously: we teach the child the new skill and he uses it everywhere. But we should not rely on this happening; especially with handicapped children. We have to teach the child the new skill again in different surroundings and at different times, and we have to let other people teach him. If this sounds a very long drawn out process, it should be said that the child normally learns more quickly with each application, so that in the end teaching becomes a matter simply of showing the child what is expected in a new situation. So it may take six months to teach a child to feed himself ice-cream with a spoon. It may take even longer—feeding yourself with ice-cream is a very complicated skill. But it may then take only four months to get on to other foods, and only two months to learn to do it at Granny's house as well—and so on, with increasing confidence.

Once a child has got to this stage, it is tempting to think that the teaching is over—that the child has learnt the skill. But skills that have been learnt can also be forgotten, and there are two important steps to take to prevent this happening.

1. Provide an opportunity for practice

This sounds so obvious we cannot imagine that we could forget it; and with our example of feeding, it is unlikely that we would. But circumstances can change (change of staff in a school or hospital, a new baby at home), so that we feel perhaps that the child is taking too long to feed himself and start to feed him again as a 'temporary measure'—and then find we have to teach him to feed himself all over again.

This kind of setback is more likely to occur when we are dealing with activities that do not come up every day. So a better example might be teaching a child to play with bricks by building them into towers. This might have been generalised so the child can build with blocks of various sizes, can use plastic or wooden blocks, and can build towers at school, at home and even for the doctor or psychologist when being tested! At this point it might seem reasonable for the parent or teacher to relax—cross 'blockbuilding' off the list of tasks to be learnt—and go on to some other task with the child. This we can do. But we must also remember to let the child play with blocks now and again, and notice and reward towers when they are built. If blocks are put away while we concentrate on the next task, the child may lose his skill altogether after a while.

This loss of skill is particularly likely to arise when special equipment has been used to train a particular skill. So we should make sure that the child's everyday environment contains toys or other objects with which he can practise whatever skills he has learnt. When parents or teachers are told about the importance of a 'stimulating' environment, it is this aspect that is the most important. It means offering the child toys or games which help him to continue to enjoy doing what he has previously been taught to do. This leads to the second important way to prevent skills being forgotten.

2. Remember to reward skills after they have been learnt

We base our teaching methods on the idea that behaviour that is rewarded is encouraged, and behaviour that is ignored or punished is eliminated. Yet so often, once a child has mastered a skill, we forget to reward him for it, perhaps because we have turned our attention to something else. We are then surprised when he stops using the skill altogether.

Sometimes we are reluctant to reward the child for doing something we know he can do, so though we might be happy to use a reward when we are actually teaching a skill we feel resentful at using it once the skill has been mastered. The root of this reluctance is probably a misapprehension about the nature of reward. We all feed, dress and toilet ourselves, play and talk to one another without, it seems, needing continual rewards. Yet the truth is that we are being subtly rewarded all the time—we take pride in being like others of our own age, in being 'grown up' or independent; we enjoy people paying attention to us; and we get pleasure from being creative or mastering some new skill. Sometimes these kinds of rewards will be sufficient for the handicapped child too—to make them so should be one of the goals of our teaching, to make the child responsive to the normal environment. But a feature of many handicaps is just this inability to respond to ordinary rewards. In these cases we must remember to continue to reward the behaviour at least now and then—gradually doing so less often, while encouraging the child whenever possible to get pleasure from the mastering of the skill itself.

One way in which we can help the child to develop interest in the task for its own sake is to use equipment which is attractive and has a number of possibilities for play. In other words we need to select toys which will themselves reward the child, rather than toys which rely on the teacher, parent or other adult to provide continual reward.

We need, however, not become over-anxious about some drop-off in skill after a task has been mastered. It is natural that when you and the child are concentrating on a particular task it will be performed as carefully as the child is able—provided that he wants to do the task, that is that the reward is enough. If you and the child then move on to something else there may be a slight deterioration in the earlier skills, simply because the child is learning the new one. Such deterioration can be tolerated, and need not mean that the child is losing ground, provided that it does not last too long and that it picks up again once the child is not having to work so hard on the new step. This is most likely to happen if he is progressing well on the new skill, and you are still remembering to reward the old skill when it comes up.

We have stressed that skills need to be taught because the handicapped child does not generally learn by 'picking things up' as the normal child appears to do. But this is not to say that the handicapped child never learns spontaneously, and it is very important that he be given an opportunity to do so if at all feasible. This is important because it means that the child will be rewarded for learning by the same kinds of things that make it worthwhile for the normal child to learn—pride in achievement, for instance—so he will be more likely to retain the skill without any particular effort on our part. It is also important because, no matter how dedicated we are, we cannot 'teach' the child in this concentrated way throughout the day.

So we must try to arrange that, during periods when the child is not being specifically taught, he is in a situation where there are at least opportunities for him to practise his skills by himself, and perhaps advance them a little. This does not mean overwhelming him with equipment but arranging what is available so that it can be readily used. If you want to encourage the child to reach out and touch objects, for instance, suitable objects should not only be within reach but they should also be such as to reward him for his efforts—they could make a noise (a musical ball, perhaps) or fall over (a toy that can be pushed over and come bouncing back). When you are teaching the skill you can offer him rewards, but when the child is left alone the toys can be chosen to help substitute for you. Interesting toys will not only help the child in mastering new skills, but will also help keep him happy.

It sounds demanding to have continually to think of what the child can learn from the situation he is in; but it is really a question of the parent or teacher acquiring a few basic teaching skills themselves, which then become a habit of thought. Applying them is a matter of routine. Once you have learnt to recognise what skills the child has, what he can learn next, and what you can use to help him learn, it is obviously best to get toys at the right level for him, and it is often just as easy to put him where he can benefit from his environment as it is to put him elsewhere.

Here are some examples which may help illustrate this point. In one classroom study we had a little girl who was not only severely mentally handicapped but was also suffering from athetoid cerebral palsy: she made continual involuntary movements and had tremendous difficulty in looking at what she was doing, so that as she reached for something her head automatically turned away, and if she looked the arms were flung out to the side. It was a matter of priority that she should learn to overcome these movements, which, though apparently involuntary, can usually be controlled by teaching. She was being taught, in twice daily sessions of 20 minutes each, to hold on with both hands to a bar held between her and the teacher, and to watch the teacher's face at the same time. During these sessions the teacher would sing 'Baa baa black sheep' whenever the child managed to both retain her grasp and look at the teacher, and stop singing the moment the child either turned her head away or loosed her grip on the bar. The little girl was very fond of 'Baa baa black sheep' and did not seem to tire of it.

This training obviously relied heavily on the teacher's presence, and could not be continued when she was not available. During periods when the little girl was left to amuse herself, therefore, she was not given the bar or put in reach of it. Our reasoning was that if the bar had been accessible:

(1) she might have practised the skill—looking at the front while she held the bar—but since she would get no reward for doing so, she might well have become discouraged. This would make it much harder to teach the skill in the actual training session;

(2) or she might have grasped the bar without looking in its direction—this being her normal way of grasping objects —and so have reinforced the very involuntary habits we were aiming to get rid of.

In this case it was not a good idea to give the child the same apparatus to use when we were not there to reward her or control the situation. What we wanted was something to reinforce the same skill, but not to interfere with the training periods. So the child was fitted with a pair of brightly coloured stretch bands over her hands, so that her eyes were attracted to the movements of her hands. This reinforced the general aim of getting her to follow the movements of her hands, but it was sufficiently different from the 'learning to look while grasping' situation not to interfere with it.

It should be emphasised that relying on the stretch mittens alone would almost certainly not have been enough to overcome this major handicap: if the child had been able to learn so readily, she would not have been severely handicapped. The concentrated training periods were essential to establish new behaviours. The general environment could be planned only to help reinforce those behaviours and broaden their use.

The question of who does this concentrated training must depend on individual circumstances. For very young children it is likely to be exclusively the parents or care staff of a hospital or home. But older children may attend schools or specialist centres, and where the school or centre is taking prime responsibility for the actual teaching sessions, it is obviously very helpful if the 'back up' environment—home—can be used to reinforce the lessons. Some parents will be very happy to work daily on a particular task with their child, perhaps because it helps to have something definite to do with an otherwise difficult child, or because they want to be directly involved with his education. Other parents, once the child is in a school, are thankful for a much needed rest and feel that when the child is home he too needs a rest. This is an individual decision. What is important is that everyone with direct responsibility for looking after the child should know what he is capable of now, and have an idea of what to teach him next or of what needs reinforcing.

A note on 'experts'. The child may come into contact with people from many different disciplines and with very different views on what is most important for him: physiotherapists for instance may stress the physical side and the parent or teacher may be told that this is priority—nothing else can be attempted until the child has learnt to cope with his physical problems. Sometimes this may be a matter of simple fact. You can hardly teach a child to feed himself if he cannot grasp an object and bring it to his mouth. But at other times the statement may need further examination. For instance parents may be told that unless the child learns first to sit in the 'correct' position, 'primitive' swallowing reflexes will be encouraged and the child will never learn to swallow and chew properly. This is common and indeed sensible advice given to many people caring for the cerebral palsy child. But if, as sometimes happens, the child has difficulty in feeding and indeed appears to hate all food, it could be argued that a higher priority was to teach the child to tolerate and even like the food: perhaps by using singing, music, kisses, to reward the child for taking food, regardless of sitting position. Learning how to place food to avoid gagging, and how to hold or sit a child to reduce tongue thrusts, is of course very valuable; but much depends on the child himself learning how to cope with food, and this in turn has much to do with whether he has learnt to enjoy the end product of all this effort.

There is seldom a single 'correct' solution to problems of this kind. The parent or teacher must listen to the advice she gets from whatever source, then test the advice from her own experience after considering all the factors involved.

Some people of course may be left entirely on their own to look after a child, while others are bombarded by a confusing array of 'experts' and therapists. Some may be tempted to welcome all offers of 'help' or treatment uncritically, either in gratitude for being recognised at all or in the hope that each new 'therapist' will somehow provide a key that has eluded the others. 'Experts' and therapists will indeed prove very valuable, but their contribution must be weighed against the effort involved and the alternatives available. On the face of it, for instance, a weekly visit to a therapist in a clinic or centre, which involves a longish journey there, an uncomfortable wait, 15 minutes' treatment and then a journey back again might seem of little benefit to parent or child. Yet the parent may learn enough about practical handling techniques from that 15 minutes to keep her going through the week. Or she may get valuable moral support for continuing to work with her child. Such factors can be evaluated only by the person concerned. If in doubt about the importance of a particular therapy, ask yourself the following questions:

(1) If he were not going to the music/art/hydro/speech/ movement therapists for this period, what else would your child be doing?

(2) Does he enjoy going, or do you enjoy taking him, or both?

(3) Does what happens with the therapist or 'expert' help you in dealing with him for the rest of the time?

(4) Do you understand what she is doing and why?

(5) If he seems to benefit from the treatment is there any way he could get the same benefit in an easier/quicker/ cheaper/more enjoyable way?

(6) If he hates the treatment (or you hate him going, or taking him) and shows no immediate benefit, how convinced are you of the long-term benefits? Sometimes, of course, unpleasant treatments are necessary to avoid even greater unpleasantness later on, but the old idea does seem to linger, that treatment, like medicine, must be horrible to do you good. It is worth checking treatments that you or your child find particularly painful or unpleasant, just to see if the same result could not be achieved using better methods.

The person in day to day care of the handicapped child, then, must have the ultimate say in his programme, for it is that person who must take responsibility for his overall development: this is so whether the person is a teacher, parent, nurse or a member of care staff in a hostel. No doctor seeing a child on a six-monthly basis, or psychologist or specialist adviser on infrequent visits, can hope to do anything but offer the most superficial guidance. The person in daily contact with the child must plan the programme and see that it is carried out. Help can be gleaned from a variety of sources, but these must be coordinated and used within the child's programme to gain maximum advantage.

PLANNING A PROGRAMME AT HOME

How do we put these suggestions into practice? What kinds of things can parents do? Are there special things which parents should do? Are there special things which parents can do which teachers and other people cannot? How much teaching should the parent try to do?

In our experience of work with parents we have seen a full range of involvement. At the one extreme there are parents who take over the whole of a child's education, covering all of the areas of need with great competence, and some workers argue that all parents should become educators. But this is clearly unrealistic. Many parents do not want to take over from other professionals. If there are several children in the family and both parents work, it is just not possible for the parents to go this far. So at the other extreme we have worked with parents who have focused on only a single problem and solved it. Participants in parent workshops often say that their greatest benefit in fact has been in getting more insight into how their children think, feel and behave.*

* In running workshops we have felt that one of the benefits to parents has been the sheer fact of contact with teachers, social workers, speech therapists and psychologists who not only are prepared to help, but who also find the job of working with their children enjoyable and intellectually stimulating. It is clearly significant to the well worn problems of 'dissipation of guilt' and 'acceptance of handicap' when professionals can assure parents in this way that their children are worthwhile human beings, and not a burden to be carried by long-suffering saints.

In general we would feel that parents could consider what they do and what they plan to do under three general headings.

1. Teaching of skills

Ranging from self-help skills through play and communication skills. Here the parent could begin by thinking through what the child does at home, and examining first of all which parts of the child's day cause problems or friction. So, if mealtimes cause a problem, teaching of self-feeding may be an area to earmark as a priority. Or if the child does not play on his own or play constructively with his brothers or sisters, we may need to teach him new games.

Almost certainly the child can do with some improvement in communication skills. Home is an ideal setting for helping the child to develop his communication.

2. Getting rid of problem behaviours

Problem behaviours at home can be very serious indeed. With some problems parents need help with adaptations to the home or other aids (see Chapter 15). Other problems arise because the child does not have necessary skills. In this case the child can be taught the skills. In other words, getting rid of problems goes back to the teaching of skills.

3. Providing stability

The mentally handicapped child must find a lot of his world very confusing. Like any child he has needs for love and affection. If he cannot express these, we may have to bring them out for him. And in any case they must be met. Second, compared with the child with normal speech who gets a great deal of security from the fact that his parents can explain the world to him, the child who cannot understand is at a special disadvantage. How does he understand for instance that his mother is coming back when she goes into hospital? Or how does he know what is happening when he goes to the dentist? Parents can be reassured that the vast majority of children can take separation experiences and hospital trips. But far fewer problems emerge if we bear in mind that the handicapped child's needs include all the normal needs, the great difference being that he requires more help in understanding threatening or difficult situations. One way in which the child can be helped is by keeping his school informed of hospital trips or separation experiences, so that any disturbed behaviours in school can be met with extra attention and reassurance.

4. Providing a range of experiences

Parents are in a unique position to provide the child with a whole range of experiences which can help stimulate and develop his interests. They can involve him in household activities: for example washing up, cooking, cleaning, gardening, do it yourself jobs, washing the car. . . . It is only a question of thinking out the way in which the child can participate. The idea here is to give the child experience, not to teach him how to do the job himself, so letting him throw the grass clippings about may be messy but if it is an original game it has potential value. Trips to the park, to the shops, on trains and buses, out in a car, to a farm or zoo, to the beach or swimming pool or cinema can all be tried periodically. We are not suggesting that you build your lives around the child, but that you integrate him into a normal family pattern and give him the same weight as other family members when deciding what to do.

The value of all these experiences is to awaken or foster new interests in the child. It is very easy to slip into seeing the handicapped child as someone *to* whom things are done. Sure enough, we have to teach him a lot; but all human beings can determine the direction of their own lives to some extent. So parents might do best first to follow the child's own interests. They can also foster new interests across a very broad range of fields. Attendance and other allowances should enable the family to spend a bit more money on toys and trips than they need do for a normal child.

Information about any newly awakened interest can then be fed back to the school with great benefit to the teaching programme.

If the parents decide to set up a formal learning programme at home, its format will obviously depend on what is to be taught. General rules include the following.

It is a good idea to keep sessions short, up to 20 minutes, and to have them at the same time each day.

Begin with one session per day only. You can build up later if necessary. Don't try too much at first.

Try to involve older brothers and sisters, if they are normally expected to help with looking after their handicapped brother or sister. Work out a session with the older child, supervise him doing it a few times and then leave him to it. *But* always take a keen interest and ask the older child afterwards what they have been doing. We have found that older children can often be given responsibility for minding a handicapped child, and that they may prove very good indeed as teachers, and offer good ideas of their own. You can be very proud if your older child plays creatively with his handicapped sister or brother. Show him your pride, it will be a reward in itself.

You should also bear in mind that you may be able to get additional help from your local parents' organisation, from the social services department or your child's school. These possibilities are discussed in Chapter 15.

RUNNING A PROGRAMME IN A RESIDENTIAL UNIT IN THE COMMUNITY OR HOSPITAL

Many of the ideas for setting up a programme at home apply to work in a residential unit or hospital also. But there are differences. Workers in residential units are professionals who often have specific training in care and education of the mentally handicapped, so we can expect a more uniform standard of programme planning and accountability for achieving goals of programmes, than we can expect among parents.

In our experience the success of the programmes depends to a large extent on the attitude to them of the unit as a whole. It must be committed to a developmental programme rather than to care or containment. This commitment shows itself in building into the jobs of workers in the unit a requirement to work on programmes, to undertake regular reviews, to involve outside consultants as advisers and to set explicit goals for individual children. We have also found that the staff in the unit need to work out a detailed timetable of who will be responsible for what and when. An unbuttoned informal approach can look good, but results in chaos, a lot of busy work and rapid abandonment of the programmes!

It is also clearly desirable for staff in short-stay residential units to work closely with parents. A programme involving an integrated home–residential unit component is often the only effective way of cracking problems such as incontinence, or extremes of behaviour disorders.

RUNNING A PROGRAMME IN SCHOOL

The idea of having separate one-to-one teaching sessions with children often strikes teachers either as undesirable or impractical. They will argue that the most effective teaching and learning goes on in the classroom, that group teaching should be used throughout, and that in any case limitations on time and staff make individual sessions impossible.

Admittedly the approach outlined here requires a rethink of the way in which many teachers operate; but teachers whom we have worked with have found that reorienting their teaching can be both possible and satisfying entirely within the framework of the normally staffed classroom.

The reason for our approach should be clear by now. We see the goal of teaching as being to provide the child with skills through which he can learn effectively in a good educational environment. And we would like to free the child from those behaviours which limit his development. But we feel that we can do this only by teaching the child those skills which he does not have or cannot learn in a good educational environment. If he is unable to take advantage of a good language environment, for instance, we should see it as our goal to teach him how to do so. The child will then take it from there. If further blocks or problems arise, the teacher should again intervene, analyse, and guide the child over the difficulties.

The natural starting points for teaching, then, are the good educational environment—a classroom equipped to encourage development—and the individual teaching session, in which problems emerging in the classroom can be pin-pointed, analysed and dealt with. The next step in the sequence is to generalise the new behaviour: from the session to the classroom and then to the home, the park, the shops or wherever else the behaviour is important. We would see this last step as involving joint parent-teacher work, though the teacher may have to take

C

on some of the work in generalising new behaviour herself, or call on other relevant professionals to cooperate with this section of a programme.

Reorganisation of the classroom to include daily sessions with each child requires first, either that there should be more than one teacher/helper in the classroom or that the other children are able to get on by themselves when individual sessions are going on. If there is help, and most classes seem to have at least one helper, the nursery nurse or teaching assistant can supervise activities whilst the teacher is running her sessions. The ideal system is for teacher and helpers to work out an integrated scheme in which the two or three people in the class all know what the aims of the programmes are and what progress children are making. In this way the child being taught to use Morgenstern toys in an individual session can be encouraged to use those he has already learned to use in a group session run by the helper. Or the nursery nurse or assistant can take over some parts of an overall programme, for instance a self-help programme, within the general scheme of classroom activity.

It is clear also that some timetabling is essential. It has been our experience that timetabling can be satisfying for teachers and helpers alike—everyone knows what they are doing and can see the direction of development. But teachers often do fear that it will restrict the spontaneity which is necessary if teachers are to respond to the changing moods of the class, or to take advantage of the weather when it is very hot, or it suddenly snows. What must be kept in mind, though, is that it is easy to change the timetable when there are only a few people involved. If each session takes 10 minutes or so, it is possible to get through eight in two hours if the organisation of equipment is reasonably slick. So the teacher and her helpers can on occasion decide to reorganise the day, and maybe get through all the sessions in the morning and go out in the afternoon. In addition there are often children whose programmes are just finishing, or who are going along so well that one day missed will not be much of a problem.

Quite often teachers are hedged round by events arranged for the children by other people. The physio comes on Tuesday morning, there's riding on Wednesday afternoon, swimming on Friday morning, the people with the inflatables come on Friday afternoon. The teacher seems to be reduced to a sort of minder whose job it is to make sure that children are available for other people to do things with!

If this is happening, the teacher should consider carefully the benefits to each child of these activities. If she feels that any child could benefit more from being in school with her, then it is her responsibility to make sure he is there.

This again raises the question of relationships between the person in overall charge of a child—in this case a teacher—and other professionals. We have already suggested that it is only the person in daily contact with a child who is in a position to assess his needs overall. Therapists, psychologists, psychiatrists, educational advisers and others who have contributions to make to the child's programme should thus be seen as *advisors* to the person with daily responsibility, and not as dictating or directing a bit of the child's programme. To allow one person to direct one bit of the programme, and another to direct another, contradicts a basic principle of our approach: that the child must be considered as a whole. His programme must be planned so that each component fits with others to create an overall pattern of developmental teaching.

CONCLUSION

In this chapter we have emphasised the need to construct a programme for an individual which reflects the child's needs and the constraints of his environment. We have pointed out that teaching needs to be carried over from one environment to others in which the skills are relevant. We have outlined the kinds of arrangements which we have seen working or have been involved in establishing in various contexts. Our central theme in this is that the parent, teacher, nurse or care staff have the responsibility for balancing a child's programme and for interpreting the input of advisers such as physiotherapists, speech therapists, psychologists, psychiatrists or educational advisers.

5: Developing Rewards and Interests

The following series of chapters deals with the content of teaching. Each chapter will begin with a discussion of the area to be concentrated on. It will go on to show you how you can assess a child's behaviour; and then to give a series of examples, most of which are short case histories. We will show you how we decided on and built up our programmes for teaching in each case. You may be able to adapt some of these programmes for your own children or, better, make up your own, using the principles we describe.

INTERESTS AND REWARDS

Our first area to concentrate on is that of developing rewards and interests.

In order to develop, the child must have needs and interests so that his environment can give him the incentive to learn.

We will begin by talking about rewards, and ways of identifying them. Then we will suggest ways in which rewards can be developed. Once the child has developed a range of things he likes, we want to encourage him to express his preferences: to teach him to choose. We will see that the capacity to choose is very fundamental.

First, making choices is not only a useful educational activity, it is also vital to development; for if, as we are suggesting, the child will develop if we observe and foster his interests, then the ability to express preferences is fundamental to the success of the programme. Then, at a different and more philosophical level, we would see the right to make choices as a fundamental right of any living organism. We allow the child to realise himself more fully by teaching him how to choose.

From a discussion of choice we will move on to talk about self-control. Again we will show that this is not a behaviour which develops only in older children. It has its origins in very early development. Again, we can teach the child important elements of self-control which can help him to master his environment.

DEFINING REWARDS AND PUNISHERS

In Chapter 2 we saw that the basic approach taken by many educationalists to the development of the handicapped child puts great emphasis on the consequences of the child's actions. These consequences may be things which the child likes, rewards; and things which he does not like, punishers.

How do we decide what the child likes and does not like? We can start by making a list of the things which the child appears to enjoy, such as eating jelly babies, being swung on the swing or being cuddled. But we have to be careful not to read too much into the child's behaviour. In order for something to qualify as a preference, the child really should show clear evidence of moving toward it. Reaching out and picking up a piece of Marmite toast when it is offered, for instance, probably shows preference. So may *not* spitting out a type of food, if he usually spits food out. But passively holding an object without looking at it when it is put into his hand is doubtful evidence. And even more doubtful is the assumption that a child likes something because *all* children like it.

Social rewards

There are several kinds of rewards and punishers. Here are some social rewards and punishers:

	Reward	*Punisher*
Physical contact	Cuddling	
	Stroking	
	Tickling	Slap
	Rubbing noses	Rough handling
	Kissing	
	Rough and tumble play	
Bodily expressions	Smile	Frown
	Hold out arms to child	Shake fist

	Reward	Punisher
Speech	Gentle speaking in quiet voice	Angry tone, shouting, speaking sharply
	'Yes', 'Good boy', 'Good girl' in enthusiastic tone	'No', 'Bad boy', 'Bad girl', in harsh tone
Attention	Playing with the child with a toy or something else he likes	'Sitting over' the child by stopping him doing most things he wants to do
	Being with the child	Withdrawing positive attention by going out of child's presence

This list does not include all possible social rewards and punishers. And we must be very careful to note that what may be a reward or punisher for one child may not be for another. So *most* children find the adult speaking in an angry tone punishing; but some children only find it funny, and will eagerly repeat the piece of behaviour that has led to the 'punishment'. And any teacher in a normal school can tell you of the child who seems to behave in a naughty way just to get teacher's attention.

The list is arranged to reflect increasing social development. Some events, like being cuddled or having the skin stroked, are usually rewarding from a very early stage. And being roughly handled or slapped is usually aversive equally early.

Response to smiles or to an angry tone of voice, on the other hand, probably involve some learning. Certainly responding to 'Good boy' or 'Nice girl' depends on learning. The theory is that the child learns that 'Good boy' has pleasant associations because it is normally followed by being cuddled, kissed, fed or some other basic reward. Similarly, 'Bad girl' may well be followed by rough handling or even a slap.

The effectiveness of attention as a reward, and withdrawal of attention as a punishment, also depends on learning. Adult attention is probably powerful in this way because the adult has control over events or things which the child finds attractive. But it may also be that the child finds that his ability to get the adult to attend is rewarding for another reason: He may enjoy his own mastery in the situation. He has been able to understand how to influence the very complicated and powerful person of the adult. This desire to understand and master things is a very fundamental motive which also shows up in the child's interest in toys and pets.

It will be useful at this stage to write a list of the social rewards and punishers your child responds to. Don't forget to try out the rewards to check your ideas. And parents and teachers may find that children like different things at home and school, so it will be useful to pool information.

Food and drink as rewards

A second category of reward is food and drink. Most children like sweet things, but the individual child also has particular preferences—for strawberry mousse, for instance. The child may also like meats, vegetables, or savoury things. We have come across children who have *very* specific preferences, in one case for *half* sausages, and the child liked nothing else. Crisps, raisins, and Marmite toast are often popular.

Again, explore what the child likes and then make a list of five or six really preferred things.

Sensory rewards

Sensory pleasure too can act as a reward: playing with a particular toy, cuddling a piece of soft material, being allowed to sniff a perfume, hearing special pieces of music played, seeing lights flashing on and off on a Christmas tree, riding in a car, watching television, playing with water in the bath.

Again you need to be careful to make sure you have clear evidence of liking. If he is ambulant, does he run toward water when at the seaside? Does he smile and make happy noises when the TV is on, try to see it more clearly by turning the controls, or cry when it is turned off?

Quite often the list of rewards and punishers we can produce for a very delayed child is very short—there may even be no preference at all! If this is the case, don't be dismayed. This chapter is designed to help you to develop a few.

First, if you cannot produce much of a list, then we would suggest that it might be a good idea to spend a few days more, just searching. In our experience the child who has *no* preferred activity is rare. Usually it is a child who has been in a subnormality hospital for a long time and who may therefore have had very little normal stimulation.

One approach which may help to identify at least preferred activities is simply to watch the child in a free environment surrounded with a few toys. If you find that he spends all his time banging, then this is by definition a preferred activity, and the opportunity to bang may be usable as a reward. In extreme cases we have had to let children rock or hand-flap as a reward because that is the only thing they appeared to like doing.

Easy and difficult rewards

When you have your list of rewards, you can divide them into those which are easy to use and those which are difficult. An easy reward is one which the adult can manipulate easily. A crisp is an easy reward: we can give the child a small piece of crisp as soon as he completes a simple puzzle, and we can give him 20 or so in a session without satiating or boring him.

On the other hand a difficult reward is one which takes a great deal of time or effort to provide. Going for a car ride would be a difficult reward. Such a reward can be used at the end of a session, or later, with children who can show understanding of the relation between current behaviour and future rewards.

It is often useful to have two or three easy rewards and a difficult one available in any session. This allows you to give the child a choice of reward, and thus to maintain his motivation and prevent each separate reward from losing its potency.

ASSESSMENT OF THE CHILD'S RESPONSIVENESS TO REWARD

We will consider first the development of the child's interest in material things. There are several possible levels of responsiveness to rewards.

Table 1. Responsiveness to material rewards
(1) Avoids most events and experiences.
(2) Indifferent to all experiences.
(3) Will respond only to difficult rewards.
(4) Approaches only a few good rewards.
(5) Approaches several good rewards—but with long delays or inconsistently.
(6) Approaches several good rewards.

1. Avoids most events and experiences

The child may avoid experiences. He may eat only a restricted number of foods, and these passively. He may cry when exposed to music or light boxes. He may push adults away. This child would need an extensive programme to reduce his avoidance reactions and develop new responses. (Example 1 page 78.)

2. Indifferent to all experiences

This is the non-reactive child who seems indifferent to everything. See Example 1 page 78.

3. Will respond only to difficult rewards

Some children are hard to reward because they like so few things, and those they do like are difficult to work with. For instance a child may like to be left alone to sit under a table and rock, or he may like being wrapped up in a blanket and put to bed. The child is not going to learn much under a table or in bed, so the rewards are hard to use in learning situations. See Example 1 page 78, and Example 2 page 80.

4. Approaches only a few good rewards

The child might like squeezing a squeaky toy and eating jelly babies—and nothing else. The main problem here is that the child will probably satiate rather quickly: he will get bored with the rewards and they will become useless. See Example 1 page 78, and Example 2 page 80.

5. Approaches several good rewards—but with long delays, or inconsistently

The child may respond well to a series of rewards, but with a variable delay because he does not always realise that the reward is available. You can work quite easily with this kind

c*

of child if you are using rewards which you deliver directly—turning on music for a few seconds or popping a piece of sweet in his mouth. But when the reward is less immediate—letting him play with a toy or giving him a cup to drink from—he may not respond immediately. This will make his learning less effective because *he* is delaying his reward. See Example 3 page 82.

6. Approaches several good rewards
The child will respond promptly to, say, ten easy rewards. This is an ideal learning situation.

If the child scores at the highest level of functioning we can say he has enough rewards for most teaching programmes.

The second part of our assessment concerns responsiveness to adults and other children. The assessment is laid out in Table 2. We will begin with responsiveness to physical contact.

Table 2. Responsiveness to physical social rewards
(1) Avoids physical contact.
(2) Indifferent to physical contact.
(3) Responds to physical contact but does not initiate it.
(4) Physical contact a reward for learning with one adult or child.
(5) Physical contact a reward for learning with several adults and children.

1. Avoids physical contact
The child moves away when approached or touched. He may even cry. Unfortunately, this response is not as rare as one might think. It is not uncommon to find children who are undergoing some of the more vigorous forms of physical therapy, for instance, actually afraid of physical contact. In these cases we need to teach the child that physical contact can be pleasurable (see Chapter 13). See Example 1 page 78.

2. Indifferent to physical contact
The child does not appear to notice physical contact. See Example 1 page 78.

3. Responds to physical contact but does not initiate it

The child responds by quieting, or smiling, when an adult or another child touches, strokes or cuddles him. But he does not initiate physical contact, by moving towards adults or children, or by squealing or calling out. He has not yet learned, in other words, that what he does affects a situation. So this is what we need to teach him. See Example 1 page 78.

4. Physical contact works as a reward for learning only with a particular adult or child

When physical contact is used as a reward the child does learn new tasks, but this works with only one person. This can be tested by using a programme of the type described in Example 8 page 89.

5. Physical contact works as a reward for learning with several adults and children

The child has learned that several people can cuddle or kiss him in a way which he enjoys. This is the ideal.

We turn now to responsiveness to what adults or children say. This assessment is laid out in Table 3.

Table 3. Responsiveness to verbal rewards and punishers
(1) Indifferent to verbal rewards and punishers.
(2) Responds to verbal rewards but not by learning.
(3) Learns with verbal reward. One adult.
(4) Learns when verbally rewarded by several adults or children.
(5) Responds to verbal punishers but not by learning.
(6) Learns with verbal punishment.

1. Indifferent to verbal rewards

Saying 'good boy' or 'very good' or 'no' and 'stop' have no effect on the child's behaviour. See Examples 4 and 5 pages 82 and 84.

2. Responds to verbal rewards but not by learning

The child smiles when you say 'good boy', or clearly enjoys being cuddled, but his response is 'silly': he takes social reward as an invitation to throw things, or to start rough and tumble play, or simply to smile back and laugh. See Examples 6 and 7 on pages 86 and 87.

3. Learns with verbal reward, but with one adult only

The child responds only to one adult by learning when rewarded verbally; so he may 'do anything for his mother' but be impossible to handle otherwise. Here the child needs a programme which encourages him to respond to other people, so that he can learn from them too. Look at Example 8 page 89.

4. Learns when verbally rewarded by several adults or children

This should be the goal for teaching, and the ideal.

5. Responds to verbal punishers but not by learning

'No' or 'stop' simply produce a laugh or are followed by 'silly' behaviour (as in the similar reaction to reward above). If your child behaves like this, look at Examples 6 and 7 on pages 86 and 87.

6. Learns with verbal punishment

As we saw in Chapter 2, learning by punishment training is very slow and uncertain. Nevertheless, when combined with reward training, it can be a help. We need to establish a response to 'no' or 'stop' which can at least be used to get the child to calm down. This is the goal. Look at Example 5 page 84.

By now you should have some idea where your child stands in relation to the ideal conditions for teaching: that is, conditions which will allow you to use physical contact, verbal rewards and verbal punishers to teach. You should also have an idea of how much you are actually going to have to teach 'social responsiveness' in order to reach 'ideal' conditions.

There is also a wider value in social responsiveness which should not be overlooked. Responsiveness to adults and other children is not only an essential condition for the learning of skills: it is crucial for later development in general. Social responsiveness as we have analysed it leads the child towards an understanding of how other human beings work—so that they can become interesting for their own sake. We will see this in particular when we talk about Communication in Chapter 9.

This general development in turn leads the child to identify himself as a boy, modelling himself on brothers or his father, or as a girl, learning that her models are her mother and sisters. Only if there is a substantial relationship built up on social interaction, both positive and negative, can this identification occur.

A special word should be said here about physical contact. There are people who feel that a great deal of cuddling, kissing and stroking of the child is too soft an approach, appropriate to tender loving care but not to teaching. There are, however, very good reasons for seeing physical contact as critical to good teaching.

In normal development the child learns to relate to other people in many ways; and part of his early learning is how to touch and hug other children in such a way that they will interpret his approach as friendly and find it pleasurable. This early learning is crucial for later relationships, for the expression of tenderness in general, and for showing feeling through physical contact in particular. Many normal children and adults have difficulty in expressing physical affection. Since the handicapped child may have difficulty in learning in all spheres, there is no reason to believe that he will not have problems in this area as well. So part of our goal in teaching him should be to teach him to show affection appropriately.

And there is a further aspect of physical responsiveness which is important. Mothers, fathers, brothers, sisters, teachers and nurses have feelings too! One of our fundamental ways of relating to children is through physical contact. So if the child pushes the adult or other child away, or does not snuggle properly when he is cuddled, one of our basic approaches to the child is being punished. This can lead to feelings of dejection and grief because we are rejected, and to a fundamental feeling that the child really is very 'different'. We may come to feel that we have no bonds at all with him, and maybe never can have. This reaction can obviously lead to a vicious circle: the child rejects us, we find it hard not to reject the child, and so on. Teaching can play a part in breaking this circle, and allowing loving relationships to grow.

EXAMPLES OF TEACHING SITUATIONS TO DEVELOP REWARDS

The first examples relate to the development of the child's interests in material and sensory experiences. Examples 4 to 8 are more concerned with the development of social rewards.

Example 1. Assessing and teaching basic responsiveness to material rewards

(1) Create a situation in which the child is awake, as alert as possible, but not distressed. The child should be in a quiet, distraction-free environment. If he has a rest in the afternoon it may be a good idea to hold his first session at the end of the rest period, when he has not been stimulated for some time.

(2) Select an experience which most children find positive and interesting: being sung to very quietly, having the face stroked, tasting a sweet substance such as honey or a savoury substance such as Marmite, watching changing lights (in a low-powered torch with coloured filters, or a few Christmas tree lights flashing against a background of silver paper) or listening to a quiet rattle. Select an experience which is low-key, gentle but nonetheless interesting.

(3) Assess the effects of the events on the child. Present them very gently, with slightly increased intensity if he appears not to notice. Details of presentation are described under step 4. Does he avoid by turning away or by crying, or is he indifferent or interested? If he approaches, you have found something you may be able to use as a reward, or something to interest him in itself. In the case of avoidance or indifference you need a programme.

(4) For the child who shows active avoidance of most things, we are going to have to begin by teaching him that the experiences are not threatening or unpleasant. This is done by first finding the level at which he appears to accept the new event: for example, if he avoids singing, he may accept it if you sing very quietly indeed. We would then sing quietly for five minutes per day for three or four days during the session period. We would then increase the intensity of the singing very slightly. If the child reacts badly, we may have to reduce intensity again. However, it is very important that we give the

child enough time—in this case ten days or so—to get used to the event. If we use two or three possible rewards in the session (singing, tasting and stroking, perhaps), we might notice progress with one. This will encourage us to keep going.

For the child who is indifferent to all or most rewards, we would introduce possible rewards in the same way. We would not have to be as careful in presenting the rewards initially, but we would use the same principles.

(5) How do we know we are having an effect? There are several ways in which we can assess progress. For example, the following sequence was used with a very handicapped child when we were looking at development of taste:

(i) A drop of new substance, for example condensed milk, was put on a teat and the teat put in the child's mouth. This was done five or six times a day for three days.

(ii) After three teat presentations, on the fourth day the teat was put on the child's lip, so that the child now had to lick her lip to get the milk.

(iii) When the child showed she would do this, the teat was put to one side of the child's mouth and about a quarter of an inch away. The child now turned her head to get the milk.

(iv) The teat was put further and further away, until the child had to move her head two or three inches to get the milk.

This sequence is important because it showed that the event was pleasurable to the child, and also that she would learn a useful response to experience it.

Another example, which brings in a further important principle, involves a child whose interest in visual stimulation was minimal. Several objects were tried, including a toy windmill and a box of Christmas tree lights, but the first object to which he showed any response was a bunch of red feathers threaded with glitter paper.

We continued to present all the objects to the child, though he showed little response except a slight following of the red feathers. But within a week he was clearly tracking the feathers, and showing some eye movement to the windmill when it was moved across his line of vision. The response requirement was gradually increased over a period of a month, so that in the end the child would turn his eyes and head to look at the feathers and windmill.

With other children one might hope to find spontaneous reaching. If reaching does not occur it can be taught, once we have established a reward. (See Chapter 7.)

The principle embodied in this example is that we try to extend the range of things that the child is interested in. So don't use just one thing in the session, use several. This will keep both you and the child interested.

These examples, using taste and visual stimulation, can be adapted to involve other senses: a range of noises can be used, or the child may be given tactile or kinaesthetic experiences. Tactile stimulation would include stroking or patting the child, or warming your hand and putting it on his cheek or hand. Mild tickling could be tried, then you can tickle him a little harder and see if you get a good response.

Kinaesthetic stimulation is a response to movement in our limbs or body. This form of stimulation may be crucial for a child with any degree of floppiness or spasticity (see Chapter 13). The aim is to teach the child that he will get pleasure from exercising his limbs. You may start by raising and lowering limbs, or bending legs and arms. In doing this begin softly and build up. And always try to get the child to do more and more for himself.

Example 2. Getting inside a child's interests
The child may have very limited interests indeed. He may be interested in only one toy or one piece of cloth, which he carries around all the time and plays with in a stereotyped way. We could use the opportunity to play with the toy as a reward to try to build up new responses. The alternative is to try to modify the interest from within. This is the classic approach of child-centred teaching.

Two examples will illustrate this. The first involves a little girl who was 'obsessed' by her hands. She would put her hand palm down on the table and examine her finger nails and fingers with great concentration. All attempts to shift her were resisted.

One day her teacher put colour on one of her finger nails. At first she objected violently, but then she quietened. The next day the teacher tried again, again resistance, then acquiescence. Over the next weeks she had her finger nails coloured all the same colour, then different ones. The child began to offer her hand for the nails to be coloured, then to ask for the other hand to be coloured, then to select colours.

The next task was to wean the child from her obsessive staring, on to other tasks. This was done in the same way, by gradually extending the child's interest to other situations.

The second example involves a little boy who was interested in pretty well nothing! Then one day he showed interest in a Matchbox car in someone else's home. He was allowed to take it home with him. He played with it by banging it and eventually smashing it. His parents bought him another, and then another, and another. He would carry these around with him and play with them, usually by banging them. They would get broken but were usually replaced.

The point is that the cars could be used as a basis to extend his play. They could be taken and hidden under a pillow where he would find them, and once he had learned the game, he would give them back to be hidden again. Getting new cars became a basis for social behaviour. He showed he knew his way to the shop by taking his parents to it. He learned that he could have only one car at a time in the shop (the Attendance Allowance helped toward buying them).

Observing him playing, his parents found that he began to match similar cars on the basis of colour and shape. This helped to guide buying: a new car could match an existing one, or start a new series.

His parents noticed that the cars were never spontaneously rolled down slopes: in fact their wheels were apparently ignored. So this offered a further possibility for getting inside the interest: a simple slope was set up with a short piece of board. The crashing proved interesting, but it took a long time for the child to develop any real fascination with the rolling of the car on the slope.

In this example, as with the first, the child was very hard to deflect from his central interest. What teachers and parents had to do was to exploit the interest in order to develop new concepts and ideas.

These examples appear different in some ways from our

clearly formulated targets. But the principles are basically the same. The objectives are held in mind all the time, and teacher or parents work continuously toward them, formulating short-term targets, and experimenting continuously in order to try to break through.

Example 3. 'He doesn't know I'm giving him a reward'
Tommy was a child who would not work at one task for more than a few seconds unless it was very interesting to him. He tended to flit. This flitting showed up when he was being rewarded. He would put a puzzle piece in place, stack a block and then, when given his reward (a bit of apple or pear), appear to be completely unaware that he was being rewarded. He would be staring away or looking round aimlessly. He was being rewarded by having the reward put on a dish in front of him, with a simultaneous 'Good boy'.

We decided to revise the way in which his rewards were given, in order to ensure that he perceived them as rewards for the response we wanted him to make. The first step was actually to put the food in his mouth. The teacher sat near. When Tommy did it right she said 'Good boy' and simultaneously popped the fruit into his mouth. At first he seemed surprised— his mouth was never open when the fruit came. Then he gradually learned to anticipate. This stage was crucial because it showed that a connection was being made between successful completion of the task and reward.

The next steps were very quick, since now Tommy was looking toward the teacher when she spoke. It was easy to move to the position where she held up the fruit for him to take, and then put it on the plate for him to pick up.

As we have already noted, if we use rewards like singing or music, or if we cuddle or kiss the child, *he* cannot delay the reward.

Example 4. Learned rewards
We have up to now been talking about children who start off with no responses we can use as rewards. If the child does have *something* which he responds to, then our task is much easier. What we need to do now is increase the number of rewards we

can use, by associating the existing reward with whatever we want to use as a new reward.

The most obvious new rewards we might want to develop are social rewards. We will take as an example developing a response to 'Good girl' and smiling, but the same principle applies to other social rewards: being stroked, spoken to or cuddled.

Verbal social rewards work initially by giving the child the information that other rewards are following. To a non-verbal child, 'good' is a neutral word. But if 'good' is followed by something pleasant, then, in time, it becomes associated with the pleasant event and rewarding in itself.

This suggests several ways in which verbal rewards can be 'created'. One is by talking to the child whilst cuddling or feeding him—provided of course he likes cuddling and food. But we must get the order right: the verbal reward, 'good', must come first, followed by the cuddle and food. Only this way can we be sure that the word will become a signal for the reward.

So in feeding the child we might

(a) Load the spoon.
(b) Pause and get the child to look at us.
(c) When he is looking say 'Good boy'.
(d) Then give him his spoonful of food, accompanied by a cuddle and a smile.

This type of programme has one or two important features. First, it aims to make 'good' a reward through becoming a signal for food. Cuddling and smiling are associated with food but do not signal it. They too may become rewards. The second point to notice is that the first three steps are carefully timed. The spoon is loaded but *there is then a pause*. This pause is introduced to prevent the child from predicting the food coming from seeing the spoon loaded. If we simply filled the spoon and put the food in the child's mouth immediately, there is no reason why the child should give any significance to the word 'good'. The pause means that the child has to attend to the adult. He gets rewarded for that. And 'good' is the signal that food is really coming.

Once we have used 'good' in this way for a time, we should test to see whether it is being accepted as a reward. Does the child respond by smiling or looking pleased when you use it in other settings? Try to build up 'good' in several settings, associating with different kinds of reward. This way it will become associated with a whole range of good things.

Once 'good' is established, we should continue to back it up with other rewards or it will lose its power to reward. We must be sure to keep the association with reward high even when the word is being used as a reward for new learning in itself.

Learned rewards can be developed in many other situations. For instance, when a material reward is being used to develop dressing skills, for instance, the parent or teacher should always use a social reward just before offering the material one. Social rewards, especially verbal ones, are especially useful because they can be given immediately the child responds correctly. This produces the best possible feedback to the child on the correctness of his responses.

Example 5. Learned punishers

There are also social punishers to which the child might learn to respond. The commonest is 'no', with 'stop' as an alternative. In Chapter 2 we said that 'no' and other punishers can be used effectively with rewards in teaching the child new behaviour; and we pointed out that in addition we do need a way of stopping the child—for instance, from doing something dangerous.

The principle involved in establishing 'no' is the same as that in establishing 'good'. We associate the word with established concepts. 'No' would be associated with some unpleasant event: this might be any of a range of punishers, from withdrawing attention or taking a drink away (both examples of time-out), to smacking and physical restriction (both examples of punishment training). The example we shall describe uses a form of physical restriction.

Anthony could do a number of simple play tasks; but he was a child who threw things. The programme to teach him to respond to 'no' was set up in a teaching session where he was being taught to sort objects by size. He would sort three or four objects, then throw one or two over his shoulder—for no clear reason other than that he liked doing it! He had plenty of opportunity to throw acceptably in other situations.

It was, happily, quite possible to predict when Anthony was going to throw. He would pause and look up before he did so. His appropriate sorting was rewarded with small sweets, but 'no' had no effect on his behaviour. He appeared not to understand that it was connected with disapproval. He had been smacked in other situations, and would cry if smacked.

Our target was to get Anthony to stop throwing when he was told 'no', and to reduce his throwing in general. In teaching, the adult continued to sit near the child. Whenever she saw that he was going to throw, she said 'no' very sharply (as she had done, unsuccessfully, before), but now she caught hold of Anthony's throwing hand and held it firmly on the table while she counted slowly to ten (one a thousand two a thousand three a thousand etc.). Anthony did not like his hand being held down. He struggled at first, trying to pull his hand away. The teacher held on firmly and did not release his hand until about five seconds after he had stopped struggling. (If she had released his hand while he was struggling, he would simply have learned to struggle when restrained!)

The use of restraint was gradually faded out by loosening restraint as the child struggled less, until in the end only a touch of the hand was necessary, in addition to the word 'no'.

If Anthony succeeded in throwing, the teacher said 'no' sharply and took the task away for 30 seconds. This, like the ten-second restraint, had the effect of reducing reward in the situation, because whilst his hand was being held or the task was withdrawn he could not get a reward.

After 15 pairings of 'no' with restraint, the power of 'no' on its own was tested. On this, and two subsequent occasions, after 30 and 42 trials respectively, Anthony threw, after which he paused and then went on sorting. By this time the restraint has been reduced to a touch.

Once 'no' is established in one situation it should be tried in others. New teaching may be necessary in other settings: for instance Anthony seemed to realise that 'no' could not be backed up in settings where he was at a distance from the adult. So another teaching programme, using removal from the situation, had to be used to establish a 'no' which would work at a distance.

The balance of yeses and noes. We have already emphasised that in setting up a programme, we must be very careful to get the balance of positive and negative, rewards and punishments, biased well in favour of rewards. In Anthony's case, we could not allow the number of noes to rise above 9 or 10 in a single session, for instance, because he had a session lasting around 20 minutes, of which only three or four minutes could be allowed for the 'no' programme, if we were to keep within our limit of 20 per cent negative experience overall in a teaching session. You may remember that this is what we suggested is as much as a child can take before the danger arises that he will begin to react against the teacher and find the whole session aversive.

Example 6. 'Silly' behaviour

Some children respond to social rewards, but do so in a way which we have described as 'silly'. The child may smile, giggle, fall about on the floor, play rough games. Usually, the child has learned that such behaviour is effective in another setting. The child is transferring behaviour which may be completely correct in one setting, to another where it interferes with learning.

There are three ways of dealing with this. One is to ignore the inappropriate behaviour altogether, if we do this, however, we run the risk that the child will not be learning because we are not rewarding him in the way he has grown to expect. The second way is to go along with him. This may make learning slow, but if we have no alternative rewards we may have to do this. The third is to use material reward in addition to social reward, and to combine this technique with ignoring silly behaviour.

The child in the example we are going to describe was blind. He did not walk, although he was physically capable. When spoken to or praised he stood up, smiled, held out his arms and circled on the spot. But when he was called, he simply went on circling. He had learned that if he got up and circled when his name was called, people came to him and picked him up. This way he did not have to risk walking. The target was to get him to walk forwards when called.

It was noticed that he liked to hear a handbell being rung,

and would move toward this. So a teaching programme was set up where he was rewarded for walking an increasing number of steps (up to 40), while the teacher said, 'Good boy, Johnny', and then rang the bell once for each step. When he had reached the required number of steps, he was given the bell to ring himself. He was also cuddled and swung round, all of which he liked very much.

The ringing of the bell was dropped out progressively over trials. 'Good boy' was kept in for each step until the whole of a walk was rewarded only verbally.

So by pairing a verbal and sensory reward, an inappropriate response to the verbal reward was gradually eliminated.

Example 7. Trapping the adult

Children frequently learn responses which force an adult into behaving in the way the child wants. Very often the adult feels he has to give in to prevent the child or someone else from getting hurt. In these cases the child is responsive to reward, but the adult cannot use this fact to the child's benefit.

Several short examples illustrate a variety of such situations:

Leila screams loudly and repeatedly when she knows meals are on their way. She stops when she gets her food. The staff hurry to give her her food and give it to her before anyone else in order to quieten her.

Jan gets hold of another child's hair and holds it ready to pull hard whenever an adult comes near. When attended to she smiles and releases the child's hair. Adults in this situation attend to Jan very quickly in order to stop the other child from getting his hair pulled.

Andrew hits his head against the wall in a playful fashion but with increasing severity when he has failed to get adult attention. When the adult does attend, he smiles and plays appropriately. The adult attends quickly to prevent the child hurting himself.

When being taught, Hazel refuses to perform appropriately until she is rewarded. When rewarded she performs well, but frequently stops—and will not begin until she is 'bribed' again. The adult bribes her because he needs to keep the session going.

In each case the problem is the same:

(1) The response of the child is unacceptable.

(2) The response is designed to get a reward from the adult.

(3) In order to stop the unacceptable behaviour the adult must reward. He is trapped and coerced into rewarding.

Sometimes these behaviours are very difficult to change. Three possible remedies can be used, usually together:

(1) *Reduce the chances of the response occurring*, by keeping the child out of the situation which leads to the behaviour.

(2) *Teach the child alternative responses* to get his rewards in the situation.

    The children in several of these examples suffer from the fact that they have only limited ways of getting adult attention. And these ways are not good ones. The answer here is to teach them *new* ways of getting attention. One good way could be to come over to the adult and get hold of his hand. In all cases this response would need to be prompted. This was done with Jan and Andrew.

(3) *Stop rewarding the unacceptable response.* Clearly we must do (2) and (3) together. To stop rewarding before the child has the opportunity to get rewarded by other means would probably fail. And it would be frustrating for the child.

With Leila, several steps were taken to reduce the screaming:

(1) The length of time she had to sit waiting for meals was reduced.

(2) She was rewarded with attention and sweets when she sat quietly waiting for her meal.

(3) Attention and sweets as well as lunch were withheld for 30 seconds when she screamed.

So she was punished by having food taken away and attention withdrawn if she screamed, and was rewarded with attention and food for quiet sitting and for eating. The few additional sweets she got did not affect her appetite for dinner.

For Hazel, the child who was being bribed by the teacher, the strategy concentrated on solutions (2) and (3).

(1) No changes in the general situation in the classroom.
(2) The teacher switched to an easy task for a short period—this meant that the child got a high level of reward whenever she worked.
(3) When the child stopped work she was ignored. Tantrums were recorded, Hazel was not at physical risk. When Hazel was quiet she was prompted once every 30 seconds to respond, but no free rewards were given.

In this case most weight is put on getting rid of the bad behaviour by not rewarding it.

The strategies described were all at least moderately successful. Leila's screaming declined, though she still has a tendency to scream. Jan stopped pulling hair and Andrew stopped banging his head when taught to approach adults directly, though Andrew would still 'threaten' at times after six months. Hazel's problem was wiped out within 20 sessions.

Example 8. Generalisation of responsiveness

Quite often we come across children who are responsive to only one person. This can be a very complex problem, but we can offer some advice to help overcome it.

In the first place we quite often find that, although the 'new' teacher says that she is doing exactly the same thing as the 'accepted' person does, she actually is not. If there is this apparent failure in the child to generalise his response to new adults, it is worth watching the 'accepted' parent or teacher very closely to see exactly what she is doing and then copy it exactly. There are many ways of tickling, for instance!

Second, the child may simply not trust strangers. Here a gradual build-up of trust is necessary involving play which does not 'push' the child at first, but which is aimed to show him that you are friendly and rewarding.

A third possibility is that the child has learned certain habits of interacting with one person which he is now transferring to another. He may believe that adults are for smiling at rather than learning from. If this is the case, he will have to learn more appropriate ways of interacting, before he can be taught anything else. Example 6 page 86 suggests a strategy which can be used here.

CONCLUSION

In this chapter we have discussed the basics of teaching, the establishment of rewards and interests. If rewards have not been developed, we will have great difficulty in teaching the child. So unless the child can be scored on the ideal on all three assessment tables, we should try to include in our early teaching programmes some teaching in this area. Even if the child scores well, we should see the development of interests as crucial for his general development. Through observing how the child behaves in a rich environment, we can get crucial cues as to how we may be able to push his teaching further ahead.

In the next chapter we shall continue the theme of developing the child's interests. We shall see that this leads us to some very exciting ideas on development.

6: Developing Choice and Self-Control

In the introduction to Chapter 5 we pointed out that choice is fundamental to development. Only if the child can express his choices can he tell us what he prefers. And if we accept that we need to follow the child's own interests in fostering his development, he must have some way of telling us what he prefers.

Choice involves deciding on one of several alternatives and staying with that alternative. This involves a good deal of self-control. As we shall see, we can teach the child self-control through choosing situations.

ASSESSMENT OF CHOOSING AND SELF-CONTROL

Table 4 lists the stages in development of choice and self-control.

Table 4. Choosing and Self-Control

(1) The child prefers some activities to others.

(2) The child is unable to stick with his choice even if the adult helps by putting other things away.

(3) Chooses: Stays with his choice until he has completed the activity if he cannot have access to alternatives.

(4) Chooses and shows self-control. Can resist temptations even if alternatives are readily available to him.

(5) Self-control: Rewards himself in settings where he has performed well.

(6) Self-control: Punishes himself in settings where he has done something wrong.

1. The child prefers some activities to others
Here we know that the child prefers some activities to others, because he shows pleasure in being fed with one type of food

but not with another. Or he reacts with pleasure to being swung on the swing but is merely passive when put in his cot. However, the child does not show consistent choice when allowed to pick amongst activities himself. See Example 1 page 93.

2. The child is unable to stick with his choice even if the adult helps by putting other things away
When offered a selection of things he likes, he usually chooses in the same way. But he will flit from one thing to another. For instance he will pick a puzzle to play with, but before completing it he will look for and start playing with a stacking toy. Children of this type are often said to be 'hyperactive' or 'lacking in concentration'. An alternative way of seeing the problem is that the child has not learned to make a choice and stay with it. See Example 1 page 93.

3. Chooses: Stays with his choice until he has completed the activity if he cannot have access to alternatives
Having chosen a puzzle he completes it. Having chosen an ice lolly he eats it before trying to get ice-cream. But the adult has to help him by putting the alternatives away. If this is not done the child will switch choices. See Example 1 page 93.

4. Chooses and shows self-control. Can resist temptations even if alternatives are readily available to him
The child chooses and completes an activity even if others are readily available to him. He may also react to interference, such as taking the thing he has chosen away, or putting alternatives out of sight in order to help him to control his behaviour. Example 4 page 95 discusses self-control further.

5. Self-Control: Rewards himself in settings where he has performed well
The child may clap when he completes a puzzle or go and get a drink when he has dressed himself. Self-reward can be verbal but does not need to be. See Examples 2 and 3 pages 94 and 95.

6. Self-Control: Punishes himself in settings where he has done something wrong
A child who has been smacked for throwing may learn to smack

himself after throwing an object. A child may bang an object on the table and then shout angrily if he has been shouted at for banging. We would not consider that teaching a child to punish himself is a good thing. Self-punishment is not necessarily effective in stopping behaviour, and *may* lead to self-destructive behaviour. See Example 4 page 95.

TEACHING CHOICE AND SELF-CONTROL

Example 1. Developing choosing and self-control

Karen flitted from one activity to another in the classroom although she could play appropriately in several settings.

The target of the programme was to teach Karen to control her flitting.

The teaching involved a daily session lasting 10 to 20 minutes. The child was seated with the teacher in a small individual teaching room. At first she would not sit for more than a few seconds. A combination of social and material rewards for sitting and playing for increasing periods of time, and time-out in the form of ignoring her when she got down from the table, got her sitting and playing for the whole session within two weeks.

But she would switch rapidly from one activity to another when given five interesting pieces of play equipment.

The strategy used to teach choosing and self-control was as follows:

(1) The teacher laid out the five tasks and then said 'Look, Karen, you choose'. When Karen chose, the teacher pushed the other toys away behind a screen. Karen was rewarded for playing with the toy for a minimum of two to three minutes by social rewards. The alternatives, minus the first preference, were then all offered again and Karen was allowed to choose. An extra activity was put in to keep up the numbers. The same procedure was followed until the end of the session.

The idea behind this part of the programme was to teach the child that when she made a choice she had to stick with it. At first she would push away some bits of equipment after a few seconds. If this happened she was required to sit until two minutes had elapsed. She was not rewarded during this time.

(2) When Karen was playing consistently throughout the session, after three weeks of sessions, the procedure changed. Instead of the teacher pushing the alternative toys away, Karen was prompted to do it herself, and was rewarded when she did it. She caught on to this quite rapidly, doing it spontaneously in the second session. This already showed the development of a degree of self-control, although the teacher was still rewarding her.

(3) The third phase in this programme was to teach the child to tolerate having the alternatives before her. First one and then other alternatives were left on the table, and Karen was rewarded for playing without touching them after she had chosen. Teacher rewards were then gradually phased out.

(4) The final phase in the programme involved generalisation of the new behaviour to the classroom. This was only partially successful. Karen would select a toy with guidance, but could 'maintain concentration' only if she was allowed to sit at a desk without other toys around or on it.

Example 2. Self-reward

The simplest examples here involve material reward. The basic procedure involves two steps:

(1) The child is rewarded for a response by being given a sweet or drink by the teacher. It is best to use a fairly easy task or series of tasks, which the child can complete quickly and which have clear end points: such as completing form board or posting box puzzles. This is important because the child must be able to know for himself when he has been successful.

Once the child has reached the stage of completing each puzzle easily, we can move on to step 2.

(2) The sweet or drink is put within the child's reach at the *beginning* of the puzzle. If he reaches for it then, cover it and say, 'No, do the puzzle'. When he has started to do the puzzle take your hand away. At the end of the

puzzle, prompt him to take the reward, if this is necessary. Experience with this situation suggests that the child will be cued to take the reward by completing the puzzle. If the child keeps reaching for the reward after the first couple of trials, he can be given time-out—the puzzle and the reward are withdrawn for 20 seconds or so.

Once the child has learned to control his self-reward with one sweet or drink available, put two or three in front of him, making sure he takes only one at a time.

At this stage it is useful to stand or sit behind the child, as a step towards fading yourself out.

When the child will reward himself only when he has completed his task, the task can be changed or made more difficult.

Example 3. Problems of self-reward

We have seen children who have learned to clap themselves in self-reward, in imitation of adults who have rewarded them by clapping. Interesting as it is, this behaviour is very difficult to control. The child can reward himself for inappropriate behaviour! If we teach the child to reward himself using material rewards, we can control the situation reasonably well.

Example 4. Self-control

We will not illustrate a programme to teach for self-punishment, though quite frequently children do learn to punish themselves by smacking or by hurting themselves in other ways. Aside from the undesirability of these responses, the problem with this kind of 'punishment' is that it does not reliably lead to better behaviour. As with other punishment situations, the 'bad' behaviour is not *replaced* by better. In addition, teaching the child to punish himself, or for that matter just punishing him, may lead to him punishing himself excessively and becoming self-destructive.

Teaching a competing behaviour at the same time that you reward self-control, on the other hand, can be very valuable in dealing with self-destructive behaviour.

An actual example may make these points clearer.

One child tended to get into a mood which began with his being noisy and bad tempered and culminating with him hitting and scratching himself, gouging his eyes and banging his head. His teacher could predict the sequence exactly, including the moment when he would start hurting himself. In desperation she restrained him by lacing him into a hammock at the beginning of the sequence. She found that he calmed down after a time and could be released. Then the interesting thing happened. At the beginning of one sequence *he* came to *her* and indicated that he wanted to be restrained. This she did. After that he had no more 'attacks' without coming to her first. Gradually the frequency of attacks and the need for restraint declined. But this only happened as he learned other skills.

This was in effect an instance of the child punishing himself for self-destructive behaviour by getting himself restrained. The problem was that while he was restrained he could not do anything else, so the key to success involved the teacher in building up the child's alternative classroom behaviour between times.

We can thus try to teach the child to switch to behaviours which compete with the undesirable behaviour. The last step of the choice programmes we described above illustrates this process. The child is rewarded for making a choice and then putting alternative toys or material rewards away. Putting the toys away is a behaviour which competes with playing with the alternative toy or eating the sweets. So the child gains self-control, and replaces an undesirable behaviour with a desirable one.

Another example arises when a child is excluded from a classroom in order to cool off when he has done something unacceptable—essentially the same strategy as the use of time-out. Once the child has learned that he will be excluded for unacceptable behaviour, he can be allowed to put himself into time-out. So when he feels he is going to flip he can ask to leave the classroom in order to cool off. Care must be taken to make sure that cooling off time is not more pleasant than class time, or the child will learn to use this as a way to get out of the classroom! But if these precautions are taken, the child can take himself off to cool down and return when he is calm. Once the child has acquired the general strategy of replacing unacceptable behaviour (like hitting other people) with acceptable (asking to go out to cool off), he is likely also to learn other ways of cooling down. He may imitate other children's responses to anger or frustration in order to deal with these emotions himself.

Experience with these procedures for developing self-control suggests that the earlier the child can interrupt the sequence of build-up of violent reactions to frustration, anger or temptation, the better will be the result. So in teaching self-control we should observe the sequence of build-up very carefully. Teaching should then begin by interrupting the sequence with time-out or prompted withdrawal at the earliest point at which we can definitely predict a bad outcome.

CONCLUSION

This chapter on choice and self-control appears to have taken us a good way beyond the simple question of rewards and interests. What we would stress is that choosing and self-control are very important and basic behaviours which we can and should teach the child early in his learning programme. All the children described in this chapter are severely handicapped, and all of them have been successfully taught to improve their capacity to choose, and to control their own behaviour.

7: Finding Out about the World

It is very difficult to imagine what the world must seem like to a baby a few days or weeks old. His waking hours may seem like a blur of sounds, shapes and colours, of light and dark. He feels distress when hungry or uncomfortable, and contentment when fed and warm. All else is confusion.

Somehow, over the first few months of life, the child begins to find order in this confusion. He begins to recognise that there is some consistency and sense to his world. He begins to realise that he is not the total world but part of it. Rather than feeling that all he sees is within himself, he is now able to look outside and see shapes and objects as something different from himself. He comes to realise that parts of this world can directly affect him and that he can affect the world. He begins to associate events. He sees his parents as objects connected with food and comfort. He comes to realise that he can exercise a certain amount of control over these things. Crying will sometimes bring food and comfort.

This stage of early development, the process of ordering the world, is probably the least understood of all the processes of development and learning. But what we do know suggests that the child needs to follow a series of steps in order to reach a particular state of understanding; and that the order of these steps is important. For instance, the child cannot associate his parents with food and comfort until he is able to see his parents as different from other things—they are not just part of the blurred background of his room, but something separate. He needs to be able to focus his eyes in order to see the difference; and he needs to be able to hear differences in sound before he can recognise the sound of his parents' voices.

It is not within the scope of this book to examine infant development in detail. What we hope to do, however, is to give some guidelines as to what to look for in your child's behaviour as an aid to understanding his development. By seeing the way your child responds to various experiences you should be able to tell how much he does understand of the world. You should then be able to tell what is likely to come next in his development. This will help you to know how best to play with your child, what games he is likely to understand and what he is likely to find confusing.

Having emphasised that the development of understanding about the world occurs in a definite order, we must also stress that no two children develop in the same way. Normal development is very difficult to define, and though it is helpful to think of it as taking place in an orderly manner, it is easy to oversimplify. The child looks at things and events at random. He slowly builds up his picture of the world, as a result of his experiences of seeing and hearing and touching. Who can guess how many times a child needs to touch an object before he realises that it is the same object he has seen from his cot every day? He needs to learn that looking at an object and touching it provide him with different information about the same object.

Thus though the development of abilities needs to occur in order—there is no way for instance that the child could possibly learn that the object he feels and the object he looks at are the same object, until he can handle the object and look at it at the same time—how *many* times this looking and touching needs to occur will be different for each child.

This variation is also true of the number of different objects a child will need to handle and see before he is able to predict what an object will feel like just by looking at it. At first he will remember the sight and the touch of only those objects he experiences very frequently, such as his bottle or teddy. Then, as he learns how to move about in his cot and to reach out and grasp objects, he will be able to experience a greater variety of objects. He will learn that some things taste and feel similar, but look different. In order to learn this he must be able to reach and grasp, to look at what he is reaching for, to look at it when it is in his hands, and to take his hands to his mouth.

Consequently we can be fairly safe in saying that a child will need to be able to do certain things before he is able to do other things. However, we cannot predict how well and how frequently he will use these skills, nor how much he needs to use them in order to teach a particular understanding of his world. This will vary from child to child.

This leads us to the problem of what we expect from a handicapped child. Much will depend on the nature of his handicap, but even then it is dangerous to generalise. Mentally handicapped children are slow in developing their understanding of the world. It may be that they are physically able to move around, reach and grasp, look at objects and so on, but choose not to. Hence they themselves are limiting the amount of experience they have of the surroundings. They may not be as eager to explore their world and experiment as other children.

On the other hand your child may be very active and spend much time handling objects, sucking and chewing them, yet have failed to move on to anything more advanced. His experience of handling, looking at and sucking objects has had little effect on his understanding of the world.

More often than not you will find that his handicap is a result of a combination of both these problems: lack of desire to experiment and do things for himself, and slowness in actually learning from this experience.

Children with other handicaps, or combinations of handicaps, will be limited in other ways. If your child is severely physically handicapped, he may have difficulty in reaching and grasping objects, or may have problems in moving to an object to find out what it is, what it feels like and tastes like. Children with poor vision are able to explore objects only when they are immediately at hand. Even if they have no learning difficulties, they are receiving much less information about their world than children with normal sight, so their understanding of the world will develop more slowly (though this does not mean that it will always be incomplete).

As parents and teachers of handicapped children we need to think of ways to help compensate for the child's lack of experience, or lack of ability to benefit from experience. There is, of course, no possible way that we can predict how well a young handicapped child will develop, nor what effect a particular handicap will have on him, but what we can do is to offer some general pointers as to how development should take place, and how to help this development.

Example 1. Looking at objects

In order for children to begin to understand the world about them they need first to have some way of collecting information. Most children have the ability to see, hear, touch and taste, and these four senses are the tools that they will use. But children do need to learn how to use their senses.

Learning how to look at an object, and see it as different from its background, is probably one of the first abilities to develop in the very young child. It is not, however, an ability that children are born with. If you observe a very young baby, you may be able to trace some of the steps he takes as he learns to look at things.

Table 5 shows a possible sequence of steps. Most children will pass through these with no difficulty, but this is not true of every child. Difficulties may arise as a result of damage to the eye or optic nerve, or to the parts of the brain which are concerned with sight. In some cases medical examination or other forms of assessment can reveal the cause of the problem and determine the extent of the damage and the possibility of it being rectified.

It is often the case, however, that nothing can be seen to be wrong, in which case you may have to teach your child to use his visual abilities. The sequence of steps shown in Table 1 will act as a guide to this teaching programme.

Table 5. The ability to look at an object

(1) Does your child change his facial expression or become more excited or more calm when a bright object (such as a torch covered with red tissue paper) is brought near his face? His eyes may move around or look away, but does he seem to be aware of something near to him?

(2) Does your child seem to make an attempt to look in the direction of an object? His control may be poor so you may notice that his eyes keep drifting away from the object and he needs to make frequent adjustments to the direction of his looking.

(3) Is he able to look at a weak pencil torch for three seconds or more without wavering his eyes?

(4) Is your child able to look at a bright but non-illuminated object, such as a small car or feeding bottle, without wavering his eyes? If he is able to do this you can probably assume that he can look at and distinguish objects from their background.

The procedure for teaching will, of course, depend on the age of the child, and on whether he suffers from poor head control or not. If he does, the first step in planning the programme will be to find a position which enables your child to keep his head relatively steady. Young children could be placed on their backs in a cot, but older children will probably be more comfortable in a chair with some form of head support (rolls or wedges have been used successfully with some cerebral palsied children).

Step 2 is to find a suitable reward. This will of course vary from child to child. A feeding bottle, singing, food of various kinds can be considered. As we have seen already, reward will act as your way of telling him that he has done well, and is also a way of motivating him to do it again.

The final step in planning will be to select suitable objects to use in the teaching. In the assessment chart in Table 5 we suggested that the first object to be used should be one which can easily be distinguished from the background: a torch covered with tissue paper is ideal to begin with. When your child becomes proficient at looking at this, change to bright non-illuminated objects such as a small car, a mirror or a ball of tinsel.

Always try to work with the object placed before a dull, uniform background. This will ensure that there is a good contrast between object and background.

The starting point for teaching will depend on what your child is able to do now, according to the assessment chart in Table 5. The technique, however, remains the same for each of the steps. Prompt your child to turn or lift his head in the direction of the object. If necessary hold his head in this position and bring the torch or object to within about two feet of his face. Depending on which stage you are teaching at the time, reward immediately you see your child behave appropriately for that stage. For instance if you are teaching at stage 1, reward your child when you notice he has become aware of the object in front of him. If you are working on stage 3, wait until he has looked directly at the torch for about three seconds and then reward.

Example 2. Looking from one object to another
When your child is able to look steadily at an object, your next consideration should be to assess his ability to look from one object to another. This introduces the idea of being able to choose what he wants to look at, and leads on to being able to explore larger objects visually. Table 6 gives a possible sequence of stages for this.

Table 6. Visual exploration
(1) Using objects which you know to be of interest to your child, hold one about two feet away from him and wait until he is looking at it. When his attention is fixed on the first object, bring the second object slowly into his field of view. Does he glance from the first to the second object?
(2) Assuming that both objects are equally interesting to your child, is he able to look from one to the other when both objects are held still?
(3) An important application of this ability to shift attention, is to be able to look at different parts of the same object. For instance, do you notice your child looking at different parts of your face when you come close to him?

There are many important implications in these steps. If your child is able to achieve stage 1, he is making use of the edge of his field of view. He also knows how to control the movements of his eyes enough to be able to turn them, and bring the new object into focus. If he moved on to stage 2, he clearly has this ability fully under control, and also shows an awareness that two or more objects can exist at the same time. Stage 3 demonstrates that he is able to, or at least moving towards being able to, build up a total picture of something from its component parts. This is obviously an important step. It provides the basis for seeing similarities and differences between objects, and for learning to recognise objects or the faces of familiar people. It allows him, in fact, to start building up ideas about the world around him.

Teaching these skills will follow a similar pattern to that described in the above programmes. For stage 1, use two interesting objects and place your child in a position where support for the head can easily be given. Hold one object about two feet away from him, and wait until he is looking at it steadily. When he is, bring the second object slowly and quietly into his field of view. Reward him immediately he glances from the first to the second object. If he fails to look at the second object until it is at the centre of his field of vision, or if his gaze wanders from the first object to nothing in particular, begin again.

You may find that your child tries to reach for the objects you are using. If this happens do not discourage it, because you may be able to use the objects as additional rewards for glancing from one to the other.

Stage 2 is a natural progression from the above. In this you will require your child to glance from the first to the second object and back again before you reward. You can develop this situation by increasing the distance between the objects, or by requiring several changes of glance as he improves his skill.

Stage 3, visual exploration of an adult's face, is a very natural teaching situation which most parents discover without the aid of a book. However, it puts the behaviour you require from your child into the context of a learning sequence. This sequence demonstrates the types of skills your child needs to learn before he is able to achieve stage 3. Reward your child by smiling and talking when he looks at your face and glances from eyes to mouth and so on.

Example 3. Looking at moving objects

The final section on looking at objects concerns the ability to follow moving objects with the eye or with head and eyes. This ability should begin to develop as, or shortly after, your child learns how to shift his glance from one object to another. Most parents notice the development of this skill when they see that their child is able to follow them about the room with his eyes.

Table 7 shows a possible sequence of stages. Your child will begin by being able to follow regular and predictable sideways and up-and-down movements. He should then progress to following irregular and unpredictable movements.

Table 7. The ability to follow a slowly moving object with the eyes

(1) Present an interesting or brightly coloured object about two feet away from the child. When he is looking at it steadily, move it slowly sideways for about six inches. Does he follow the movement with eyes or head and eyes? Is he able to repeat this when you move it in the other direction?

(2) The same as above, but moving the object upward, and then downward.

(3) The same as above but making a small circular movement with the object. You may notice that it is difficult for the child to follow this movement for a complete circle. If your child is able to follow most of the movement, this is satisfactory.

(4) Make the object move in a series of slow but irregular curves away from and towards your child. If he is able to follow this type of movement for five seconds or more, visual following should present no problem.

An essential part of teaching these skills is to use objects which your child is interested in. A feeding bottle, a piece of biscuit or a favourite doll could well be suitable; or a coloured torch could be used, with the biscuit or bottle being given as the reward for successful following.

When beginning to teach any one of these steps, present the object about two feet away from your child. Wait until he is looking steadily at it, and then move it about six inches. Reward him if he succeeds in following it with his eyes. As he learns what is required of him, begin to make larger movements and vary the distance at which you present the object. If he is able to move head and eyes to follow the object, all the better. But some children, particularly cerebral palsied children, have great difficulty with head control, so if this is the case, concentrate for the time being on the eyes alone. This will mean keeping the movements fairly small.

Example 4. Combining vision with other abilities

We are now going to discuss how hearing, sight and touch combine to give your child a meaningful impression of his world. We have already spoken of the importance of being able to look at something and reach for it, and of being able to look at it while it is being handled. Only when your child is able to do these things will he understand the meaning of what he sees in terms of physical dimensions and texture.

Having to reach for something helps him learn about distances and perspective. Certain objects will appear small because they are some way from him. Others will appear large because they are close. Unless he has attempted to reach for a distant object and found it impossible to touch, he will be unable to understand this idea of perspective. In time he should learn to take account of more of the many clues which we use in making judgements of distance, but to do this he will need to experiment and explore. Reaching and grasping is the first step in this process.

In addition he will need to learn how to use hearing to locate an object. When he hears a noise he will turn to see what made it, and then perhaps reach out in its direction. For children with sight problems turning and reaching is particularly important. They may need to be taught how to locate the direction of sound, and to reach in that direction.

Another important function of your child's early attempts to reach and grasp is that they will provide the beginnings of his ideas of cause and effect. For instance, if the child reaches for an object and knocks it over, it may disappear from view. By reaching for and knocking the object over he has altered his immediate situation. Or if he succeeds in grasping a squeaky toy or rattle it may make a noise. He may not at first associate the noise with his holding of the object, but after several attempts he may come to realise that, again, he has had an effect on an object in his environment. Learning to reach and grasp will represent the beginning of your child's understanding of cause and effect.

Table 8 shows a possible sequence of behaviours leading to visually directed grasping. Assess your child to see what stage he has reached in this sequence. It is possible to teach each of these stages. However, from stage 3 onwards it will be necessary for your child to be able to look at objects in the manner we described in the previous section. Consequently you should see this section as following directly on from the previous one in terms of a teaching programme.

Table 8. Visually directed grasping

(1) Is your child able to grasp small objects that are placed in his hand?

(2) If your child touches an object, will he sometimes grasp it? At this point it is not necessary for him either to look at the object when his hand touches it, or to lift it to his eyes or his mouth when it is held in his hand.

(3) If an interesting object is within your child's reach, does he grasp it if he can see both his hand and the object at the same time?

(4) Does your child reach and grasp for an object if the object is placed in front of him, and his hands are to the side? This is a more advanced stage than stage 3, as he will now grasp even if he is unable to see the object and his hand at the same time.

(5) Does your child have some idea of how far objects are away from him? You will be able to judge this by looking at the way your child attempts to reach and grasp objects placed at varying distances. He will grasp objects that are within reach without attempting to move his body forward. He will move his body forward when grasping objects just outside his reach. He will not attempt to grasp objects that are placed too far for his reach; or he will stop attempting to reach for an object when it is moved away from him. He may revert to pointing at it or crying if it is something that he really wants to hold, such as a feeding bottle or biscuit.

(6) Does your child move his body forward to help him grasp an object which is out of reach? This is the final step in the development of visually directed grasping.

As in the previous section, you will need to find a comfortable position for your child to work in. A sitting position is likely to be the most effective, although some physically handicapped children may work better over a roll or wedge. The other essentials are an effective reward and a number of small interesting objects. Coloured cubes, about an inch along on each face, coloured rods or pieces of cloth will probably be suitable to begin with. However, as the teaching progresses and your child becomes more skilful at reaching for and selecting objects, you may notice that he begins to show preferences for certain types of objects. If this happens, use these preferred objects whenever possible.

Example 5. Grasping

Teaching the first stage in Table 8 should be a simple prompt and fade process. Place a small object in your child's hand, fold his fingers around the object and hold his fingers closed. Praise him while he is holding the object, and if you have selected an edible reward, such as a piece of biscuit or a drink of milk, give him this reward after about 10 seconds. When he has finished his reward, remove the object from his hand, pause for a few seconds and then begin again. At the beginning of each attempt say something like 'Hold the block, Peter'. As the session progresses fade your prompt by gradually reducing the amount of support that you give in keeping his hand closed.

By the end of step one of this stage you should have faded the prompt to the point where he needs assistance only in closing his fingers around the object. Once this has happened he will continue holding the object until after he has been rewarded.

You must now concentrate on fading the prompt necessary to get him closing his hand around the object. Do this by placing the object in the palm of his hand and then giving his fingers a push in the right direction for closing. The feel of the object in the hand and the prompt to begin the closing action should now be enough cue for him to continue until his hand is clenched. Fade the initial push that you need to give to his fingers, until you reach the point where the feel of the object in the palm of the hand is enough to make him close his hand around it.

By the end of this stage you will have taught your child to

make the basic grasping response. Before you move on to teaching the next stage, make sure that this grasping action occurs when you use a variety of objects. If you taught the first stage by using a small cube, try it now with several other different shaped objects, such as a rod or piece of cloth. This is a necessary check to ensure that generalisation of the skill has taken place.

Example 6. Looking at the object and grasping it

Assuming that your child is able to look at objects, he should now be ready to move on to stage 3 in Table 8. This will involve prompting him to grasp the object while he is looking at it. You can arrange this in two ways. You can either hold the object, òr place it on a surface: which you choose depends on the position of the child during the session. The important point is that the object is presented immediately in front of him. Move his hand to within a few inches of the object, and, when you are certain that he is looking in the direction of the object and his hand, say 'Hold the block, Peter' and prompt his hand to close over the object. If your teaching of stage 1 has been effective, he should grasp it when he feels it touching his hand. Praise him as soon as he grasps the object, and then reward him for holding it for five seconds or more.

When you prompt him at the beginning of this stage, hold your child's wrist or forearm. As the teaching progresses, gradually fade the prompt of lifting his hand to the object, and allow him to finish the action on his own. As you fade the prompt, require him to do more and more of the final part of the action. By doing this you should reach the point where all that he needs to grasp the object is a touch of his wrist when you say 'Hold the block, Peter'.

By the end of stage 3 your child should readily grasp and hold small objects when they are near to his hand.

The remaining stages in this section should follow on naturally. Stage 4 will require you gradually to increase the distance between his hand and the object before starting each attempt. Where this distance is such that he is unable to see both the object and his hand at the same time, you may need to prompt him to bring his hand into the same field of view as the object. The teaching aim of this stage will be to fade this prompt so that eventually he will move his hand towards the object when you say 'Hold the block, Peter'. By this time, of course, he may be reaching for the block as soon as it is placed in front of him.

Teaching stages 5 and 6 will be extensions of the previous steps. Your child should now be able to reach and grasp for objects placed in front of him without the aid of a prompt.

Begin to vary the distance between his hand and the object. Use one object at a time, and for the first attempt put it close to his chest. If he succeeds in grasping it, reward him, and then place the object to one side, and so on. As the teaching progresses move the object out to a point which requires him to stretch in order to grasp it. Move to this point gradually, all the time interspersing long reaches with short reaches.

When he is used to turning his body slightly to reach the object in one position, and stretching to reach it in another, begin to place the object just outside of his grasping range. If he stretches his arm, finds that he cannot reach and gives up, prompt him to move his body as well as his arm in the right direction. Repeat this position over a number of attempts and fade the prompt to his body.

A programme such as this should help your child to judge grasping range, and also teach him how to move towards an object which is beyond grasping range. Once he is able to achieve this, he should be proficient at visually directed reaching and have the basic skills necessary for developing exploratory play.

SOUND, TOUCH AND SIGHT

So far in this chapter we have spoken of ways to teach your child to look at objects, to grasp objects, and to reach for objects that he is looking at. We now need to consider the basic skills involved in hearing. These are obviously important skills because of their implications for language development (see Chapter 10 on Communication). Appropriate response to sounds will also help with general awareness of his surroundings.

Table 9 gives a sequence of possible responses to sound. At the simplest level your child demonstrates that he is aware of sounds, but he makes no attempt to investigate the sound or seek its source. In stage 2 he will turn in the direction of the sound. If he looks at the person or object that made the sound, then he is clearly able to combine visual skills with hearing skills. Stage 4 takes him a step further. Once he has seen the object which produces the noise he will attempt to reach for the object. The success of this venture will depend on how advanced he is in the skills described in the previous section.

If he is able to reach and grasp, or attempt to reach and grasp, an object after he has heard it making a noise, hearing has become an important key to exploring his surroundings. There is now a link between touching, hearing and sight, and he can begin to learn that the same object can appear attractive, feel good to hold and even produce interesting noises.

Table 9. Response to sound

(1) Does your child change his facial expressions or become more excited or more calm when a sound is made near to him?

(2) Does your child attempt to turn in the direction of the sound when a noise is made near to him?

(3) Is your child able to turn to the sound and look at the object or person that made it?

(4) If your child turns to look at the object that made the sound, will he attempt to reach for it?

Example 7. Teaching response to sound

If your child makes only a minimal response to sound, it may indicate that he has hearing problems or that he needs to be taught that sounds are a significant part of his surroundings. In order to teach your child to respond to sound, you need to collect together a few toys such as a rattle, a bell, a small tambourine, and find an effective reward.

The programme will be best taught in a quiet room. Work from behind your child so that he is unable to see your hand movements. Make a noise with one of the instruments, to one side and slightly behind him. If he makes no response, prompt him to turn his head in the direction of the sound, and then reward immediately. If, after several attempts, he is still making no spontaneous effort to turn, try using a different instrument. As long as you detected at least a minimal response to sound in your assessment, this procedure should eventually teach him to turn in the direction of the sound.

There are several problems with running this type of programme:

(1) You need to ensure that you produce sounds on either side of his body. But try not to do this as a regular alternation of left, right, left, right. Your child may be quick in picking up this pattern. Change the position at random.

(2) Once your child has learned that by turning his head he receives a reward, he will be able to turn to either side with a one in two chance of being correct. This turning may be unrelated to his hearing the sound. Thus in a session he can receive a good number of rewards for merely turning his head.

(3) An extension of this situation may develop, and your child may spend the whole session trying to turn towards you because he has initially been rewarded for turning.

A solution to this last problem is for two people to act as teachers. One can sit in front of the child and keep him attending to the front. The second person can work from behind and produce the noises to one side or the other. If a correct response is made, or the second person prompts the response, the first person can then reward. Because the reward always comes from the front the child may be less tempted to keep turning, except when the sound is produced.

However, it is often difficult for one parent or teacher, let alone two, to find time enough to work for a quarter of an hour with one child. So if only one person is available to teach, try some of the following suggestions:

Once the child has begun to turn without prompt, reward only when he turns in the correct direction immediately the sound is made. Keep the length of the sound short, between one and two seconds. Ignore whatever responses he makes if he delays for longer than about two seconds after the sound has finished.

If he makes an incorrect or delayed response, prompt him to turn his head forward and wait for about fifteen seconds before starting again.

Vary the time between the end of one attempt and the beginning of another. This will make it difficult for him to predict when the sound is due. Consequently his only cue for responding will be the sound.

If he is making repeated attempts to turn without waiting for the sound, prompt him to face forward and wait until he has settled down before beginning again.

In order to help you decide how consistently he is responding, try making out a list of lefts and rights before you begin. Then during the session keep to this order and make a tick or a cross beside each position according to whether he made a correct or incorrect turn. This is better than trying to remember what happened, and it may also show whether he has a tendency to turn only in one direction. This information will help you to decide when he is ready to move on to the next stage.

CONCLUSION

Again in this chapter we have been talking about very fundamental abilities which are high priorities in development. Visually directed grasping is fundamental to a whole range of other behaviours, from development of understanding of depth, to exploratory and creative play.

In the next chapter we will go on to see how these fundamental abilities fan out in the child's development of ideas about objects and people.

8: Developing Ideas about Objects and People

Having covered some of the basic skills your child will need in order to investigate his surroundings, we must now look at the application of these skills as a means towards understanding the world. One important milestone is the development of an awareness that objects and people continue to exist even when they cannot be seen or heard. Very young children will handle and suck objects when they come to hand. If they drop the object they will make no attempt to find it. They will continue to move their hands until they find something else to take its place.

As the child's ability to look at things improves, he will begin to recognise familiar people and objects. Other senses are also important. He will learn to associate sounds with particular toys, and voices with particular people. He will slowly construct a picture of sameness and difference in his surroundings.

Once he has this idea, he is in a position to understand that objects and people can continue to exist even when he is not aware of them near him. But he will still need a great deal of experience to confirm this. In his play he will notice that toys can be lost and found. If he catches sight of a partly hidden toy, he may recognise it as his. By moving his head or moving a cover he can make the whole toy appear; then by making repeated movements he can make it appear or disappear at will.

Many games which young children play are based on this idea. Throwing favourite toys over the edge of the table or out of the cot, to be picked up over and over again by mum, can provide hours of fun; as will peek-a-boo. These sorts of games are part of the child's reconciliation of appearance and disappearance with continued existence. This is called the attainment of object permanence—the idea that objects have permanent existence even though you cannot see or hear them.

Once these ideas are established, the child's style of play is likely to change. Up until now he has been dealing with immediate situations in his surroundings. He played with things that he could see, or that were at hand. If favourite toys were not visible he would make do with others. He cried because he was uncomfortable and not because he wanted to attract his parents' attention. But once he realises that objects have a permanent existence unrelated to his own being, his activities become more purposeful. He begins to search for things which he has lost during play. This gives him more control over what he learns and how he learns. If he gets bored while playing with one type of toy he can stop and look for another. Crying will become a way of communicating with his parents rather than an expression of discomfort only.

The idea that objects have a permanent existence thus provides the child with a most important foundation for understanding his world. So it is necessary to ensure that he has as much opportunity as possible to learn the concept. This refers not only to the way that you teach and play with your child, but also to the way that you provide him with his own toys and possessions to be kept near him at all times. Children who spend their early life in hospitals or children's homes may lack this form of security. They are likely to have many different people looking after them, and they may have few toys of their own. The way they begin to learn about people and things is likely to be different from that of a child brought up in his own family.

OBJECT PERMANENCE

In Table 10 we have provided a series of tests which should help you to judge whether your child has an idea of object permanence. Each of the stages requires him to look for an object which has disappeared, and all but stage 5 require him to reach for the object.

If your child fails to reach for the partially hidden object, it is an indication either that he no longer recognises the object, or that he is not interested in it. You can test this by uncovering the object to see whether he will then reach for it. If he fails on several attempts to reach when it is partly hidden, but does

reach when it is uncovered, it is likely that he has yet to develop
an understanding of object permanence.

Table 10. Object permanence

(1) Find an object which your child will readily reach
for (a toy, a piece of biscuit, feeding bottle). While
your child is watching, if you partially cover the
object with a piece of cloth, will he now reach for
it?

(2) Will he attempt to reach for it if the object is
completely covered by the cloth?

(3) Will he reach for it if you hide it and then stop
him reaching for a short period of time (5
seconds)?

(4) If you have two pieces of cloth and hide the object
under one, will he reach for the correct cloth to
find the object?

(5) If you move quietly behind your child will he
follow you with his head and eyes as far as he can,
and then turn to find you on the other side of him?

Example 1. Teaching object permanence

Assuming that there are no problems with his ability to look,
reach and grasp, teaching object permanence should be
straightforward. Use an object which you know he will be keen
to reach for, and a piece of plain cloth as a cover. Place the
object immediately in front of your child at a distance which
will require him to reach forward to get it. Allow him to reach
for it once or twice without using the cloth, and once he has the
idea of what is required cover the edge of it with the cloth. If
you are using something small, like a sweet, at first merely place
the cloth to the edge of the sweet.

As the teaching progresses cover more of the object. With
large objects, such as a doll or a bottle, you can teach by slowly
covering more and more of the object. Small objects are
difficult to cover gradually, so you may find it easier to prompt
the child to remove the cloth, then fade the prompt.

Continue teaching in this way until he will reliably reach for
the object under the cloth. Now change the cover. Use different
coloured cloths or pieces of paper. Hide the object behind or

under other things. You may find that you need to teach the process again with new covers, because the behaviour you taught in the first place became a response to the particular cloth rather than a response to the hidden object. However, by using a variety of covers, and perhaps a variety of objects, it should be possible to evoke a response to the objects.

Once you have established this simple hiding and finding game, you have not only provided your child with a skill he can use when playing by himself, but you will find that a great many teaching possibilities will lead from it. By teaching stage 3 you will be demanding not only an idea of object permanence, but also the ability to remember the position of the object for a short period of time. Stage 4 introduces the idea of choice. Allow him to watch you hide the object under one of the two screens, and wait for two or three seconds before letting him respond. If he goes to the correct screen first, allow him to have the reward. If he goes to the wrong screen, remove the reward and start again. This becomes a test of object permanence, observation and memory.

There are two directions to take from here. You could teach him to persist in searching for objects or you could teach some form of simple discrimination.

SEARCH

Teaching your child to search for hidden objects is a natural extension of the idea of object permanence. When a child persists in searching for something which is lost, it is a clear indication that the idea of object permanence is firmly established.

Example 2. Searching for an object
A simple test or teaching situation would be to arrange two or three screens or crumpled cloths on a table. Show your child that you are holding an interesting object in your hand. Pass your hand under or behind each screen, leaving the object under one. Your child has to look for the object. Of course he has a good chance of finding it immediately, but if he fails, see whether he gives up or moves to the next screen. If he stops after the first attempt prompt him to lift the correct screen. By

using the technique of prompting and fading the prompt you should find that he will learn to persist when looking for a hidden object.

A useful second stage in this programme is to build in a delay between hiding the object and allowing him to search. This, in fact, brings the teaching closer to a real life situation. Now your child will have to remember what he is looking for and where it is likely to be found. He is no longer responding to an immediate problem, seeing the object hidden and searching for it. Introduce the delay gradually. Begin by hiding the object, and stop him reaching for two or three seconds. As he learns how to deal with this, increase the length of delay until you reach a point where he can cope with about twenty seconds and still find the object. If he can achieve this you have taught him a very useful strategy for dealing with his surroundings.

DISCRIMINATION

This is the ability to see differences or similarities between objects. If you have two beakers of the same size and shape, but of different colours, red and white for instance, and you consistently hide the sweet under the red one, you can teach your child to choose the correct beaker. When he is able to do this he is demonstrating an ability to discriminate between red and white. Alternatively you could use two beakers of the same shape and colour but of different size. You could consistently hide the sweet under the large one. In this case he will be discriminating between sizes.

Learning to see difference and similarity between objects is an extremely important skill. It forms the basis of the child's ability to order and categorise his surroundings. However, it is likely that children do not notice differences until these differences are made meaningful in some way.

Objects differ one from another along many dimensions and we use these as a basis for identifying them. Thus, in order to be able to identify reliably, a child may need to be aware of the object's size, shape, colour, texture and even perhaps its taste, the sound it makes and whether or not it moves.

In real life objects differ in many ways. A billiard ball and a ripe apple may be about the same size, red and round. But the ball is more symmetrical, it is very hard and colder than an apple and it smells different. It is also likely to hurt your teeth if you mistake it for an apple.

In order to discriminate between an apple and a billiard ball a child needs to be aware of these different dimensions, and to take account of several dimensions at once. Mentally handicapped children often find it very difficult to discriminate in terms of more than one feature at a time. Consequently when teaching a child to discriminate it is best to begin with one difference at a time. We have suggested using beakers of various colours and sizes because these represent a convenient method of teaching.

Example 3. Teaching discrimination of size, shape and colour

When selecting the beakers always ensure that they are different in only one respect—size, shape or colour. If they are different in more than one respect, you will be unable to tell which difference your child is responding to.

Over the first few attempts show your child which beaker you are placing the sweet under. This will act as his prompt. When he has got the idea of taking the sweet from under the beaker, put the sweet under while he is not looking. At this stage your target is that he should respond to the same beaker each time, using only its colour or shape as a cue. If he gets the choice correct he will be rewarded by finding the sweet. If he gets it wrong, do not let him go on to the other one. Take both the beakers away, wait a few seconds and start again.

A problem we have frequently encountered when using this type of programme is the child's tendency to respond to the position of the beaker rather than to its colour or size. Thus you may find your child going mainly for the beaker on the left, or mainly for the one on the right. This is the same problem as we described in the programme concerned with location of sound. Try to work out a similar solution by randomly alternating the side on which you present the correct beaker.

Example 4. Developing the programme

When you are satisfied that your child is discriminating between two beakers, for instance he always lifts the red one regardless of which side it is on, you can extend the programme in a number of ways. You could replace the white beaker with an orange one. Still keeping the sweet under the red he now needs to learn how to tell the difference between red and orange rather than red and white. In this way you can work your way through a series of colours. You might then try changing to size by using the same red beaker and introducing a larger red beaker. He is now to learn that the difference between the beakers is not one of colour but of size.

As you can imagine there are many variations on this theme. With careful planning you can direct the programme to teaching a range of skills, leading up to the beginnings of a language programme. A very simple programme for teaching the child to understand language uses this type of problem. Instead of being guided by a visual cue the child is guided by sound cue, 'red' or 'white'.

Example 5. Teaching discrimination by touch

Peter was a blind five-year-old. Up to the time we started working with him, he showed little or no play behaviour. He was unable to walk and showed no interest in exploring the world with his hands. He had no speech, and his understanding of others' speech was limited.

We planned two teaching programmes. One aimed at developing the use of his hands for exploring objects. The second aimed at teaching him to feed himself (discussed in Chapter 11). The two programmes were complementary in that they both concentrated on encouraging Peter to use his hands in a purposeful way. They both also involved the skills of search and grasp.

Although Peter rarely used his hands to explore, he had no problem with grasping when he touched an object. We planned a simple discrimination programme to help him become aware of objects, and of the differences between objects.

The first step was to find a suitable reward. This was not difficult as Peter often had biscuit mashed in warm milk when he arrived at school in the morning. He ate this with relish. Consequently, we ran the programme in the morning and used this as his reward.

Step 1: Preliminary teaching. Because Peter was blind and as yet unable to search with his hands, we needed to use objects that could be confined to one spot on the table. Pegs in a peg boat seemed to fit this requirement. The boat was six inches by three inches by three inches, and it had five half-inch holes. The pegs were half an inch in diameter and about five inches long.

Before we could begin to teach Peter to discriminate between objects we needed to teach the basic response of lifting the pegs from the boat. We did this by placing the boat in front of him, guiding his hand to the peg and prompting him to lift it out. After each prompt he was rewarded by a spoonful of biscuit.

Because he was unable to see when it was time for the next attempt, we said 'Give me the peg'. We hoped that he would learn to recognise this phrase as a cue for his next try.

The prompt of guiding his hand to the peg and lifting the peg out was faded within seven sessions. By this time he would move his hand along the peg boat, grasp the peg and lift it out when we said 'Give me the peg'. He released the peg after he had been given his milk and biscuit.

Step 2: Discriminating between rough and smooth. Now that Peter was able to lift out a peg we decided to introduce the discrimination task. The first discrimination was to be between a rough and smooth peg. We covered one peg with baking foil and left the second as smooth wood. Before each session we made a list of left/right positions, as described in the previous section.

Peter was now presented with the boat containing two pegs, and was asked to give the smooth peg. We used a system of prompting and time-out to teach him to ignore the rough one and lift out the smooth one. On some attempts, if he began to lift the rough peg, we would hold it down in the boat. This forced him to move his hand to the smooth peg and lift it out. He was rewarded for this. On other attempts he was allowed to lift out the rough peg and he received no reward.

Over the first six sessions the number of unprompted correct responses was variable. They averaged fifteen out of thirty, which was no higher than might have been achieved by chance. From session six to session ten the unprompted correct responses remained consistently at eighteen out of thirty.

During sessions eleven and twelve he was correct twenty-six times out of thirty, without a prompt. Peter was now clearly able to discriminate between the foil-covered peg and the smooth peg.

Step 3: Discrimination with a wool-covered peg. We followed the same procedure for step 3, but we replaced the foil-covered peg with one wrapped in wool. Peter was still required to remove the smooth peg. During the first session he got fifteen out of thirty correct without prompt. In the second session he made only four errors, and in the third session he made only one error. This demonstrated very good generalisation from step 2.

Step 4: The three pegs. We were now able to give Peter all three pegs: the foil-covered, the wool-covered and the smooth. With three pegs, he could not, as he had with two, place a hand on each and lift out the correct one. He often had to touch all three before making his choice. Thus this task required him not only to discriminate but also to search.

During the first three sessions he made between ten and thirteen errors in thirty attempts. (Remember there was now a two in three chance of him making an error.) During the fourth and fifth sessions he made only six errors in each. In the seventh he made four, and in the eighth he made only one.

We felt he had made good headway in discriminating between rough and smooth, and thought it appropriate to change the type of discrimination.

Step 5: Shape discrimination. The two objects we selected were an inch-square wooden cube and a wooden ball about an inch in diameter. For this discrimination the textures were the same and the sizes were similar. Shape was the critical difference. We covered the peg boat with plasticine and moulded holes for the ball and the cube.

We asked Peter to remove the cube, and followed a similar teaching pattern to that used with the pegs—time-out and prompt. Over the first three sessions he made between ten and twelve errors in thirty attempts, and over the next four sessions built up to no errors. This was very rapid learning compared with step 2.

Step 6: Discriminating between hot and cold. As a final step in this stage of the programme, we decided to teach discrimination between hot and cold. We used two plastic bottles about three inches high and half an inch in diameter, and filled one with iced water and one with warm water. They were moulded into the peg boat in the same way as the cube and ball.

Over the first three sessions Peter averaged fifteen errors out of thirty. This improved slowly, and in session seventeen he made no errors. It seemed to take him much longer to learn to discriminate between hot and cold than between rough and smooth, round and square; but this was not entirely a function of slower learning. Problems with the equipment contributed to the difficulty. The bottles slipped out of the moulds more easily than the pegs or the cubes, so sometimes Peter grasped the incorrect bottle in order to feel it, and found that it had come out of the boat by accident. This we counted as an error. Therefore he had to learn to be careful when touching the bottles, which was not an intentional part of the programme. Also the difference between the hot and cold decreased as the session progressed, and we usually had to stop at least once to refill the bottles. Thus the temperature difference between the two bottles was not consistent, and the interruption certainly did not help.

The simple discrimination between texture, shape and temperature provided a very useful first step in Peter's teaching programme. There were several direct benefits from this.

(1) Peter learned how to discriminate in a number of different areas—texture, shape and temperature.
(2) The discrimination required the development of simple search behaviour. This skill increased his ability to explore his immediate surroundings.
(3) He clearly illustrated that he had reached the stage of object permanence. He would search to find things he knew should be there, even though he was not touching them at the time.

Example 6. Matching a sample

A number of the discrimination tasks which we teach children demand that they match a picture or a word to a sample which we show them.

So we might show the child two boxes, one with red marbles in it and one with blue. We then give him a red marble and say 'put it with the other red'. Or we may hold up a red marble and say to him 'show me one like this'.

There are a large number of real-life situations in which this matching skill is needed, ranging from sight testing right up to producing the right word when we ask him to imitate! Happily this very basic skill can be taught without words.

The set-up can be very simple. The teacher has a card or shallow box in which she shows her sample, the child has to point to the one in his set which is like the teacher's. Or he may be asked to put his card or object into the teacher's box. The child can have any number of alternatives to choose from, but it is usually sensible to begin with only one or two.

The steps in teaching are as follows:

(1) The scene is arranged from the first so that the child can get the idea of what he is to do. He has one object and the teacher has an identical one in her box. He is then prompted to put his object in her box, and is then rewarded for doing this. Prompts are then faded until he is doing it on his own.

(2) When this behaviour is established, two objects are introduced. The child now has to learn to look. Hold his sample next to yours and ensure that he looks. It may be valuable here to prompt correct responses at first, or when the child makes an incorrect response to say 'no' and introduce a delay before the next try. Use the two objects in random order so that the child does not know what is coming next.

(3) Once the child has learned this basic two-item discrimination, the game can be extended to include any number of items.

One school we know has developed the matching game into a Bingo game in which the children delight. Using a simplified Bingo system can help the child to learn to match a wide variety of shapes, and as the child becomes more skilled he can begin to match letters too, or items with abstract links, such as 'hand' and 'glove'. The matching to sample game is well worth teaching.

Example 7. Doing simple puzzles

One of the stock pieces of equipment in the home and school is the jigsaw puzzle.

How do we teach a child to do a puzzle? The answer is that it is an exercise in backward chaining, teaching the last step first.

Say we have a simple four-piece puzzle. We begin by putting the completed puzzle in front of the child and removing one piece. We place this piece at the edge of the puzzle, so that the child needs to move it only an inch or so to get it in. If necessary we prompt him to push it in, then reward immediately. Note that he is rewarded when he can see the whole puzzle.

Next we fade the prompt for putting the piece in. When he is doing it without need of a prompt, move on to the next step. Remove piece one and a second piece. Prompt him to put the second piece in, and then leave him to fit the first without prompt. Fade the prompt for the second piece. Use this procedure for pieces three and four.

You will find that this general strategy works well for virtually all puzzles and posting boxes. Be careful, however, that the child is looking at what he is doing. Use a simple puzzle, if possible one with a picture of a real object he can recognise, so that he can see himself as 'constructing' the object.

EXPLORATORY PLAY

The purpose of teaching the skills we have discussed in this section is to provide your child with a means of finding out about his world. If your child is able to look at an object and reach for it, he then needs to do something with the object. He needs to explore its possibilities. He needs to find out what happens if it is squeezed, shaken, thrown, dropped, what it tastes like, what noise it makes and so on.

Having done these things he will be able to classify the object along the dimensions we spoke of in the discrimination section. This will enable him to build up concepts of various objects. Thus, although two cups may be different in certain respects— colour for instance—they will also have many features in common. A set of concepts about objects and activities is necessary before any meaningful thought can take place.

Therefore exploratory play is a key to the child's intellectual development.

We have already suggested that mentally handicapped children are usually less spontaneous in their play behaviour than the normal child. They are likely to need help in learning many of the play skills, and they may need more carefully organised surroundings to ensure that they make use of the skills which they do have. There is little point in teaching a child to squeeze a squeaky toy if there are no squeaky toys available when he is away from the teaching session.

This is an important point, because it emphasises the necessity of co-ordinating the play setting with the teaching.

Table 11 lists a variety of skills which your child will need in order to explore the potential of toys and objects. He may have some of these skills. Others may need to be taught. The list also gives some idea of the types of toys and objects which should be readily available to him throughout most of the day.

The most suitable toys are those which do something as a result of an action. For instance squeaky toys, bells and tambourines will produce various types of sound when they are hit, squeezed, shaken, dropped or pushed. Boxes with lids can be opened and closed. These can be made more interesting if small objects or sweets are hidden inside. They will also rattle if shaken. Surprise boxes and picture television sets can be operated by turning handles and squeezing knobs. They provide visual displays or surprises, and sometimes music.

Table 11. Exploratory play behaviours

(1) Does your child lick, chew or suck objects? This is an early stage in the process of exploration.

(2) Does he hold objects?

(3) Does he throw objects?

(4) Does he transfer objects from hand to hand?

(5) Is he able to hold two objects, one in each hand, and bang them together?

(6) Does he hold objects and rub them against a surface?

(7) Will he bang objects on a surface?

(8) Will he shake objects? Does he persist with this if they make a noise?

(9) Does he bang hands on a surface?

(10) Will he hit a squeaky toy?

(11) Will he crumple paper to produce interesting sounds?

(12) Does he squeeze squeaky toys to produce sounds, or to see if they do produce sounds?

(13) Does your child look at objects that he is holding?

(14) Will he remove parts of an object, such as pegs from a peg boat, or tops from bottles?

(15) Does he look at the parts that he has removed?

(16) If given a small box will he try to open it by looking for the join between the lid and the box?

(17) Will he turn handles or knobs, such as those found on music boxes or toy television sets?

(18) Will he press buttons or switches, such as buttons found on a surprise box, or ordinary light switches?

(19) Will he use both hands when trying to unscrew a bottle, plastic barrels, a large plastic nut and bolt?

(20) When going into a new room will he do any of the following: move around and look at what is on the tables, open doors or cupboards to see what is inside?

Example 8. Teaching exploratory play: squeezing

Jonathan was a severely mentally handicapped child who showed very little spontaneous play behaviour. Although he was able to look at objects and reach and grasp, if left on his own with a variety of toys he just sat and sucked his fingers. He handled objects infrequently and with little purpose. At most they were picked up and dropped.

When playing with him it became evident that he did enjoy certain toys, particularly the squeaky animals, although he required his teacher to do the squeezing. Consequently we felt it appropriate to teach him how to do this.

The toys. We selected five different squeaky toys: four animals varying in shape, size and difficulty for squeezing, and a bicycle horn. Two of the animals were easy to grasp, although, as it turned out, neither was soft enough to use in the first stage of the programme. We planned to teach him to use this range of toys, beginning with the easiest of the animals and ending with the bicycle horn.

Reward. Although we had chosen to teach squeaky toys because Jonathan seemed to like the noise they produced, we provided the additional reward of a crisp for each correct squeeze. It was easy to phase out the reward once he had learned all the necessary skills.

Step 1. We chose a small round policeman as the first toy. In order to produce any noise Jonathan needed to hold him firmly round the middle and squeeze. If he grasped the helmet or feet nothing happened.

During the first session Jonathan was prompted to hold him correctly and squeeze. He was rewarded for each attempt. During the second session we began to fade the prompts, and by the end of that session he was grasping correctly. (It was still necessary to support the policeman while he attempted to grasp. If the policeman fell over Jonathan was unable to stand him upright.) However, he still required the prompt to squeeze him.

This procedure continued for five sessions, with still no attempt at a squeeze from Jonathan. If he was given no prompt he would sit and hold the toy firmly. So we decided to find a much softer squeaky toy which produced a noise at a mere touch. After two prompted attempts with this toy, Jonathan held and squeezed it with ease.

We ran two sessions, sixty attempts, using this easy toy to ensure that the grasping and squeezing were well established. During the following session we tried the policeman three times. We slipped it in between attempts with the easy toy. Jonathan made no attempt to squeeze it although he continued squeezing the other.

Over the next three sessions we introduced the policeman more frequently. Occasionally we left Jonathan holding the policeman, with no reward. On other occasions we prompted him. Towards the end of this third session Jonathan squeezed the policeman once with no prompt. During the following session he squeezed it twice again with no prompt. During the next two sessions there were no successful squeezes. However, in the session after that, the eighth since we had brought back the policeman, he squeezed it six times. This session was made up of seventeen attempts with the policeman, and thirteen with the easy toy.

During the ninth session we used the policeman twenty-seven times and Jonathan produced only one unsuccessful attempt.

Step 2. It had taken eighteen sessions to get Jonathan to squeeze the toy. The aim of step 2 was to fade out the prompt which we gave to the top of the toy while he grasped and squeezed it. During this stage Jonathan developed a new behaviour. Whenever we failed to hold the toy down while he squeezed it, he would either pick it up and shake it or pick it up and suck it. Although these two behaviours appear on our list of exploratory play skills they were not appropriate for the teaching session. Consequently we had to use a combination of prompts and time-out to eliminate them. It took us a further nine sessions to do this.

Step 3. Jonathan was now able to squeeze the toy with no help at all, as long as it was placed upright and in front of him. In order to make the squeezing appropriate in an unsupervised play situation, we had to teach him to pick up the toy when it was on its side.

We now had to reintroduce prompts. These prompts were not to help him grasp and squeeze but to show him how to stand the toy upright. The prompts were faded over eight sessions. By the end of this time Jonathan was able to squeeze the toy without prompt, regardless of how it was given to him.

Step 4. In order to be sure that the squeezing would generalise to play in the classroom and home, we now had to phase out the crisps as a reward. We did this first by requiring him to make two or three successful attempts before he got a crisp. Gradually we required him to do more for each crisp. In addition we began to place the toy at different points on the

E

table. Sometimes he would have to stretch forward to reach it, and at other times he would have to move to his left or right.

The results of the programme. It took us many weeks of work to teach Jonathan to squeeze this toy. However, the programme ensured that he could use this behaviour under most conditions. In order to see whether it generalised to unsupervised play, we observed him playing with a range of toys, including several squeaky animals that he had not seen before. Over a ten-minute period he showed very little finger sucking, a lot of squeezing and squeaking, and several other good exploratory behaviours that we had not taught. Had we finished the programme at the end of step 2 it is unlikely that such good generalisation of the skill would have occurred.

Example 9. Teaching exploratory play: twisting and opening

Joan was a severely mentally handicapped child who, like Jonathan, had little or no spontaneous play behaviour. If left alone with toys she would amuse herself in several alarming ways, some of which caused her to do damage to herself.

Unlike Jonathan, she showed no interest in toys when an adult played with her. Consequently we had to select a series of toys to teach without being able to refer to her particular interests. We planned to teach her to use a musical box operated by turning a handle, to open a simple plastic box containing a sweet, and to unscrew a barrel.

Step 1: The musical box. Having found a selection of sweets and drinks that she liked, we began by teaching the musical box. It was necessary to teach two behaviours: the first was to hold the box with one hand, and the second was to turn the handle with the other hand.

We began by prompting her to grasp the box and then to hold the handle between finger and thumb. During the first session she was prompted through every stage of the task. One hand was held firmly around the box and the other was held on the handle. After several turns she was rewarded. During the second session we began to fade the prompt for turning, by exerting less pressure on her hand while the prompt was given.

By the fifth session this prompt was faded to the point where she would grasp the handle firmly, and we would push her hand gently round, allowing as much opportunity for spontaneous movement as possible. During this session, out of thirty attempts she made four very small spontaneous movements. These were immediately rewarded.

During the next session this number of movements improved to twenty-three out of thirty tries. Again they were very small movements, but she was clearly showing that she knew what was expected.

Over the next twelve sessions we concentrated on getting her to make larger movements. At first she was rewarded whenever she made a half turn, then when she made a complete turn and so on. By the end of the twelve sessions she was turning up to ten times before she received the reward.

There were no problems in fading the prompt to hold the music box. While we were working on her turning, she began to pick it up and hold it spontaneously. This was not planned and it effectively eliminated one of the steps.

Step 2: Screw barrels. The barrel we chose was about three inches long. Joan was allowed to select a sweet or crisp and put it in the barrel. We then closed the barrel and prompted her to hold it. The action for opening it involved a twist of the wrist. This was also prompted and Joan was then allowed to find the sweet.

The prompts were faded, and by the end of the sixth session the only prompt she required was assistance with placing her hands on either side of the screw thread. Over the next two sessions we managed to fade this.

However, by the time she was making the complete response without prompt she had learned that the barrels could be opened fairly easily merely by squeezing them and pulling them apart. Although this was an interesting discovery on her part, it was an inappropriate action for the task in hand. We therefore had to go back to prompting her to twist. It took a further six sessions to fade this. By the end of this step in her programme she had learned to turn the handle of a music box and unscrew a set of barrels.

Step 3: Opening the box. Having learned the complex action of unscrewing a set of barrels, opening a simple box with a hinged lid presented no problems. Joan managed to find the non-hinged side on her first attempt without the need for demonstration or prompt.

The results of the programme. As with Jonathan, we were interested to see how well these play skills generalised to unsupervised play. We observed her playing with a range of toys she had not seen before, although some were similar to the ones we used in the teaching sessions.

She had been taught a wider range of skills than Jonathan, and consequently she used a greater variety of exploratory play behaviours during the observation. She produced none of her alarming self-injurious behaviours: investigating objects seemed to have replaced them.

There was no doubt that this programme had been effective in rousing her interest in finding out about things. But this was obviously only a first step. We now had to ensure that she increased her range of exploratory skills. Also we needed to provide her with the best opportunity to use these in the classroom. Providing suitable equipment and toys, and organising a teaching programme for the classroom, followed the individual session work.

CONCLUSION

In this section we have covered the development of one of the fundamental ideas about the world, that of object permanence. Without this concept the child will be limited in the way that he explores the world, and understands the function of objects and people within it.

We have also discussed two important skills: the ability to search for objects which are hidden or lost, and the ability to look at the various properties of objects and see them as different or similar. The ability to search for objects will develop only once the child has an idea of object permanence. This has significant implications for the child's play skills. Until he has the ability to search for objects, he will be able to play only with what is at hand. He will not look for things to interest him. When teaching search behaviour it is also important to aim at developing a memory component, so that he will do more than search for things which are immediately lost or hidden: he will remember where he lost or last saw an object, and search for it there.

Being able to look at differences and similarities in objects is also very important. If he can recognise that there are differences in colour, shape, size, texture, taste and temperature, he will begin to classify.

Teaching discrimination in the way we have described will help to make these differences meaningful. The child should then be able to apply this skill to his everyday life.

This application can be seen in the way the child explores his world. In Table 11 we have listed a number of exploratory play skills. Some are very basic, such as sucking and chewing objects. Others are more advanced, for instance looking for the lid of a box and opening it.

Many handicapped children develop these skills slowly. Others reach a certain point in development, but fail to advance. We have illustrated two programmes to teach the child new skills, and seen that both were effective in increasing the children's exploratory play in and away from the teaching situation. Teaching the child to learn for himself is probably the most effective form of teaching that a parent or teacher can provide.

9 : Ways of Communicating

As we have already seen, responsiveness to other people is a crucial step in development. In this chapter we shall consider the early stages in the development of communication, and in particular we shall look at ways of communicating which are not usually stressed in books about development. Most books tend to stress speech only, and even to suggest that until the child learns to speak he cannot be said to be communicating.

Nothing, in our view, could be further from the truth. A great deal of human communication is non-verbal. We point with our fingers, indicate with our eyes, we use different facial expressions, we use hand gestures to show our feelings, and sometimes to show the size and weight and shape of things. We also use written words or pictures to tell people what we want.

Over the past few years teachers and researchers have come to recognise that severely handicapped children often develop non-verbal ways of communicating for themselves. Such codes, however, may be restricted, and understood by only a few people. So the really exciting breakthrough has been the realisation that we can *teach* the severely handicapped person to use non-verbal signs or symbols, and thus to communicate his needs more effectively.

Our lay-out in this chapter will be rather different from that in other chapters. We will concentrate on describing the various alternative systems of non-verbal communication; and on analysing what each requires of the child. In the next chapter we will draw together these requirements into an assessment system, and go on to discuss specific programmes to illustrate how different forms of communication can be taught.

BASIS OF COMMUNICATION

For communication to take place, four basic conditions are necessary:

1. The child must have something to communicate about

At the simplest level, he must have some basic needs—for example the need for food or warmth, the need to see something or to change his position. At a slightly different level, he may have 'ideas'—be aware of people, sensations or objects. If the child does not have needs or ideas, he will have nothing to say. Happily there are very few people, even amongst the most profoundly handicapped, who have absolutely nothing to communicate about.

2. Given something to communicate about, the child now needs to realise that he can communicate

We have quite often met handicapped children and adults who simply have not learned that there can be any connection between what they do, and how parents, teachers or nurses respond. So a child might throw a toy in frustration because he does not realise that he can 'ask' an adult for help in getting it to work (for instance, by taking it to the adult). Or he may cry when he hurts himself without directing this to his mother (for instance by going to her to get something done about the pain). Later we will talk about a child who allowed objects to be taken from him without protest; yet when he was taught to ask for them back (by leading the teacher to where they had been put), he soon showed that he had strong preferences—he had simply been unable to show them.

3. The child needs some means of expressing his needs or ideas

Even if the child has well-defined needs which he can identify, and does know that he can communicate with other people, he needs to have a *means* of communicating. Not having a means of expressing needs and ideas can be very frustrating indeed. In our experience this frustration underlies bad behaviour in at least some handicapped children; in others, who appear to have learned to accept their inability to express themselves, it leads to passivity. With both groups, teaching some means of expression can produce very rapid advances indeed. This is where the use of sign language and other alternatives to speech has been particularly successful.

4. The child needs some means of understanding what other people are trying to communicate to him

This condition is clearly necessary for two-way communication. In a very simple sense, whenever we respond to the child we are 'communicating' with him. The child cries—we attend to him by turning, looking, and possibly saying something. At this simple level, the child's realisation that when he makes a noise or does something, people regularly respond in ways he can predict, is part of the process by which he learns that *he* can communicate (see point 2 above). But when we are trying to get the child to do or to understand something, we usually need a more complex 'language'—for example, to respond sensibly to the instruction 'under the chair', he has to be able to identify an object from a word and to identify relative positions of objects (on, in, under etc.) from words.

It is generally accepted that learning language involves a constant interplay between learning to understand words or other means of communicating, such as signs and learning to use these means. Learning to understand usually comes first— the child learns the names for objects, people or events from his parents or teachers. Once this has happened the adult encourages the child to use speech expressively—to name things correctly, mainly by imitation. On the other hand, teachers have found that children or adults learning sign language can often express themselves in sign *before* they learn to understand other people's signs.

THE ALTERNATIVES

In this section we shall consider various communication systems which can be used to complement or as alternatives to speech. We wish to make clear that adopting one such alternative does not in any way exclude others: they are all closely related, and a child in the process of development could progress through various systems of communication.

Basic non-verbal communication

Even a very young baby will cry, coo, look at his mother's face (and his father's), smile in recognition, respond when spoken to and use a variety of non-verbal communication techniques. He also soon learns to 'refer' to objects by looking at them. The origin of this learning probably lies in the parents' tendency to follow the direction of the child's gaze, and then to comment on the object or move it closer to the child. Some workers feel that this stage of 'shared reference' is a very crucial step in development.

These foundation phases of development simply may not happen for the very severely handicapped child. In fact the failure to show the kinds of normal responsiveness which we have just described is often the first sign that their child is 'different' that parents notice.

The developing child continues to use basic non-verbal communication before he learns to use words. He uses cries to attract attention, he learns to lead other people to things he wants, and to put their hands on toys which are causing him trouble or on a door handle he wants turned. He points to draw attention to things he wants, or wants to share with other people.

Meanwhile he continues to respond with increasing understanding to what other people say to him. He also makes eye contact when he is being talked to, or when he is trying to communicate with someone else—especially when the adult is not attending properly to what the child is trying to get over.

This is perhaps the place to include a note about the teaching of eye contact. We have seen it taught as an end in itself. And there are several reasons why teaching it might be held to be valuable. If the child is making eye contact he is not looking somewhere else, so he is visually attentive. Second, if he is looking at the parent or teacher he is exposed to the person's facial expression, and has a greater chance of noticing facial expression and lip movements: the coordination of lip movements and sound may hold his attention more effectively than sound alone. He may also learn something about how to localise the source of a sound.

But making eye contact does not *guarantee* any of these things. We can 'look' without 'seeing'. We can be looking at something and attending to a sound somewhere else. So if we think that by teaching eye contact we are doing more than getting the child to look in the right direction on command, we are guilty of 'teaching by magic'.

E*

Eye contact is important only as a step in a sequence of communication, and it should be seen only as a step in teaching.

Verbal communication

From the very earliest stages of development, we see the origins of verbal communication. We have already mentioned responsiveness to parents' voices. (Among other things this is an important indicator of ability to hear.) Then, as the child makes sounds for himself, we can normally detect a gradual increase in the range and accuracy of his imitation of normal speech sounds. These changes are often difficult to hear accurately, but if we listen carefully over a period it is possible to get a reasonable idea of the child's range. Normally the child begins with vowel sounds and then gradually acquires consonants. Our assessment procedure will suggest ways in which we can check this ability.

From combinations of these speech sounds the child's first words are formed.

The first words

The child's first words serve the same purposes as do the later stages of his non-verbal communication. These purposes can be divided roughly into requests, demands and naming responses drawing attention to objects or events.

Recent research into language development has led developmental psychologists and psycholinguists over the last few years to approach the one-word stage of development less in terms of grammar and syntax than in terms of semantics: that is, to emphasise the *meaning* the child is trying to get over rather than the part of speech he is using.

This approach in terms of meaning depends on careful attention to the context in which the child makes an utterance.

The following sequence is an example of the kind of attention we mean.

Simon pushed the lorry over the table to Lenny. 'Lorry,' he said loudly when Lenny did not respond. He looked at the teacher. She said 'What do you want?' 'Lorry,' he said again, pointing at Lenny. The teacher prompted Lenny to push the lorry back to Simon. Simon smiled.

Here Simon used the word 'lorry' first to call Lenny's attention (loudly), and probably to get him to push it as well. The second time he clearly meant Lenny to push the lorry, because he pointed to Lenny and then said 'lorry'. The context provides the meaning.

This approach to early language in terms of what the child is trying to say can be carried one step further back: if we observe the child's non-verbal communication carefully, we can often predict what words would be useful to him. This gives us a very important teaching strategy: offering the child words linked with his observed needs and desires, rather than impressing an artificial framework on him.

The earliest words used by normal and handicapped children, as we have already noted, are typically demands, and naming responses. Other early responses include asking for recurrence—'more'—negation—'no'—and pointing out where things are.

Is this order of responses genetically determined? The answer seems to be a fairly clear 'no'. The fact that children typically develop these responses early is almost certainly a function of the structure of their experience. In other words, certain experiences are fundamental to development. These experiences encourage the child to learn to communicate—in order to satisfy needs. More development follows as the child extends his range of experience and makes more demands on his environment and as the environment makes more demands on him.

This idea has important implications for the education of the handicapped child. It implies that if the handicapped child lacks a challenging environment—either because his home (or hospital) environment is poor, or because he is restricted by physical handicap—his development will be inhibited. We cannot rely on maturation happening by itself.

In a study of children in a subnormality hospital we actually found that their powers of language and communication deteriorated significantly over a four-year period. The children were not degenerating physically, they were simply in an environment which they could not influence and in which they were consequently not rewarded for attempts at communication.

SIGN LANGUAGES AND SIGN SYSTEMS

Sign languages have been used as alternatives to voiced speech for centuries, the most familiar being those used by deaf people. There are two types of signing. The first is finger spelling, which uses hand signs as letters of the alphabet. Since finger spelling depends not only on knowledge of words, but an ability to spell as well, it is obviously not suitable for mentally handicapped people as an introduction to speech.

The other kind of sign language involves a hand sign for a whole word. So the signer may represent the word 'drink' by forming his hand as if he were holding a glass and then lifting it to his mouth; or 'food' by miming using a knife and fork.

It is this latter kind of signing which has been used successfully with the mentally handicapped.

Sign languages were evolved by deaf people. There are several different languages used in the world. The United Kingdom has its own sign language, as has France. The French Sign Language was imported into the United States, so the American Sign Language is quite distinct from that used in the UK.

Two main sign languages are used in the United Kingdom. These are the sign language of the deaf, now increasingly referred to as British Sign Language, and the Paget Gorman Sign System. The two languages are very different, and unfortunately in competition at present in British schools and hospitals, some of which are adopting British Sign Language (BSL), others Paget Gorman Sign Systems (PGSS). We shall outline below some of the strengths and weaknesses of each system.

British Sign Language

BSL is the historically evolved language of the deaf people in Britain—it has evolved in much the same way that spoken English has evolved, words being added to the system as they were needed. This means that BSL probably contains enough signs for all everyday usage, though the signs have never been systematically recorded. (See photographs for some examples.)

BSL was, and still is, disapproved of by some teachers of the deaf, on the ground that to teach a child a sign language will retard his development of normal speech. There is in fact very little documented evidence in support of this view, and a good deal of evidence against it.

One consequence of this mistrust is that BSL has been an underground language, passed on from child to child in the playgrounds of deaf schools, but banned in the classrooms. Offenders used to be punished by having their thumbs bound together with sticky tape behind their backs! BSL has survived and developed, but the penalty of suppression has been lack of standardisation. BSL has very sharp dialects. However, a large dictionary is at last being produced, and when this is available greater standardisation will be possible.

There are several ways to judge BSL and other sign languages from the point of view of their suitability for teaching to a child. For example, you might look at how many of the signs use one hand or two, and if two, in the same or different positions. 'Drink' uses one hand in BSL, for instance; 'book' uses two, with both hands held in the same way; and 'cake' uses two hands held in different ways. When we analysed BSL from this point of view, we found that about half of the signs examined used only one hand, 37 per cent used two hands in the same position, and only 14 per cent two hands in different positions: that is 86 per cent of the signs were simple ones.

You might also analyse the use made of movement in the language. BSL uses a great deal. About 84 per cent of all signs use movement. Sometimes the movement is a mime of the action represented, as in 'drink' or 'eat', but most often it is not representational. Whether or not the movement is representational, however, it probably serves to reinforce memory.

A third way to analyse sign languages is to look at the variety of hand postures needed. Three kinds of postures are used very often in BSL. These are flat hands, fists and 'pointing' with the index finger. These are shown in Illustration 1. Together they account for 54 per cent of all postures used in the sample examined. We know from data on normal development and from studies done at the Thomas Coram Research Unit that these three postures are the earliest to develop and the easiest for handicapped children to do and to imitate.

These comments on BSL suggest that a child would not have to have great manual ability to use the system. He could make

Figure 1. Postures involved in the British Sign Language

headway even if he could use only one hand, if he could move it, make a flat hand and a fist, and point his index finger from his fist.

A special vocabulary of BSL signs has been developed for use with the mentally handicapped. Called the Makaton vocabulary, this was initially devised by a speech therapist, Margaret Walker, and two colleagues for use in subnormality hospitals. The vocabulary consists of nine groups of signs, each group or stage comprising about 35 words, according to the latest edition available. The original idea was that the stages should be graded in difficulty and consequently the vocabulary was based on word counts. However, the vocabulary has now been so modified that there is no relation between 'difficulty' or 'frequency' of use, and the stages. The stages represent collections of signs which might usefully be taught together.

An illustrated guide to the signs has been published, and a booklet of teaching suggestions. We will comment more on the Makaton vocabulary in the next chapter (see Example 7 page 182).

BSL can be learned very easily. The average adult, with effort, can learn about 50 signs in a day course—far more than would be needed for beginning teaching. Courses are run in connection with the Makaton vocabulary, but the most accessible sources of help for those who want to learn are Social Workers for the Deaf, who may be employed by Local Authorities or by branches of the Royal Association of the Deaf and Dumb.

One reason why BSL is not popular with teachers of the deaf

is that it does not allow precise translation from spoken English to sign. BSL does not have signs for 'the' or 'a', and it does not have tense endings for verbs, nor means of directly translating imperatives, for instance. There are ways of translating tenses, for example by putting the sign for 'before' in the sentence to indicate past tense: what are missing are equivalents for tense endings such as 'ing' or 'ed'. BSL also uses different word orders from spoken English.

The problems of direct translation worry teachers of the deaf because they see them as interfering with the learning of spoken English. We will come back to the problems in the mismatch of spoken English and BSL after discussing PGSS.

Paget–Gorman Sign System
The origins of PGSS are very different from those of BSL. PGSS is a modern invention, devised by Richard Paget and developed by Pierre Gorman and Grace Paget.

The original idea behind PGSS was to produce a universal language which would combine good features from existing sign languages from all over the world. PGSS is thus highly systematised. There is an official manual describing hand postures and over 3,000 signs. Unlike BSL, PGSS is a well-controlled system in which a consistent effort is made to prevent the development of dialects by carefully controlling who teaches the system to teachers or parents, through a panel of examiners. The system is being actively developed by a group of teachers of the deaf, with additional input from professionals concerned with mental handicap.

PGSS places different demands on the child from BSL. If we analyse a sample of PGSS signs equivalent to the BSL signs already analysed we find that 49 per cent not only require two hands but require them in different positions. About the same number of signs as in BSL require one hand only (35 per cent), about 16 per cent require the two hands in the same position.

Movement is required by PGSS in only 56 per cent signs (as compared with 84 per cent for BSL). As in BSL, many of the movements depict the action they stand for; and many of the signs not involving movement are also representational.

Analysed in terms of the hand postures PGSS emerges as far more complex than BSL. Whereas over 50 per cent of BSL signs use the simple hand positions flat, fist and pointing with index finger, only about 39 per cent of the PGSS signs use these postures. Frequently used signs involve far more complicated positions—for example PGSS uses an L Hand and a compressed hand—which BSL uses not at all (see Illustration 2). We know from developmental data and from testing handicapped children that these and other signs used by PGSS are more difficult for the children to imitate. However, many children may be able to learn them effectively.

Figure 2. Postures involved in the Paget Gorman Sign System

In some cases the differences between the BSL and PGSS signs are small. 'Walk' is virtually the same in both systems, and 'up' and 'down' differ but are really quite close. In other cases the differences are as large as those between spoken English and spoken French.

PGSS is an overtly concept based language. An attempt, that is, has been made to group signs round 'basic signs'—for instance, all the signs for animals involve a basic animal sign as a constant element (a representation of an animal's head), with other elements to identify the particular animal: whiskers added for 'cat', yapping movement for 'dog', etc. The idea is that the child identifies the concept from the basic sign and then the specific animal from the added component. This idea has of course no correspondence in spoken English, where the sounds of the words for different animals give no indication at all that they belong together. We will see later that this grouping could help the mentally handicapped child considerably.

BSL, and other natural sign languages such as American Sign Language, also use some conceptual grouping. PGSS has perhaps developed this feature more systematically.

Unlike the other sign languages, PGSS sets out to be a translation of spoken English into sign. All tense endings and other grammatical features have direct equivalents in PGSS: for example 'walking' uses two signs, one for 'walk' and one for 'ing'. Word order is precisely that of English. For this reason, teachers of the deaf have been far readier to accept PGSS than BSL.

The supporters of PGSS argue that the structure of the system allows the teacher to speak and simultaneously sign all the features of spoken English. This, they argue, gives the child the best chance to learn spoken English while he learns signing.

No one, however, has yet produced evidence that PGSS is superior to BSL; nor that the child does learn spoken English as a result of learning to sign in the way suggested.

American Sign Language

American Sign Language (ASL), like BSL, is a natural language, in that it has been evolved in everyday use by deaf people. It has also been shown that ASL can be learned by mentally handicapped children or adults who have failed to learn speech by normal means or special teaching. ASL in relation to BSL and PGSS produces several interesting comparisons. First of all ASL relies heavily on simple 'two hand same' signs. In about half of a group of sampled signs, ASL requires both hands to be used and both hands to make the same postures. Once again a 'natural language' proves to be simpler than PGSS. Similarly ASL uses the very simple flat hand, fists and pointed index fingers used by BSL, rather than the more complex PGSS postures.

ASL differs sharply from BSL in one respect. Several workers have devised ways of adding to ASL in order to include those 'parts of speech' which are needed to bring it in line with spoken English. So people in the USA are not faced with choosing between a natural language which cannot be translated precisely into spoken English, and a language which can be translated but is contrived.

Which system should we use?

This question cannot be answered simply. BSL has the apparent advantage of requiring simpler signs and hand postures. PGSS has the advantage of mirroring spoken English and possibly also of being more explicitly concept based.

People favouring BSL point out that it is the natural language of the deaf and so is actually widely in use. In addition, because it is a natural language, it is more likely to be adapted to everyday needs and to clarity of expression. They also point out that it is easy to find teachers.

BSL supporters also argue that there is nothing to prevent the teacher signing and speaking, to teach spoken English word order; and that verb endings and other grammatical refinements in any case are less important to the mentally handicapped than the ability to get the essence of an idea across. And at least one British school is taking the lead from American groups who have modified American Sign Language by adding signs for tense endings, and devised similar signs to add to BSL.

Those favouring PGSS, on the other hand, will point to the greater clarity and standardisation of the system and to its concept-related basis. They see the system not as an end in itself but as a means to teaching spoken English. Though the signs may be complex, children and teachers can modify the signs to 'baby' forms, just as they do with spoken English.

We tend to favour BSL because of its relative simplicity and widespread use. However, choice in any individual case would need to take into consideration which system was being most commonly used in the locality.

What skills does the child need before he can learn to use sign language?
We will go into the problem of assessment more fully in the next chapter. Here we will say only that, at the simplest level, before he can begin to learn to use sign language, the child should be able to use at least one hand with reasonable freedom of movement of the hand and arm. If he can do this we can begin. We can prompt him to make a response and follow it by reward. (Even this simple level does assume that the child can see or hear the cue for reward, and of course that he has needs which we can refer to.)

Why should the mentally handicapped child learn sign language more easily than speech?
The teaching of sign language is a new development that promises to be a major breakthrough in the education of the

handicapped. We already have evidence of children and adults who have never learned to speak, learning two or three hundred word vocabularies in sign and learning to communicate quite complex ideas effectively. Not all children can do this, but it seems that many can.

One reason why signing may succeed where speech fails is that many mentally handicapped people have a degree of deafness which may have gone undetected. The methods of diagnosing deafness in the handicapped are often very crude and inefficient.

Another reason is that it is a good deal easier to prompt a child to make a sign than to say a word. This prompting may prove crucial to the first step—the understanding that the child *can* communicate—that enables him to take off. (Example 1, page 174)

On the other hand it may be that teachers are better motivated when they teach signing rather than speech. Signing is new and fashionable. Similarly, it may be that a new approach enthuses the child. He may have been bathed for ten years in words which he has been unable to follow, so that he has lost interest. In a new medium, he breaks through and for the first time in his life can understand and communicate. His enthusiasm is roused, and eventually generalised to attempts to understand and use spoken words. This may explain why many children spontaneously develop speech within the context of a signing programme: the signing simply focuses them on speech as a meaningful activity.

The pattern of normal development offers clues to the success of signing with many children. There is some evidence suggesting that gestures develop earlier than words. In normal children this communication is often ignored by the parents; but in deaf children of deaf parents it is encouraged, and the children appear to learn to use signs quickly, and to put two 'words' together earlier than speaking children do.

Similarly, several theorists, Piaget included, have argued that speech develops from a basis laid by internalised action, and that gesture—the part representation of the action—may predate speech. So in learning a new concept the child learns the relevant physical response, and, in internalising it, attaches the words to the action sequence. In our society, only words are normally acceptable as a means of general communication. But the work of Piaget and others points to action-related and pictorial signs as a possible means of communicating more basic than, but just as sophisticated as, speech.

There is also evidence arising from research among the mentally handicapped, that the handicapped have fundamental problems with spoken language; but they have far fewer problems with visual representations. Many normal people find it easier to think in pictures and picture sequences than in words, and it is possible that many severely mentally handicapped children and adults have an exaggerated form of this tendency. Brain damage in the auditory analysing areas may have caused massive problems with speech; while the same people, if concepts are represented in visuo-spatial terms, may be able to function at a much higher level.

So it may be that sign languages are easier for the mentally handicapped to handle than are words.

The symbol systems which we will talk about next presents another insight into the nature of mental handicap. One of the problems in language processing concerns sequencing: that is, the handicapped child often has difficulty in placing words in the right order in a sentence.

Normal people meet the same problem with larger units. If we are trying to remember a sequence of events or points in an argument, we often have to write the sequence down or to use a mnemonic aid like remembering the sequence of objects around a familiar room and then attaching a point to each object. We then recall the objects in order, and this helps us to recall the sequence of points. It is possible that some of the new teaching methods provide the handicapped with a similar mnemonic aid through which they can overcome their problems in sequencing. We will see later how this might be happening.

For the moment let us repeat that there are several good reasons why sign languages and other visual symbol systems should be useful with the handicapped. It is possible then that teachers have been doing the wrong thing in trying to get the mentally handicapped to learn speech as their first line of communication. Like the deaf, they may find it easier at least to begin with a sign language. Speech, if it develops, can come later.

USING OBJECTS, PICTURES AND SYMBOLS

So far we have considered ways of communicating in which the child makes the words or signs himself. In the case of words and of signs the child has to remember what to say or do. He has to learn and produce the form of expression.

One of the easiest forms of communication simply requires the child to touch or point to what he wants. So the child who wants a drink picks up a cup, or the child who wants a toy points to it. This method requires the child only to know what he wants, to have the idea that he can communicate his needs, and to have learned to touch or point to an object. This way of communicating is obviously especially valuable for people who have great physical difficulty in speaking or making hand signs.

There are several different systems which use this simple principle.

Communication boards

At the simplest level there are communication boards. These are boards which have on them objects, or pictures representing things which the child likes or needs. So a typical board for a physically handicapped child might have pictures of a cup, plate of food, toilet, bed, favourite toys, the garden, and the car. The child then needs a means of indicating which of the things he wants. He may do this by pointing with a finger or his hand; by pointing with a pointer attached to a head band if his head control is better than hand control: or even by pointing with his eyes if that is all that he can do.

If the object itself is on the communication board—a cup, for instance—the child can very easily learn the connection between pointing or touching and the satisfaction of his wish, since the object he touches is itself directly involved in satisfying his need. But this form of communication is also very limited. For instance how does the child indicate he wants to go to the toilet? So we need to move fairly quickly into the principle of one object representing another. We can make this transition by using miniatures, scale models of the objects concerned. However, miniatures are again limited, and are best used as an introduction to pictures. So a child who likes going into the playground could be provided with a photograph, or line tracing from a photograph.

This idea can obviously be extended to cover a lot of special needs and likes. But as the child's range of experiences increases we may have to move from the very simple level of 'I want' to answers to questions such as 'do you want x or y?'. The system can take this into account, but the child may have to be taught to understand these various different questions. We will go into this in the next chapter.

Rebus system

A rebus is literally a representation of a name or object by a picture. The term has a more specialised meaning following the development of a system for teaching reading by Woodward and his associates. Their idea was that children might find it easier to learn to read if they read in picture sequences, the words being inserted gradually. The system consists of a series of pictures and simple symbols. For instance 'run' is represented by a stick figure running, 'tree' by a picture of a tree. Words like 'on', 'in', 'up' are represented by a black dot related to a box (see Illustration 3). The illustration also shows examples of abstract symbols.

Rebus is convenient because it presents a standard set of picture forms for concrete objects, and standard ways of representing the ideas embodied in prepositions, verbs, etc. The big disadvantage of the system is that it soon gets complicated. Because the intention is to allow a quick way to translate from picture to written forms to speech, the system is based on the sounds of words. For example OLD is represented by a picture of a bald man with a beard, a fair pictorial representation. SOLD is represented by putting the letter S to the left of the OLD symbol. This clearly makes good sense if the child knows the concept SOLD and uses the system only to get the sound of the word. However, the point of using a pictorial system with a severely handicapped child is usually to provide him with a system in terms of which he can think. Combinations of letters and symbols, or symbols and symbols, to represent new ideas is more likely to confuse than to help.

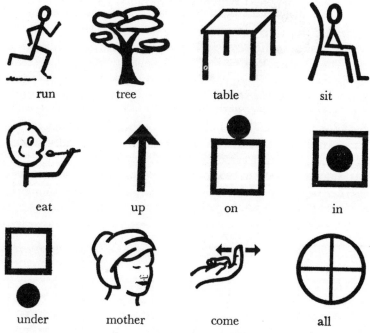

Figure 3. Rebus symbols

Blissymbols

The Rebus system was developed with the idea of helping children to learn to read. The Bliss system on the other hand was set up with the idea of providing a universal written means of communication. Once again it was not set up with the handicapped in mind, so, as with Rebus, the system is not perfectly adapted for their use.

The basic idea of Blissymbolics is that pictures represent ideas. Blissymbols tend to be more abstract than Rebus. The illustration shows symbols for 'man', 'woman', 'father' and 'mother' (Illustration 4). The difference between 'man' and 'woman' and 'father' and 'mother' is that the latter pair include arms, a 'roof' or 'cover' which symbolises protection. The cover, man and woman signs are all elements which are used in different combinations in other words.

Other symbols show how abstract concepts are represented.

For instance, the heart symbol is always included when emotion is involved in the idea. Each of the other elements shown in the illustration has a constant meaning across symbols.

The Bliss system seems rather abstract and complicated at first. The symbols look very abstract, and the idea of representing similar ideas through different combinations of the same elements in pictures would seem unlikely to help the severely handicapped. However, many children, especially very severely physically handicapped children, have shown that they can in fact learn to use Blissymbols with great ease. We really cannot tell which child will respond until we try.

It may be that, as with the sign languages, the classing together of similar ideas with similar signs is of particular help to the mentally handicapped.

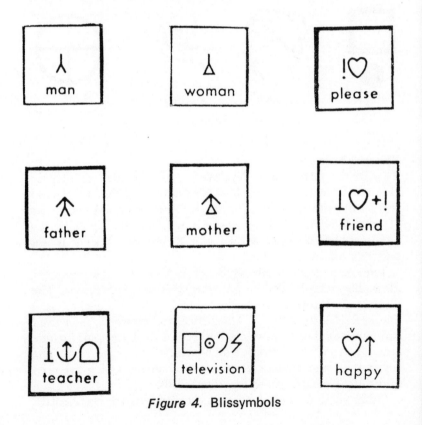

Figure 4. Blissymbols

Used at a simple level Blissymbols are fairly simple in form. As the elements are built up to represent more complex ideas, however, they can get very complicated indeed. The illustration shows symbols for 'teacher', 'television' and 'friend'. Each is built up from the elements of the system and is included in the recommended first hundred words.

Faced with examples like this, teachers often ask whether it would not be simpler to teach the child to identify written words! However, if we look at the equivalent words, we usually find that they are even more complicated than the symbol, and they do not include the visual clues to meaning.

In learning to communicate through Bliss, the child may begin with a small number of symbols selected on the basis of his needs, likes and dislikes. The symbols are drawn on a large sheet of card which is then attached to a board, just like the communication board. When the child wants to communicate he points to the symbols. A very proficient child may have several hundred symbols he can use, and may also make up his own.

In order to make communication possible with people who do not know the system, the translation is always written on the card underneath the symbol. This means that the child *may* be learning shape of the written word at the same time as he is learning or using the Bliss system. We say *may*, because without special teaching there seems no reason why the child should abandon the Bliss system, which he knows, in favour of a more difficult system.

Premackese

Communication boards and the Bliss system are very well adapted for children who can only point or indicate the location of a symbol. If the child wants to put two or more words together, for instance, in describing an object, 'big ball', he points to the symbol for 'big' and the symbol for 'ball'. If his sentence is 'big ball in box' he would point to four symbols in sequence.

These systems are like signing in this way. If the child wants to put a series of ideas together he has to plan his sentence in his head and then produce it in the right order.

Many mentally handicapped people find this task very

difficult. Their words tend to come out in the wrong order or no order, and so they fail to communicate.

Another system can help with this problem. This is a system devised by David Premack and developed by Joe Carrier, and Ruth Deich and Patricia Hodges in California.

The system involves using plastic plaques to represent words. The child is initially taught to use individual plaques to represent words for objects, events etc. When he has acquired a basic vocabulary, he is taught to lay out the plaques in order left to right to represent words in a sentence. Obviously the sentences are very simple at first. For example the child may say 'teacher give drink'.

The main point about the Premack system is that it offers a framework in terms of which strings of words can be laid out and checked before the child communicates. The child does not have to plan and remember and produce the sequence at the same time.

The provision of a framework within which word order can be planned is also a feature of other systems. A reading scheme 'Breakthrough to Literacy' involves the child in making up sentences out of words in much the same way as the Premack system does. We have seen several mentally handicapped children who have found it easier to use the framework provided by 'Breakthrough' than to speak sentences. Similarly, we have seen children who have learned to sign and to write very simple words, who can communicate more effectively through writing than through signs.

The disadvantage of the Premack system lies in its origins. Premack's original purpose was to investigate the acquisition of language by chimpanzees. For that reason his plaques were deliberately non-representational: he did not want to give cues about meaning from the shape of the plaques. But if we are trying to set up a system which is as easy as possible to acquire, we might well argue that it would be better to use representational symbols.

The Premack system includes a specific provision for planning of sequences. Although it is unique in this within the systems which have been used with the handicapped, there is no reason why other systems should not incorporate the physical framework used by Premack.

What do we need the child to do in order to learn to use Bliss or Premackese?

To start a child on a Bliss programme, we must be able to identify at least two needs or interests which we can meet when the child asks, e.g. 'kiss' and 'drink'. In addition, the child must be physically able to indicate in some way which of the symbols he is referring to—by pointing with the hand, foot, a pointer attached to a headband, or eyes. And that is all. As with signing, we can see later whether the child has the ability to 'represent' in any complicated way. For the moment all we are asking is that the child should make a simple pointing response.

The requirements of the Premack system go a bit further. Here the person needs to be able to place the plaques in a frame. This needs more motor control than Bliss, although there seems no reason why some automation of the system should not be possible. Once again, however, at the simplest level, the requirements of the system are very few and there seems no reason why it should not be tried with any child who can reach the minimum criteria of showing needs and interests which can be manipulated, and having minimal physical skills.

Does the child need to have reached the level of symbolic thought to be taught to use these alternatives?

Research workers and educationalists interested in the development of young children and the mentally handicapped sometimes argue that the child should be capable of 'symbolic' thought before he can use language. This view draws a distinction between a simple response to a situation, for instance where the child sees a cup and makes a sign 'cup', and a more complex process where he has the 'idea' of the cup as a symbol.

It is argued that you can see the difference between a child who is pre-symbolic and one who comprehends symbols, by observing their play. The child who has reached the symbol stage will play 'pretend' games: play teaparties, play with dolls, play with cars making car noises, steering them, pretending to fill them up with petrol—all activities making clear that the child is able to imagine the real-life events.

Symbolic play is important for a number of reasons. The

question we have to ask here is whether the child needs to have reached the level of symbolic play before we try to teach him a language system.

Our answer is a definite 'no'. Normal children begin to develop speech well before they first show symbolic play. Second, even if the child is not capable of symbolising he can still learn to communicate in a very important way: he can tell us that he needs a drink or is tired. This ability alone will make a big difference to him and to us. Third, the pre-symbolic use of a communication system almost certainly helps the child to move on to the symbolic stage: the 'words' taught can become the symbols which he then uses in symbolic play.

Coramese

As we have seen, each of the systems seems to have something in its favour. And all share the feature that they use a single visual symbol for a word. All signs and symbols can be accompanied by the spoken word, and the pictorial symbols by the written word.

The sign systems have a very substantial advantage in that they do not require the child to carry anything round with him in order to communicate. This is an obvious advantage with the ambulant child, although less important if the child is confined to a wheel-chair.

The Premack system includes a specific provision for planning of sequences. Although it is unique within the systems which have been used with the handicapped, there is no reason why other systems should not incorporate the physical framework used by Premack.

The different systems obviously make different physical demands. Signing requires that the child should be able to use at least some basic hand postures. This may be beyond some children suffering from severe physical handicap, although we have seen some children in whom the effort to communicate has led to more control over their hand movements. The Premack system requires the child to place plaques in an order. Again this may be difficult for the severely physically handicapped, but a simple electronic device could allow the child to put up a Premack or Bliss sentence on a display, and then to correct it.

We have evolved a compromise system which capitalises on

the positive features of each. We will assume that we are dealing with a child with enough hand control to make simple signs.

Given such a child, we go for signing accompanied by speech as the basic medium of communication. The child is asked initially to sign only, speech comes later in ways we will suggest in the next chapter. When the child has acquired a working vocabulary of say 30–40 signs we try to combine them. If the child shows good evidence of being able to combine signs, we can move on to more complex combinations. If not, or if the child gets stuck, then we move into pictorials.

First of all, signs are associated with pictures of signs and objects. The child is taught to make the sign by being shown a large picture of his parent, teacher or himself making the sign. Using a mirror should help him to identify his own signs. Once this step has been completed for a range of signs, new signs can be taught by showing sign and picture for a new object or situation, thus extending his vocabulary.

We can then move into the use of a Premack-type framework for teaching word order. The aim is to allow the child to use a mnemonic aid to structure his sentences.

This proposed system aims to draw together the best elements in other systems, but it is still in process of experimentation. Many problems remain to be solved. Research is currently under way at the Thomas Coram Research Unit which, we hope, will provide guidelines for its development and future use with the handicapped.

CONCLUSION

In this chapter we have discussed a number of alternatives to speech as means of communication. The use of these systems offers new hope for at least some mentally handicapped children and adults. There are few 'qualifications' needed by the child before you can begin to teach him to use one of these systems, and there are clearly possibilities for major advances in teaching in this field.

See Appendix for addresses of organisations from whom you can find out more about usual communication systems (page 303).

10: Teaching the Child to Communicate

In this chapter we will discuss ways of assessing the child before and during a communication programme. We will then go on to discuss some examples of teaching programmes.

There are many methods of assessing speech and communication skills. Some of these are very formal and require the child to cooperate with the psychologist or speech therapist doing the test. Others involve observing the child in play, or interviewing the parent, teacher or nurse who knows the child best.

Each method has its advantages. Standard tests such as the Reynell will tell us how much the child understands and uses speech in a set test situation. This allows comparison with other children. However, in order to be successful in these test situations, the child has to know how to play the game of being tested and he also has to be prepared to cooperate. Since many young or severely handicapped children do not fit these requirements, they will show up badly.

Less formal methods are more useful in these cases. We can often discover a good deal more about how the child communicates and what he understands by watching him interact with his parents or teachers for a couple of hours. Talking to people who know the child well can also give important clues. For example a child we worked with used several words to get people to do things: she would say 'out' when she wanted to go out, 'up' when she wanted her parents to get up in the morning. However, she did not use words in this way at all at school. It was only by talking to the parents that we realised that this important use of words was established. In one project we also found that completely different pictures were produced from the Reynell tests on the one hand, and interviews with the parents and teachers on the other. The children showed a much wider range of abilities out of the formal test setting.

We would go so far as to say that if an educational psychologist or speech therapist does not discuss the child's communication with the parents and teachers, then he or she is not doing a thorough job of assessment. Programme planning should always begin from a basis of formal test results, observation, and discussion with people who really know the child well.

Our assessment here consists of a series of questions, and one or two tests. We suggest that you read through the list, try the tests and then keep the questions in mind for a couple of days as you play with or watch your child with other people. It is often only when you are looking out for something that you notice it.

ASSESSMENT OF COMMUNICATION

Because the behaviour we are talking about is complicated, we need a long assessment. It can be split into three sections.

A. Needs and Interests. This section covers the basics of the 'reason for communication'. This is covered in Table 12.
B. Understanding of sounds or gestures. This is covered in Table 13.
C. Use of communication. This is the most complex section. It covers seven areas. The first four are concerned with nonverbal communication, and motor imitation as a basis for learning nonverbal communication.

(1) Basics of nonverbal communication. Table 14.
(2) Communication by manipulation. Table 15.
(3) Communication by gesture. Table 16.
(4) Motor imitation. Table 17.

The next three sections concern verbal communication:

(1) Development of sounds. Table 18.
(2) Verbal imitation. Table 19.
(3) Communication by sounds and words. Table 20.

One word of caution. The assessment is not a test on which the child will pass or fail. So don't be too generous. If you are not sure that the child can do something, it is in his best interests to assume that he can't. If he can, you will soon find

out when you start teaching him. Then you can move on
confident in his abilities, rather than try to teach him beyond
his level.

Table 12. *Needs and Interests*
(1) What needs does the child have?
(2) What interests does the child have?

Needs and Interests: Answering the questions
(1) *What needs does the child have?* This can be assessed from your
knowledge of the child or from observation. If he has several
clear needs there is no need to list them fully.

(2) *What interests does he have?* Is he interested in toys, if so what
toys? Are there particular things, such as a blanket, which he
is very attached to? Are there particular people he likes a lot?

  If the child shows neither needs nor interests then we really
need to go back to Chapter 5 to see how these can be developed.
If he shows a wide range of needs and interests, we have one
basis for a communication programme.

Understanding
These questions are listed in Table 13.

Table 13. *Understanding*
 (1) Can he hear? Does he respond to any sounds?
      Does he respond to speech sounds?
 (2) Does he listen?
 (3) Can he see?
 (4) Does he attend to you when you speak or point?
 (5) Does he understand simple requests?
 (6) Does he know the names of objects and things?
 (7) Does he know words used to describe objects?
 (8) Does he understand two words together?
 (9) Does he understand three-word sentences?
(10) Does he understand complicated gestures?

(1) *Can he hear? Does he respond to any sounds? Does he respond to
speech sounds?* If the answers here are no, it does not necessarily

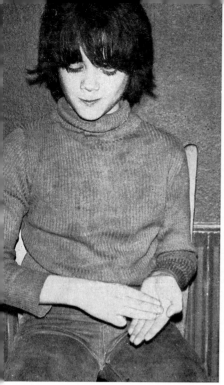

Mother — tap right hand on left twice

2. Father — tap right hand on left twice

3. Man — draw 'beard' on face

4. Lady — draw finger down cheek

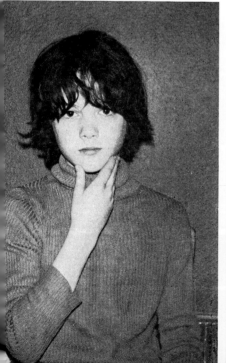

5. Baby — 'rock' the baby

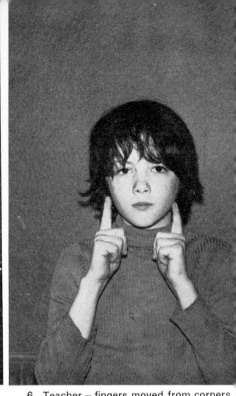

6. Teacher — fingers moved from corners mouth

7. I — me — point to self

8. You — point to other person

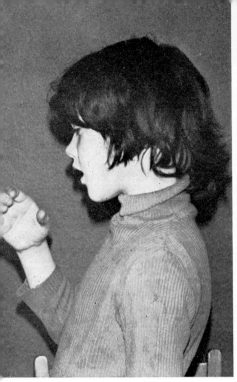

9. Drink – mime drinking

10. Eat – dinner – mime eating

11. Knife – mime cutting

12. Plate – 'draw' round plate

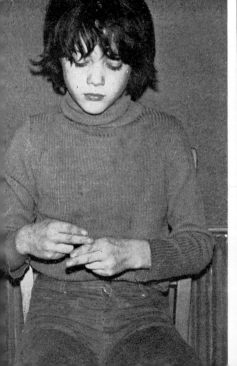

13. More — tap right hand on left

14. Sweets — remove toffee from teet

15. Hot — jerk hand away from mouth

16. Dirty — wipe right hand over left

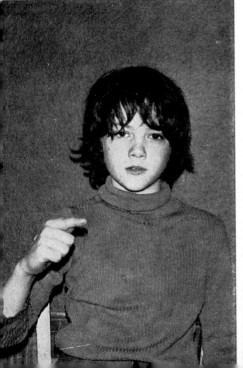

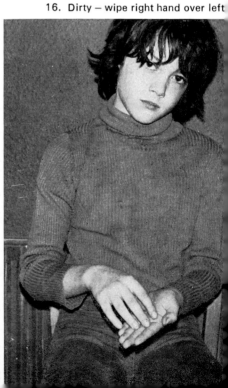

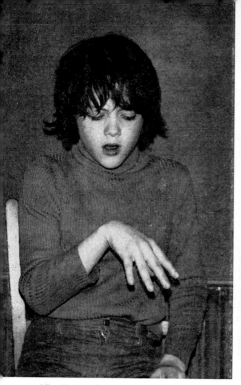

17. Hurt — jerk hand away

18. Wash — mime washing

19. Toilet — brush chest with fingers

20. Sleep — bed — lay head on hands

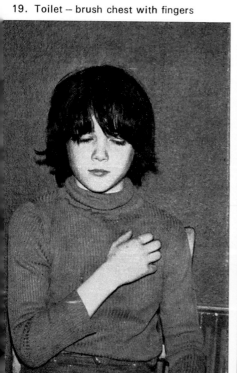

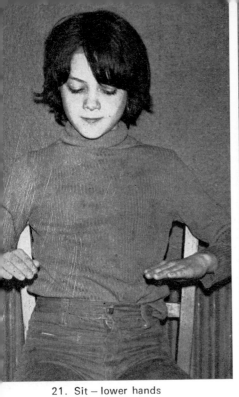

21. Sit — lower hands

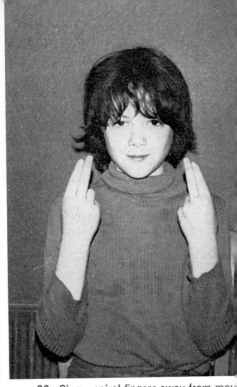

22. Sing — spiral fingers away from mou

23. Book — open book

24. Up — point upwards

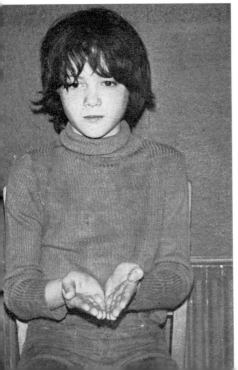

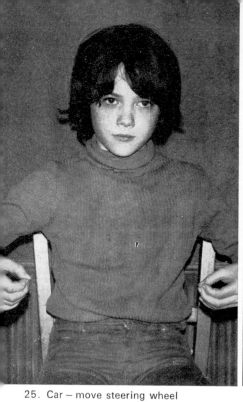

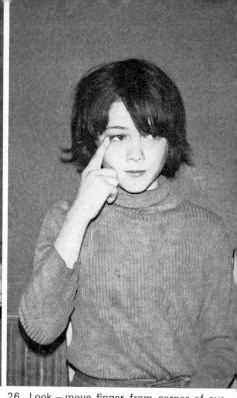

25. Car – move steering wheel

26. Look – move finger from corner of eye toward object

27. Come – beckon

28. Give – move hand away from self

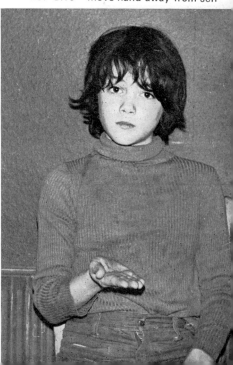

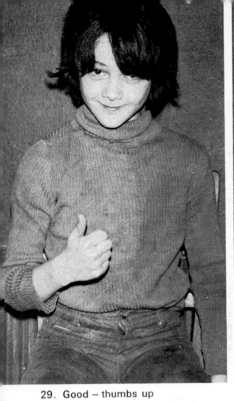

29. Good — thumbs up

30. Yes — 'nod' hand at wrist

31. No — cross and uncross arms

mean that the child is deaf. Sound may simply not mean anything to him. However, if the child's hearing has not been checked, it would be a very good idea to get it done now.

(2) *Does he listen?* Does the child listen to sounds which he makes in play, or to other people's voices? The child may produce noise, or appear to like noise, without really attending closely. He needs to acquire sharp and clear reactions to sounds.

(3) *Can he see?* This is important if gesture is to be used as part of the programme. Is his vision good enough to pick out gestures?

(4) *Does he attend to you when you speak or point?*

(5) *Does he understand simple requests?* Does he respond to requests like 'Come here', 'Sit down', 'Shush', 'Stand up', 'Stop', 'No'. If he does, which requests does he respond to? Will he respond to anyone making the request, or only to some people in some situations? Does the child respond to the words, or does he need a gesture as well? If he responds to the word, is it the actual word or is it the tone of voice used? If he responds to words only if accompanied by gesture, will he respond to the gesture alone?

(6) *Does he know the names of objects and things?* We can construct a checklist of names:

(a) Does he respond to his own name?

(b) Can he point to or get you common objects when you ask for them by name? Examples might be 'cup', 'plate', 'shoe'. Does he know the names of things which he plays with often?

(c) Can he point to parts of his body when you name them, or to parts of your body, or a doll's body?

(d) Will he go to parts of the house or to the garden or car when you ask him?

(7) *Does he know words used to describe things?* These might include the following:

(a) Hot—cold.

(b) Colours.

(c) Size: big, small.

(d) Shape: square, round.

(e) Number: one, two.

F

Finding out whether the child understands descriptive words needs quite a lot of ingenuity. We can use natural situations, especially the child's play situations, or we might have to contrive situations, like hiding a sweet under a big or small cup and then telling the child where it is, in order to get a clear picture. Remember that if the child does not respond correctly it may be that he has not learned about the attribute involved.

(8) *Does he understand two words together?* We have to be rather careful here. Quite often a child will learn to respond to two or more words as a unit. Examples might be 'Come here' or 'Stand up'. The response we are after is to a combination of two words that he understands as separate. So 'Peter gone' should provoke a different response from 'Mummy gone', 'Peter drink' from 'Mummy drink'.

(9) *Does he understand three-word sentences such as 'Daddy kick ball', 'Peter show doll'?* These represent a further step in the understanding of speech. Gather some examples.

(10) *More complicated sentences.* The child may understand more complex sentences. It would be useful to gather examples as they will give clues as to how the child may be able to learn to use language.

Ability to communicate
We will consider the development of communication through symbols, signs and speech.

Nonverbal communication

1. Basics of nonverbal communication
Table 14 covers these questions.

Table 14. Basics of nonverbal communication
(1) Can the child respond in any way by controlling his eyes, by moving his head or by using a hand or foot?
(2) Does he have changes in facial expression, such as smiling, frowning?
(3) Does he smile when you smile at him or when he is approached?

(4) Does he make a range of sounds which reflect different needs?

(1) *Can the child respond in any way by controlling his eyes, by moving his head or by using a hand or foot?* If the answer here is yes, then we can certainly consider him for a symbol programme, such as Bliss, which does not require the child to make complicated responses. If the answer is no, then we must try to teach him a method of responding.

(2) *Does he have changes in facial expression such as smiling or frowning?* If yes, these can be used in the initial stages of teaching. The child may not be 'aware' of his facial expressions, but we can use them as clues to his feelings and so get him to understand that his environment is responsive to his needs.

(3) *Does he smile when you smile at him or when he is approached?* Again this ability can be used as a starting point to show the child that his environment is responsive.

(4) *Does he make a range of sounds which reflect different needs?* Again we may be able to use these sounds to make the child aware of the responsiveness of the environment, and so to develop the idea of communication.

2. Communication by manipulation
See Table 15 for a listing of these questions.

Table 15. Communication by manipulation
(1) Does he reach up to be lifted?
(2) Does he lead or push an adult or child to things he wants?
(3) Does he bring objects to other people or take the people to the objects to ask for help in solving problems?

(1) *Does he reach up to be lifted?*
(2) *Does he lead or push an adult or other child to things he wants?* For example, he may push the adult into the kitchen when he wants a drink.
(3) *Does he bring objects to other people, or take the people to the objects, to ask for help in solving problems?* For example, he may give the adult a sweet tin and put his hands on the lid when he can't get it open.

The child at levels 2 and 3 ought to be a serious candidate for a signing programme, or for a speech programme if he can make speech sounds. If the child does not score on this section, look at Example 1 on page 174. If he scores in this section but he does not use signs or words, then look at Example 2 on page 174.

3. Communicates by gesture
Table 16 lists these questions.

Table 16. Communicates by gesture
(1) Does he communicate by giving the adult an object to represent a need?
(2) Does he show a near object which he wants by touching it, and looking at an adult or other child?
(3) Does he show distant objects which he wants by pointing?
(4) Does he use gestures to indicate any needs?
(5) Does the child mime needs?
(6) Does the child 'comment' on things or draw attention to them by pointing, even though he doesn't want them?
(7) Does the child comment by using gestures or mime?
(8) Does he nod 'yes' or shake his head for 'no'?
(9) Does he wave 'goodbye' on instruction?

(1) *Does he communicate by giving the adult an object to represent a need?* For example, the child may give a cup to his mother when he wants a drink. This is a transitional technique between manipulation and gesturing.
(2) *Does he show a near object which he wants by touching it and looking at an adult or other child?*
(3) *Does he show distant objects which he wants by pointing?* In order to 'score' here, the child should show evidence of realising when the adult is attending appropriately.
(4) *Does he use gestures to indicate any needs?* Examples might include holding himself when he wants to go to the toilet. In order to be classed here, the child should show some clear

intention to tell us something. We can infer this in several ways. For example, he may make a noise at the same time, or deliberately stand in front of you, or pull your face round so that you have to watch.

(5) *Does the child mime needs?* For example miming drinking or eating.

(6) *Does the child 'comment' on things, or draw attention to them by pointing, even though he doesn't want them?* This is the 'Look, mum' response. The child is sharing experience rather than wanting to have something. If the child does not do this look at Example 3 on page 175.

(7) *Does the child comment by using gestures or mime?*

(8) *Does he nod 'yes' or shake his head for 'no'?* This is a fairly abstract and advanced kind of response.

If the child scores on any of the items in Table 16, he is a *certain* candidate for a signing or speech programme. If he has speech sounds, then he might be taken towards speech. Either way you now want to know if he can imitate gestures or sounds. If he scores on items 6, 7 or 8 he is at a fairly advanced level of development and may well progress fast once you give him a chance. Examples 2, 3, 4, 6 and 7 should be of interest. Pages 174–179.

(9) *Does he wave 'goodbye' on instruction?* If yes, then he is aware of arm and hand positions as a means of communicating.

4. Motor imitation

The idea here is to see whether the child has the ability to imitate, as the first step in a signing or speech programme. Table 17 lists these questions.

Table 17. Motor imitation

(1) Will he imitate simple responses which you make which involve objects?

(2) Will he imitate simple responses which you make which involve your hands or body?

(3) Will he imitate hand postures which you make?

(1) *Will he imitate simple responses to objects?* First of all find a reward which the child likes, then sit beside him with a

collection of objects on the table in front of you. When the child has settled, select, say, a cup and two wooden blocks. You take one block, give him the other. Then say 'Look, Tommy, do this' and put your block in the cup. If he does not understand, then prompt him and reward the prompted response. If he responds correctly straight away, reward him and try another response: stacking two bricks together, or drawing a line on a piece of paper. If the child is successful in a range of say 10 or so imitation tasks, and he is interested and attentive, you can assume that he is capable in object motor imitation. If not, he may need more teaching to cooperate, or to imitate. See Example 6, page 179.

(2) *Will he imitate simple responses using hands and body?* Will the child imitate hands on head, clap hands, hands on knees, arms up in the air? If he can imitate in this way and is happy to, then we can go on to look at his imitation of hand postures. If not then he may benefit from some teaching in imitation. See Example 6, page 179.

(3) *Will he imitate your hand postures?* One of us (CK) has developed a simple Imitation Test, in collaboration with Barbara Reid. The test involves the 12 hand postures shown in Illustration 5. You sit beside the child and say 'Look, Tommy, do this' and show him each hand posture in order. If necessary a couple of practice trials can be used to give the child the idea. If the child gets all the responses right, then we can say quite confidently that he will be able to make most of the signs required by any sign system. If he can make only a flat hand, fist hand and index hand he is clearly discriminating but may need a lot of help with other postures. Common errors can be very informative. The child may make the right shape but use the wrong fingers. This happens especially with the Y hand. Or he may not get the correct number of fingers in the V hand, or be able to distinguish between the V hand and the 1,2 finger hand because he does not attend to the separation of the two fingers. So the test can be used to diagnose something about how the child is seeing the postures.

If the child cannot imitate more than a few signs it would probably be a good idea to focus teaching on those signs which need the postures he can do.

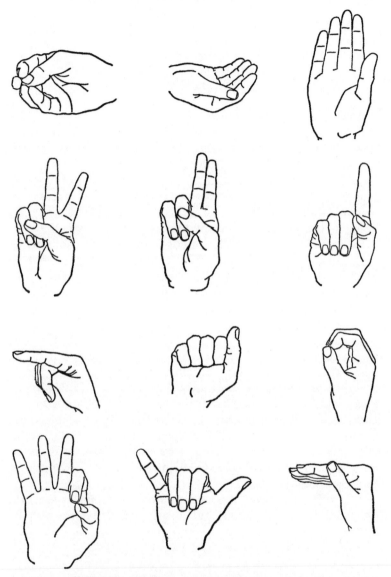

Figure 5. Postures from the Imitation Test

(1) Compressed hand. (2) Cupped hand. (3) Flat hand. (4) V hand.
(5) 1, 2 finger hand (6) Index hand. (7) Right-angle index hand. (8) Fist
hand. (9) O hand. (10) 2, 3, 4 finger hand. (11) Y hand. (12) L hand.

Verbal communication

Table 18. Development of sounds
(1) Does the child produce speech sounds?
(2) Does the child babble?

1. Development of sounds

(1) *Does the child produce speech sounds?* There is some unnecessary mystification around the business of assessment of speech sounds. It is true that really accurate logging of speech sounds requires a very good ear and a detailed knowledge of how the sounds *should* be made—sounds can resemble speech sounds yet be made in the wrong way. However, a working assessment can be made quite easily, using the phonetic list on page 169.

In the table the speech sounds are divided into vowels, diphthongs and consonants. The symbols are those used to describe the sounds in phonetics. We suggest you write down what your child's vocalisations sound like in ordinary word form first. Then get two or three people to listen and agree on a phonetic transcription. So the child might make a loud noise sounding like 'each' or 'werr'. These might be transcribed as 'i:tʃ' and 'wə:'. This method may be approximate, but it will allow you to see whether the child can produce all types of sound or only vowels and diphthongs. If we look closely at the consonants, we can see whether the child fails to produce consonants with particular characteristics, for example those involving lip motion or different tongue positions in the mouth (the alveolar, velar and dental); or those involving different types of breath control (plosive, fricative etc.); or the voiced or unvoiced sounds.

It is difficult to prompt speech sounds. Example 5, page 177, describes some techniques, but also suggests that we may be better advised not to try! Example 6, page 179, suggests ways to teach imitation of speech sounds.

(2) *Does the child babble?* Does he produce chains of speech sounds which he appears to vary? If the answer is yes, then this may be the beginning of speech. However, we cannot assume that if the child does babble then he will go on to speech without help. In any case we may be able to push his development along a bit.

THE PHONEMES COMMONLY RECOGNISED IN ENGLISH

	Phonetic symbol	Sample word		Voiced or Unvoiced	Place of Articulation	Manner of Articulation
1	i:	*eat*		V		
2	i	*it*		V		
3	e	*get*		V		
4	a	*act*		V		
5	a:	*art*	VOWELS	V		
6	o	*on*		V		
7	o:	*saw*		V		
8	u	*book*		V		
9	u:	*soon*		V		
10	ʌ	*up*		V		
11	ə:	*word* ⎫		V		
12	ə	*ever* ⎬		V		
13	ei	*aid*		V		
14	ou	*own*		V		
15	ai	*eye*	DIPHTHONGS	V		
16	au	*out*		V		
17	oi	*oil*		V		
18	iu	*due*		V		
19	uə	*poor*		V		
20	eə	*air*		V		
21	iə	*hear*		V		
22	p	*paid*		UV	Bi-labial	Plosive
23	b	*been*		V	,,	,,
24	t	*tea*		UV	Alveolar	,,
25	d	*day*		V	,,	,,
26	k	*car*		UV	Velar	,,
27	g	*give*		V	,,	,,
28	f	*farm*		UV	Labio-dental	Fricative
29	v	*very*		V	,,	,,
30	θ	*think*		UV	Dental	,,
31	ð	*these*		V	,,	,,
32	s	*say*	CONSONANTS	UV	Alveolar	,,
33	z	*size*		V	,,	,,
34	ʃ	*she*		UV	,, back	,,
35	ʒ	*measure*		V	,, back	,,
36	r	*red*		V	Alveolar	,,
37	h	*hope*		UV	Glottal	,,
38	tʃ	*chair*		UV	Alveolar	Affricate
39	dʒ	*just*		V	,,	,,
40	m	*met*		V	Bi-labial	Nasal
41	n	*near*		V	Alveolar	,,
42	ŋ	*long*		V	Velar	,,
43	l	*life*		V	Alveolar	Lateral
44	w	*win*		V		Semi-vowel
45	j	*yet*		V		,,

F*

2. Verbal imitation

Table 19 lists these questions.

Table 19. Verbal imitation

(1) Will the child blow, smack his lips, open his mouth, put his tongue out or blow through his lips when you ask him to imitate?

(2) Does the child imitate your speech sounds when you ask him to do so?

(3) Does he imitate combinations of speech sounds?

(4) Does he imitate words?

(1) *Will the child blow, smack his lips, open his mouth, put his tongue out or blow through his lips when you ask him to imitate?* This should be a game if possible. Get the child to blow on his hand, or to blow pieces of paper off a dish in imitation of you. You may get him to put out his tongue by showing him how to lick up sugar from a dish. The object, however, is to see if he will respond *without* the physical props, in other words just imitate you. The idea behind this question is to see if the child has voluntary control over the responses which are necessary in the production of speech sounds.

If he can imitate these responses, then it would be worth trying to teach him to imitate speech sounds.

(2) *Does the child imitate your speech sounds when you ask him to do so?* We can again test this fairly formally if necessary. If we take a selection of sounds from the list of speech sounds, and ask the child 'Look, Tommy, do this', we can again assess both his ability and his willingness to imitate.

If he can do this he is well on the way to being able to use speech. If he cannot do this, look at Example 6 on page 179.

(3) *Does he imitate combinations of speech sounds?* Will the child imitate sound combinations, of the kind used in words? Some children find great difficulty in blending sounds.

(4) *Does he imitate words?* When the child can do this, he is home so far as speech sounds are concerned.

3. Communication by sounds and words

Table 20. Communication by sounds and words

(1) Does he make sounds to draw your attention to his needs?

(2) Does he use any words correctly for needs or to get something he wants?

(3) Does he use these words with everyone or wherever the need arises or only in special settings?

(4) Does he refer to things by words in order to draw the attention of other people to them and share experience?

(5) Does he use a range of words like 'more', 'no', 'stop', to regulate other people's behaviour?

(6) Does he use two words together in a flexible way?

(1) *Does he make sounds to draw attention to his needs?* These may include crying, shouting, squealing. We have to be very careful in working out exactly what the child is doing when he makes noises. Many non-speaking handicapped children we have come across make a lot of noise, but the noise does not seem to be communicative. We shall develop this point further in an example, but meanwhile we can lay down some rules of thumb. If the child makes the noise only or mainly when adults or other people who help him are around, and if the noise stops or changes significantly when he gets attention or his need is filled, then we can probably say he is using the noise communicatively. If he is, we may safely infer that he has the idea of communication through sound. If not, we may try to teach him to use sound this way. This can be followed up in Example 5, page 177.

(2) *Does he use any words correctly for needs, or to get something he wants?* These may be baby words, but they must be directed at other children or adults and refer to particular situations. If yes, see Example 6, page 179.

(3) *Does he use these words with everyone, and wherever the need arises, or only in special settings?* If the answer is special settings only, then we need to set up a programme to generalise the use of the word.

(4) *Does he refer to things by words in order to draw the attention of other people to them and share experience?* If the answer is no, look at Example 3, page 175.

(5) *Does he use a range of words like 'more', 'no', 'stop', to regulate other people's behaviour?* If no, then this is a useful step in teaching.

(6) *Does he use two words together in a flexible way?* For example, can he say 'more pudding' or 'drink gone', as well as 'more drink' or 'pudding gone'.

INTERPRETING THE ASSESSMENT

The only requirement for going any further is that the child should score at least something in the section on needs and interests. If he does not, your programme should begin with the development of needs and interests in Chapter 5.

Otherwise, the really crucial sections are those on the use of communication. By now you should have an idea of where your child can fit in.

EXAMPLES OF TEACHING PROGRAMMES

Any programme for teaching a child communication needs to be carefully geared to his needs and interests on the one hand, and to his motor skills in speech or signing on the other. We feel that the child should always be led *toward* normal verbal communication. We suggest therefore that we should never lose sight of that goal, even though it may be clear from very early on that the child has not got the motor ability to produce speech. We can at least lead him toward the use of written words. For a child who has perfectly normal speech musculature, we would want always to work toward the goal of normal speech, at least by keeping open the options. We might decide to go for signing, Bliss, Premack or another system in order to begin, but we would keep the options open; for instance, by always speaking whilst signing or using Bliss, and by watching out for and rewarding any tendency on the child's part to use speech or to vocalise more appropriately. There are now many examples recorded of children who began by using signing and then, apparently quite spontaneously, started to speak. We have some ideas about why this happens (Example 6, page 179), and we can help the process by using several simple techniques described in Examples 6 and 8, pages 179 and 183.

On the other hand we would take it as a first principle that the child *must* be given some means of communication. The range of systems available is wide and can be suited to all needs. We would suggest that even the most profoundly.

handicapped child is capable of some form of communication of needs. Providing the child with a means of communication is one of the most fundamental ways in which we can give him a degree of independence and control over his environment.

The setting of teaching

We have seen that in order to learn to communicate the child must have something to communicate about (needs or interests), the idea that he can communicate, a means of communication, and, if communication is to be two-way, an understanding of our communication to him.

Given these requirements, the setting of teaching is crucial. In order to foster communication the setting must have two characteristics:

(1) It must be able to satisfy the child's needs and interests;
(2) It should require the child to communicate in order to get his needs or interests satisfied.

We said in a previous chapter that a fairly free environment with plenty of opportunity to find out about toys and people represents an ideal educational environment. But this description must be qualified in order to foster the development of communication. In a completely free classroom, or in a home where the child has free access to all the toys, to drinks, to the toilet, to the garden, *there may be no reason why he should learn to communicate*. He can get everything he wants without anybody else's help. No more encouraging to communication is the typical hospital setting, where the child has 'everything done for him'. He is given his food at particular times with no opportunity for asking for food at other times, he is toileted regularly and changed if dirty, he is allowed up at certain times, and put to bed at certain times, allowed in the garden or in the swimming pool according to a rota.

In order to teach the child to communicate, we need either to get between him and the satisfaction of a need, or to involve ourselves in his interests in order to become part of his games. These are really very simple principles. In the first case we teach the child to ask us when he wants a drink rather than allow him to get it for himself; in the second, instead of simply watching him play with his toy cars, we play with him, pushing his cars back to him or devising a slope they can run down.

(Once he is confident that we will give him the car back, we could teach him to ask us to push the car or to set up the slope.)

Example 1. Getting over the idea of communication

Bob was a child who had no means of communicating his needs or wishes. He had no speech, no gestures and did not lead people to things. If you took things away from him when he was playing, he would wander off and find something else. Occasionally he would cry for no obvious reason, but he never asked for things in any way.

We decided to try to teach him to communicate by leading the teacher to an object he wanted. We knew a lot about the things he preferred doing in the classroom, one of which was to scoot around on a trolley in the shape of an aeroplane. But you could take the aeroplane away and he would not complain or try to get it back.

The programme involved two people. The teacher waited until Bob was playing on the plane and then she took it away and put it on a high shelf. The assistant immediately led Bob over to the teacher and put his hands on her as if reaching up to 'ask for' the plane. The teacher then returned the plane and Bob was allowed to play on it for a couple of minutes. Then the whole process was repeated.

Within a few trials Bob was going readily to the teacher and the assistant could fade out her prompts. Within two weeks, with seven or eight trials per day, the teacher was able to go to different parts of the room after putting the plane away and Bob would still come and lead her to the shelf.

Bob generalised the new response to other people and situations, with only a small amount of extra teaching. Within three or four weeks he had led a child to the playground gate and put his hand on it to open it for him. And one afternoon when he clearly did not feel well he led the nursery nurse to his coat to ask her to put it on him. He then led her to the outside door. Bob had asked to go home.

Example 2. Deciding the words to use for a child with no speech or signs

Jim could communicate only by leading people, or bringing things to them. We decided to try to teach him to sign. In deciding where to start, we decided to list all the objects and situations which he enjoyed. This gave us several objects and situations which were easy to manipulate. These included sweets, drinks and tea, the opportunity to play with cars and an Action Man, and to have a cupboard open to get toys out. (Other situations, not so easy to manipulate, included going out in a car and going to the swimming pool.) We decided to begin with one object, the Action Man, to try to give Jim the idea that making a sign could substitute for leading the person. A game was set up in which the man was hidden by the teacher, Jim was prompted to make the sign, and the return of the Action Man was the reward. After he had got over his initial anxiety that his man had disappeared, the game became fun and the sign became a part of it.

This sign was then generalised to other settings, and signs relating to other needs were introduced.

The objective of the programme was to establish the idea that a sign could communicate a need. We started from the child's needs and worked from there.

Example 3. Deciding the words to use for a child with some speech or signs

There are several kinds of problem here. We will outline two.

Jim, the child in the last example, progressed well in his signing programme. But all of the signs he learned related to his needs or interests. After a time it became clear that we could not extend his vocabulary or his use of language unless we taught him to use signs in a different way. We felt that we had to teach him to use signs to describe or simply to name objects. This would take him into the phase of development involving sharing of experience—the 'look, mummy—a dog' phase—where there is no request except that mummy looks and shares the enjoyment.

A game was set up by hiding a favourite toy behind big pictures of common objects, such as a shoe, a telephone, a dog and a ball. Jim could see the toy being put behind the picture, and was prompted to make the sign for the object it had been hidden behind, whilst the teacher also made the sign and said the word. Prompts were faded, leaving Jim with a new set of words which he could use.

Generalisation was planned by ensuring that everyone who came in contact with Jim knew the words, and drew Jim's attention to the objects and named them whenever they saw them outside the teaching situation. Correct naming by Jim was rewarded.

Finally Jim began to draw the attention of adults to objects, which he named for the sake of shared experience.

Simon presented a different kind of problem. He had a narrow but effective vocabulary, with some adult words and some baby words. In addition he had many single words which stood for requests, or served to point things out to people. So he would say 'Ay' when he wanted attention or help.

Simon's programme involved several strands. He was taught new vocabulary in order to extend his knowledge of words. He was prompted to replace baby words with their adult equivalent. Finally, where he was using single words to count for two or three, he was prompted to use a fuller phrase. So 'Ay' was replaced by 'help', with the appropriate word for whatever he wanted help with.

The general principle of selection is that the programme should begin from the words or signs the child needs to use. The programme then develops in line with the increasing demands which the child puts on his environment. *But* the environment may need to be engineered in order to create situations requiring new types of communication.

Example 4. Teaching social words

One thing all children have to do is to relate to other people in a social way. No doubt in recognition of this, teaching programmes sometimes teach the child to say or sign 'please'. This is fine if the child already has some words or signs: it helps you to accept the child's requests—or demands. But the policy can misfire. In one programme the sign for please had been taught very early on. A child would sign 'please', the teacher would say 'what do you want?' and the child would then point to the object. But these children seemed to be failing to learn the names of the objects. They had learned to use the sign as a substitute for the name of the object they wanted.

The value of teaching a social response can be clearly demonstrated, however, by the example of another child who tended to be rather rough in his play. He would quite often, though accidentally, hurt other children or adults. This produced the natural response of aggression in the person hurt. Normal children learn very quickly to say 'sorry, sorry' when they have hurt another child or their parent, and this tends to inhibit aggression. But our child had not learned this. So we felt that it would be a good idea to teach him 'sorry'. The next time he hurt someone accidentally, an adult immediately prompted 'sorry' in sign language, in this case the Paget Gorman 'sorry', hitting your left breast twice just above the heart with a closed fist. The hurt person immediately stopped looking angry. The next time someone got hurt accidentally, the child signed 'sorry' quite spontaneously. The situation was clear, the motivation was high and learning was therefore fast.

Example 5. Teaching the child to make sounds

We have already seen how signs can be taught by showing the child an object, prompting the child to make the sign, and then fading the prompt. In this way we can teach the child single signs quite effectively.

There are bigger problems in encouraging the child to make speech sounds. With a hand sign we can take the child's hand and mould it to the right shape. We cannot do this with speech. If the child does not make speech sounds spontaneously we have a very hard job.

In one method that has been used the teacher in some way forces the child to produce noises, and then rewards him. For instance, she might put her arm round him and squeeze him suddenly, thereby getting him to produce an involuntary sound. This sound production is then rewarded. This technique has been used successfully to get a child making noises which have indeed led to communication, but it is not a pleasant one to use.

A second approach works only if the child makes *some* sounds in some situations. For instance, one child was found to make his only sound when music was playing. The teacher played a record which made the child vocalise. She rewarded any vocalisation during the record, then the volume of the record was gradually lowered until the child was vocalising without the record being played at all.

Another method of rewarding speech sounds is simply to wait until the child vocalises and then to reward him. This could be a very inefficient method, especially if the child does not vocalise frequently.

In addition we have come across several children who make quite a range of sounds, but the sounds are 'play' or emotional reactions, without any apparent communicative value.

Bob, the child already mentioned, vocalised a great deal. Careful observation showed that his main vocalisations were squeals, with some varied speech sounds. The squeals he produced sometimes with people, sometimes on his own; but the speech sounds always accompanied solitary play. Several attempts to change this pattern failed. The reason for our failure may have been that we were simply not clever enough to devise an effective programme to change his vocalisation. Another possible reason might have been some mysterious factor related to the way his brain worked. And a third possibility might have been connected with the fact that his rate of vocalisation throughout the day, on average one a minute, meant that the majority of his noises were ignored, simply because they were made at such a rate that attending to them all would have been impossible. So for the most part the child got attention and rewards regardless of his vocalisation, and occasionally he was told to shut up when things got too noisy. From the child's point of view, therefore, his vocalisations had little effect on his environment. Against this background the introduction of a relatively short session of reward for vocalisation would have only a small impact.

The general conclusion from our experience is that speech sounds can be difficult to prompt, and they may not be the best place to start with a communication programme in any case. This is *not* to say that we shouldn't aim to end up with speech sounds—simply that we should not feel defeated when we cannot make an impression by this route at first.

Once the child can make a range of speech sounds spontaneously, we can use other techniques to encourage him to use them and possibly to extend them. These techniques all involve imitation.

Example 6. Teaching the child to imitate

The ability to imitate can be very important in the teaching of the handicapped child. If the child does not work something out for himself, or is unable to follow verbal instructions, then the ability to imitate allows us to show him what to do.

Ian was a child who had no effective method of communicating. He was fifteen years old. He had no speech and made no speech sounds. We decided to include him in an imitation training programme. The first step was to assess his ability to imitate. A test was devised. Ian was asked to copy a number of simple responses: putting a spoon in a cup, standing up, clapping his hands, and putting an object on the floor. His first performance was very poor, but part of the problem was that he would not look at what we were trying to get him to do, and he also wandered off.

So the first step in the programme consisted of teaching him to sit down and look when he was called. This we did by rewarding him every 30 seconds or so when he was sitting. Reward was given when we called 'Ian look', and he looked at us. Reward was ensured because he was prompted by having his head turned gently, even if he did not look spontaneously. After six short sessions he was sitting and looking reliably when called.

A retest on imitation did not produce a better performance than the first. Ian simply did not understand what we wanted of him.

The next step was to teach him to imitate two simple responses: to put a small toy into a cardboard box, and to stack two beakers together. These two were picked because they were easy to do and easy to prompt. We needed two tasks because our aim was to teach Ian to attend to and watch what the adult was doing as a cue to what he should do. If we had used one task only, he would not have had to watch the adult to find out what to do.

Ian and his teacher sat side by side. The two tasks were put in front of Ian and an identical set in front of the person teaching. We then said 'Ian, do this'. The task was then demonstrated. Ian was prompted if necessary, and rewarded regardless of whether prompts were used. Gradually prompts were withdrawn. Once Ian had successfully made the responses

for three of four sessions, he was no longer allowed to correct
a wrong choice. If he made a mistake he did not get rewarded.

Ian learned fast. The first two tasks reached 90 per cent
correct and were replaced by two others. After each block of
four tasks, we tested to see if he was generalising to novel tasks.
After twelve tasks he generalised very well. At this stage he had
learned to attend to an adult when called, to watch him when
he said 'Ian do this', and then to imitate the response the adult
showed him. We showed that he would do this in different
settings and with people who were relative strangers.

Ian developed a useful generalised imitative response which
could be used to teach him new motor skills, to help in general
cooperation and to form the basis of a communication
programme.

Some children find it quite easy to learn responses involving
objects, but have great difficulty in learning responses involving
only their bodies. So a child might quite happily learn to
imitate putting a car in a box or putting two pieces of a puzzle
together, but find it very hard to learn to put his hand on his
leg or his finger on the tip of his nose. If this is the case, it can
be a big block to progress. One way round it is to teach the
child in front of a mirror, drawing attention to the similarity of
your responses and his. Another way to try is to include an
object in the response as a first step. So the first step towards
touching the top of your head might be for both adult and
child to have a hat on, or a piece of cloth on the head, and the
first response to be imitated would be to take off the hat or
cloth. A piece of cloth might be faded by cutting down its size.
Similarly, with touching your nose, you might begin with a
small piece of sticky paper stuck on the adult's and the child's
noses. The first task is then taking the paper off. Once this is
well established, the paper can be omitted, and touching will
occur instead.

Once the child has a well established tendency to imitate
object-related responses, he can move on to body-related ones.
It may be that only when these are well established will he
begin to imitate vocalisations, but it is always a good idea to try
to generalise object- or body-related motor imitation to sounds.

This can be done by including a couple of sounds in any imitation teaching session.

It is not surprising that children should learn to imitate sounds as a result of learning to imitate motor responses. Learning to imitate involves learning to attend to responses which adults make and trying to reproduce them. Many children may be quite capable of imitating sounds, but because these are hard to prompt, they do not learn that the adult wants them to imitate. Teaching them to imitate motor responses helps them to get this message. So when they have learned what is required of them, they may begin to imitate speech sounds apparently quite spontaneously. This is almost certainly one of the reasons why children so often learn to speak as a side effect of a sign teaching programme.

Once the child can imitate sounds reliably, it is possible to teach simple words. The method here is already familiar. The adult holds up an object, such as a cup with a drink in it, and says 'Look, Tommy, what's this?' . . . 'drink, say drink'. The child is then rewarded for saying 'drink' by being given a small drink. The process is then repeated until the child is imitating readily—perhaps saying 'drink' after the first repetition. At this stage the pause between 'what's this?' and 'drink' can be lengthened. Often the child will then produce the word appropriately. Or the prompt 'drink' can be faded by saying it very quietly or just saying 'd——'.

Once the child has learned in this context, each word should be used in several contexts, with several related objects, and, if possible, with several people.

A technique of developing speech sounds should be mentioned at this point. It is fairly easy to teach a child to make particular lip positions in making words because he can see what he has to do. It is not possible for the child to see how you make sounds like 'rrr' which involve a vibration of the vocal flaps. We can feel these being made if we put our fingers on either side of the windpipe just under the back of the jaw. Speech therapists sometimes use this vibration as an extra cue to the child. The adult models the sound with the child's hand on her throat, and then puts his hand on his own throat. If the child can produce the noise at all, this technique is helpful. But the child obviously needs to be very cooperative and fairly sophisticated as well as highly imitative to pick this up and use it as a cue.

One final point about teaching imitation. Speech therapists often say that teaching the child to imitate leads to echolalia— the meaningless repetition of anything the adult says. So the adult may say 'What's your name', and the child say 'Your name'; the adult, 'My name's Chris', and the child, 'names Chris', and so on. In our experience echolalia in mentally handicapped children usually develops when the child can't understand, or wants the adult to go away. From the child's point of view this is pretty effective: it is extremely frustrating to try to converse with an echolalic child, so the adult breaks off the exchange pretty quickly, or starts to help the child in the way he wants. The following conversation illustrates this. Adult: 'Phil, put your coat on.' Phil: '. . . coat on.' Adult: 'Put on your coat.' Phil: '. . . your coat.' Adult, picking up coat: 'Come here.' Phil: 'Come here' (not moving). Adult, taking coat to child and putting it on him: 'Here you are then.' Phil: '. . . are then.'

Echolalia is likely to develop only if the programme is badly planned and does not tap the child's needs. We have never seen a child develop an echolalic tendency as a result of an imitation training programme.

Example 7. Teaching signs with flash cards

Margaret Walker, already mentioned as one of the workers who developed the Makaton Vocabulary, used the vocabulary initially in group teaching. The students sit round a table with a teacher and a helper. Pictures or miniatures of objects are used. The teacher shows the picture and says 'Look, this is a ball'. She then models the response, and the students imitate, if necessary with help from the teacher or helper. Later objects may be used instead of pictures, then real life situations as well. Conversations between students are encouraged. They are asked about what they do out of the teaching situation.

This approach can be very effective when used with suitable students. Several published studies show that adult mentally handicapped people can learn to use over 100 signs in six to nine months, and this can revolutionise people's lives. However, in order to benefit fully, a candidate must have the following:

(*a*) A well developed set of ideas and concepts which allow him to identify objects from pictures or miniatures.
(*b*) Willingness to attend and to stay in a group.
(*c*) Good imitative abilities.

This type of learning is rather like the learning of a second language. The ideal student already has the concepts to which he attaches the responses that enable him to express himself.

One of the problems with the method is that it may not mesh with the child's own established needs. The child may not learn the words he needs unless parents or nurses list what his interests and needs are in advance.

The other—related—problem is generalisation. The system will not work out well unless measures are taken to ensure generalisation to settings other than the teaching setting. It may be necessary to follow up each setting the child moves in, to make sure that it requires him to communicate and that other people know what he is saying and are prepared to talk to him.

Example 8. The transition from signs to speech

We have come across several reasons why children learning signs often move on easily to producing speech: their attention is focused on speech by signs, they learn to imitate signs and therefore may be more ready to imitate speech. But there are other reasons as well. The teacher or parents may find renewed motivation when they move to signs. The adult certainly becomes more aware of the complexity of verbal statements when she is signing at the same time. Even the statement 'Will you come here, please' is actually very complicated, and if this is replaced with the two-sign 'Come here', or even just 'Come', the effect is a greatly simplified language structure which is far more accessible to the child.

At another level the child who has learned signs may be increasingly motivated to learn speech because he finds increasing frustration in not being able to communicate with people who do not understand his signs.

All of these possibilities should be thought of in using signing, for the aim of any signing programme really ought to be to get the child or adult moved on to normal speech. This may happen in several ways.

If speech is always used with signing, the signs can be used as extra cues to meaning. Several teachers have found it easier to teach 'in', 'on', 'under' and other prepositions by a combination of signs and speech, than by speech alone. In both British Sign Language and Paget Gorman Sign System prepositions are expressed by reference of the hands to one another. This gives a valuable added cue which can be faded when the child has learned the meaning of the word.

A similar example comes from a school where the teacher was using signs with speech. She found that children were more confident in learning spoken words if they learned the signs as well.

Despite these positive examples there is no doubt that children who find it easier to sign or to read signs than they find it to use speech may become dependent on signs. We can, however, devise programmes which will encourage the child to attend to speech.

The basic structure is simple. The child is taught to identify objects on the basis of signs. This may be in a formal teaching session, or in a generalised programme. The objects or pictures are then presented in groups of three or four, and the child is asked, in sign, to identify the objects; 'Show me dog' etc. If he can identify the objects by sign the same procedure can be repeated with words. If he is accurate here then there is no problem. If he is confused, he needs to be taught to identify the objects through spoken words.

This can be done again by setting up a teaching session where the child is asked 'Show me dog' etc., with the request spoken and signed (in that order) and a correct response rewarded. If the child is to learn that the word 'dog' stands for the sign, then the word must be a signal for the sign, that is the word must precede the sign. This way the child will need to attend to the word in order to solve the problem.

You can set the situation up in such a way that the adult says 'Show me dog' (word) then 'dog' (sign). The gap between the two should be only about a half second, until the child has really learned how to play the game. You can then try dropping the sign completely on occasion. These probe trials will test the child's learning of the words, and also give you the opportunity to reward the child for responding to words.

The principle behind this stage of teaching is that the word *must* be given signal value. The child's attainment of a goal must be dependent on his attending to it.

This type of session can be effectively extended if the child can also be asked to name.

CONCLUSION

In this chapter we have discussed ways of assessing the child's communication and ways of working on communication. Our central points are that there is always somewhere to start, and something that can be done to help the child communicate his needs and interests; that if we are to be effective we must start from where the child is; and that we should always move toward the most normal type of communication possible. In terms of assessment we need to observe the child very carefully, especially if he is very handicapped. The programme must be cast in the context of the child's normal life and involve all of his normal contacts if generalisation is to be achieved.

11: Learning to Feed

The skills which we are going to consider in the following chapters are feeding, washing, toileting and dressing. The teaching of these skills should be seen as an important part of the child's day in school and home. At a general level, an increase in competence in these skills leads to a corresponding increase in independence for the child, and independence should be a primary target of teachers and parents. In addition the child can learn or practise many other things during the teaching of self-help skills. For instance, during the early stages of learning to feed, the child will need to develop well controlled grasping, though it is not necessary for grasping to be developed to perfection before you begin teaching self feeding—the two skills can be taught at the same time. If the child enjoys food, mealtimes offer good opportunities for teaching skills such as grasping, since successful self feeding will be inherently rewarding.

The child may spend a sizeable part of his day in feeding, toileting and dressing. Many very severely handicapped children have to be helped with all these skills. In practice it is usually much quicker to feed and dress such a child than to try to get him to do it for himself, but this is likely to be a short-term saving, with few direct benefits for the child. It makes sense to see his daily routines as valuable teaching periods, and whenever possible to use them as such.

We shall use the same framework for the development of our programmes as we have in previous chapters. Having decided on which of the self-help skills you want to teach, there are four steps to follow.

(1) Assess what your child can do now.
(2) On the basis of this assessment, decide on a suitable aim for your programme. This can be stated in broad terms such as: getting your child to eat solid food; getting him to use a spoon without help from an adult; getting him dry during the day.

(3) Decide on what type of reward you will use in order to teach him these skills.

(4) Plan the first step in your teaching programme. This should be stated in simple and precise terms: Getting Peter to put the filled spoon in his mouth, without the aid of a prompt from an adult.

FEEDING

There are four groups of problems that we wish to cover in our assessment of feeding skills and the subsequent planning of programmes:

(1) The teaching of self feeding.

(2) Methods of overcoming feeding problems which arise from physical handicap.

(3) Methods of overcoming food fads.

(4) Overcoming problem behaviours. These are covered in the assessment table and discussed in the example programmes. However, Chapters 2 and 14 will also be relevant to this topic.

Table 21 highlights the skills that your child should have before you begin a self feeding programme. The two essentials are that he should be able to grasp the spoon, and move his hand to his mouth. Being able to finger feed is also an advantage because it clearly indicates that the child has the necessary awareness and motivation to begin using a spoon. It is not, however, an essential component.

It may be that a feeding programme will act as a means of improving your child's ability to grasp and move hand to mouth. However, if the problem is severe you may need to work on these skills before self feeding can be considered.

Table 22 considers the types of food your child eats: for instance, whether he eats a variety of foods or merely a few specific things. If the latter is the case, expanding the diet would seem a higher priority than self feeding, so this would probably be your first consideration in a teaching programme.

Table 23 considers problem behaviours. Your child may frequently refuse to eat, or have temper tantrums while you are trying to feed him. These may be closely associated with food fads and can be dealt with as a combined problem. Plate throwing and general naughtiness at mealtimes is more likely to be a problem associated with control or attention, and will probably require the use of procedures described in Chapter 14.

FEEDING ASSESSMENT

Table 21. Self feeding

(1) Does your child have difficulty in both grasping and moving hand to mouth?
(2) Does he have difficulty in either grasping or moving hand to mouth?
(3) Is he able to grasp and move hand to mouth?
(4) Does he make any attempt to feed himself?
(5) Does he finger feed?
(6) Does he attempt to feed with a spoon, but have difficulty?
(7) Is he able to use a spoon, or spoon and fork, without difficulty?

Table 22. Types of food

(1) Does your child have difficulty in swallowing food?
(2) Will he take only liquids?
(3) Will he eat only a limited number of foods?
(4) Does he eat most foods, even though they have to be liquidised?
(5) Does he eat most foods, although these need to be mashed?
(6) Does he eat most types of food he is given?
(7) Does he seem to enjoy his food?

Table 23. Problem behaviours

(1) Does your child often struggle or cry when being fed?
(2) Does he struggle or cry when being fed particular foods that he does not like?
(3) Does he have problem behaviours at mealtime? These might include throwing cutlery or plates, trying to steal other people's food, or persisting in

eating with his fingers in spite of being able to use
a spoon or fork.

THE TEACHING OF SELF FEEDING

The aim of programmes in this section will be to teach your
child to feed himself independently. In the case of a blind or
partially sighted child, or a child suffering from mild physical
handicap, your aim will be to get him to feed himself with the
minimum of assistance. The problems arising from severe
physical handicap will be dealt with in a later section.

Teaching your child to feed himself by using a spoon should
be relatively straightforward, provided he enjoys food. The food
will be his reward for learning to use his spoon, and because it
is the 'natural' reward at mealtimes you will not have to face
the problem of phasing out the reward once he has learned the
skill of using a spoon. Furthermore, mealtimes usually take
place three times a day, and this allows plenty of opportunity
for practice; they are also times when you probably give
undivided attention to your child. The regularity, the one-to-
one relationship and the built-in reward, all contribute to make
feeding an ideal teaching situation.

Difficulties may arise if your child is attending a day school
or playgroup and there is no attempt to coordinate the methods
used at home and at school. Ideally, parent and teacher should
have regular contact to discuss the current position and plan
the next step. But even if teacher and parent find themselves
working independently on the same problem, this may slow
down your child's progress, but it should not be reason enough
to stop you planning and carrying through a teaching
programme.

TEACHING METHODS

The reward

In this section we will be discussing programmes suitable for
children who are physically able to use a spoon, and who enjoy
eating most foods. The food will act as the main reward. But
you must also consider the need to use attention and praise as
additional rewards for developing the skills. It is important to

see attention acting as a reward, and use it as such. If we see food as the only reward at mealtimes, when your child fails to lift the filled spoon to his mouth and misses the food, he will not be rewarded even though his response has been appropriate. Attention in the form of 'Oh dear, Peter, what a mess, let's have another go', will act as reward to encourage him to try again. As a rule of thumb we suggest that success in the various steps in the teaching programme be rewarded with food and praise. Failure should result in no food and no comment.

The first step

So far we have assessed our child, decided on an overall aim, and decided on a method of reward. We must now face the problem of deciding on the first step in teaching the skill. In previous chapters we have discussed the value of teaching the final stage in a sequence of steps first (backward chaining). Grasping the filled spoon as it enters the mouth represents the final step in the chain, and it is the step immediately followed by the reward. As such it is the most appropriate one to begin with.

At the beginning of the programme this step may require a full prompt. The target will be to fade this prompt so that your child will eventually make this action without need of guidance from you. Start by filling the spoon and resting it on the edge of the dish. Place your child's hand around the spoon handle, and holding his hand firmly guide it to his mouth. As the filled spoon enters his mouth release your grip on his hand, so that he is the only one holding the handle when his mouth closes over the spoon. When he gets proficient at this you can start releasing the pressure of your prompt as it comes up to his lips.

The prompt must be faded slowly. At each stage you will be requiring him to move the spoon a little further to his mouth on his own, working back to the point where you will prompt him to grasp the spoon as it rests on the edge of the dish, but he will take it from there to his mouth without help. When he is able to do this you will have completed the first step in the teaching programme.

Step size

There is no accurate way of predicting step size, or length of time spent on each step. This will be largely dependent on how competent your child is at the beginning of the programme. Returning to the assessment chart, if your child is able to grasp objects, and move hand to mouth, you may find that it is only necessary to prompt for two or three spoonfuls before you feel that he is able to hold the spoon as it enters his mouth. On the fourth spoonful you may begin to fade your prompt as the spoon approaches his mouth. By the end of the first mealtime you could have reached a position where your child is being prompted to grasp the filled spoon and is then taking it to his mouth without the aid of a prompt.

Progress is likely to be much slower if your child has difficulty either in grasping or in moving his hand to his mouth. You may find that it takes a week to achieve just the first part of the step. In this case he is not having to learn only how to apply the skill of grasping to the feeding situation, but he is having to learn the skill itself.

Unwanted behaviours and time-out

Another factor which will affect your child's rate of progress is the possibility that unwanted behaviours may occur during the process of fading the prompt. The early stages should be quite straightforward, because you will be prompting his hand to lift the spoon from the edge of the dish to his mouth, and getting him to do a very small amount without prompt. Therefore he does not have the opportunity to do anything other than the correct action. However, when you have reached the stage where your child is moving the spoon several inches to his mouth without a prompt he has more opportunity to do things other than putting it in his mouth. He may move the spoon in the right direction but turn his face away, and so miss his mouth. He may drop the spoon, or turn it over and lose the food. If such behaviours occur you can use a time-out procedure.

Let us suppose that during Saturday lunch your child made good progress and towards the end of the meal consistently took the spoon two or three inches to his mouth without a prompt. As he took each spoonful he received a great deal of praise. During Saturday tea the first three spoonfuls go just as well, but on the fourth spoonful he turns the spoon over and loses most of the food. He then proceeds to take the spoon to his mouth.

If you allow him to continue he may be rewarded just by the feel of the spoon going into his mouth, even though it is nearly empty and he does not receive praise from you. It would be best to remove the spoon from his hand as soon as he turns it, and in order to make the situation very clear to him, move the dish away as well. Remain silent, turning your head away so that no eye contact can be made. Stay like this for about 10 seconds and then push the dish back, fill the spoon and start the prompt again. Repeat the procedure if the same thing happens for the next spoonful. However, if it happens on the third spoonful it would be wise to go back a step with your prompt and begin the process of fading again. Too many successive failures will not help your child to learn the correct behaviour.

In the same way that we advise teaching only one step at a time, we also feel that it is important to deal with only one undesirable behaviour at a time. Your child may occasionally turn his spoon upside down and also sometimes turn his head away. Use the time-out procedure described above to get rid of his spoon turning. While you are doing this, should he turn his head, prompt him to turn it back so that he faces forwards. When there has been a complete meal in which there has been no attempt to turn the spoon, but there are still occasions when he turns away, use the same time-out procedure to discourage head turning.

There may be some justification for using time-out to affect both head and spoon turning during the same mealtime, if both behaviours occur very infrequently—perhaps only once or twice each during one mealtime. If they occur more frequently you will be forced to use too many time-out periods and this will not provide a very effective learning situation for your child.

If you do not seem to be decreasing the number of times turning occurs, or worse, if the turning seems to be steadily increasing over the period of a week, then return to prompting more fully. It could be that your child does not understand exactly what is expected of him. Time-out is your way of telling him that he is doing something you do not like. He may get that message quite quickly, but still be confused about what he must do to please you. If he is confused about this you must return to fuller prompts in order to show him the correct behaviour.

One step at a time

While you are teaching your child the first step, there will be many things going on during the mealtime. It is quite likely that as soon as the food has been taken from the spoon he will drop the spoon. There are two things you can do about this. You can allow the spoon to drop, pick it up, fill it, rest it on the edge of the dish and prompt him to grasp it. Or, immediately the food has been taken from the spoon, you can prompt him to continue holding it, prompt his hand down to the dish, prompt him to fill the spoon, and then proceed with fading the prompt as he returns the filled spoon to his mouth. On no account worry about teaching these additional stages until you have successfully taught him to take the filled spoon to his mouth. Concentrate on one step at a time.

The next step

Having got your child to complete the first step without prompt, you must now consider what the next step in teaching is to be. You are faced with two alternatives. You can teach your child to take the empty spoon back to the dish, or teach him to fill the spoon before taking it to his mouth. Experience has shown that teaching a child to push his spoon into the food is the most difficult part of the self-feeding skill, so one could argue that this should be the last part to be taught. However, according to our backward chaining procedure, this is the next step in the sequence so it is best to concentrate on this as the second step. Once a child has mastered this activity there are generally few problems concerned with fading the prompt of bringing the spoon down to the dish.

We shall call this step 'teaching your child how to dig'. One method of dealing with it is to take his hand as he removes the food from the spoon, and prompt hand and spoon to the dish, ending the movement by digging the spoon into the food. From here he should be able to lift it straight to his mouth.

The procedure for fading the 'digging' prompt may be slightly more difficult than fading the 'grasping' and 'lifting' prompts. You may find yourself prompting the spoon from your

G

child's mouth to the dish, and then prompting the spoon to the food. At this point you will be trying to fade your prompt so that your child continues the action by digging into the food and lifting it to his mouth. However, once the spoon has reached the food he may keep his hand still until you finally resort to prompting him to dig into the food, or he may lift the spoon immediately you have finished prompting him, regardless of how much food, if any, he has on the spoon. There is no guaranteed way around this. You will have to resort to patience and very gradual fading of the prompt. A method that can be used is to move your prompt away from your child's hand to his wrist, and then along the forearm until finally you are prompting from the elbow. From here you can fade your prompt from holding the elbow during the digging action to giving the elbow a push at the beginning of the digging action. The intensity of the push can then be decreased.

The food
There are several points which may make this stage easier to teach. To begin with try to provide food which is easy to dig into, and which is easy to keep on the spoon. Jelly and peas are very much more difficult to deal with than mince, mashed potato and breakfast cereal. Also it is useful to provide a bowl or small plate with a lip. This makes scooping food far easier than chasing it over the edge of the plate.

Finally you may find it useful to provide more food than your child is prepared to eat (or you will allow him to eat). When the food is piled up it is easier to dig into than when there are only a few scraps left. After he has had enough, take the remaining food away. This may sound wasteful but it may be an effective way of helping him over the initial stages of learning to dig.

The final step
By now your child should be filling the spoon himself and taking the filled spoon to his mouth. The final stage is the relatively simple one of getting him to take the empty spoon to the dish and position it near the food so that he is able to make the digging action. It is quite possible that he will be able to do this without the need for systematic fading of your prompt. How-

ever, if this is not the case, you should use the usual procedure
of fading the last part of the prompt first. Prompt your child to
bring his hand down from his mouth to the edge of the dish,
and then allow him to position the spoon and dig on his own.
Fade your prompt in steps so that the final stage is just slight
guidance to his hand when the spoon leaves his mouth.

What next?

By now your child has the basic self-feeding skills. The next step
is to work on any improvements in style which you feel appropriate. You may need to stop him being messy when feeding,
or you may wish to slow him down to ensure that he chews his
food well. If you have followed a procedure similar to that
described above, and successfully taught him the basic skills,
you should have no problem in working out a programme to
improve his style of feeding—the same basic principles apply.

Example 1. Teaching a blind child

The feeding programme we are about to describe was used with
Peter, the five-year-old blind boy whom we mentioned in the
section on discrimination learning. We started the feeding
programme three weeks before we began the discrimination
tasks. Thus there was little difference in his behaviour at the
beginning of the two programmes.

Assessment. Peter had to be fed. He would eat only soft mashed
foods, and he made no attempt to finger feed. He was able to
grasp objects when they were placed in his hand, although he
made little spontaneous effort to grasp things or explore when
left on his own. He also had the alarming habit of spitting out
most of each spoonful of food. This occurred at home and at
school, and represented a big problem as mealtimes could take
anything up to an hour, and even then it was difficult to
estimate how much food he had eaten.

Time-out for spitting. Our first step was to stop him spitting out
his food. We proposed to use a time-out procedure which ran
as follows.

At home Peter was fed by his mother. Whenever she gave him
a spoonful of food she would talk to him and praise him as long
as the food remained in his mouth. As soon as he showed any

sign of spitting the food out she stopped talking to him, moved away from his side and began talking with his brother. She would return after a short period of time (about 10 or 15 seconds) and give him another spoonful.

At school the same procedure was used. Spitting food out resulted in his teacher moving away from him and talking to another child. Within three weeks Peter had stopped spitting. This was rapid learning, and clearly demonstrated that food and adult attention were effective rewards. The results of the programme suggested that it should be possible to teach Peter to feed himself. In order to assess the feasibility of the programme, the first steps were conducted at school only. When it was under way the programme was introduced at Peter's home.

Step 1. The programme we used was similar to that already described. The first step involved prompting Peter to lift the filled spoon from the edge of his dish to his mouth. At first, when we attempted to prompt him to lift the spoon, he brought his other hand to his mouth, and so spoon and free hand were entering his mouth at the same time. A preliminary to fading the step 1 prompt was to teach Peter to leave his other hand idle when holding the spoon. During the first part of the first meal he was prompted to keep his other hand beneath the table top. As the meal progressed Peter began to take some spoonfuls to his mouth without attempting to lift his second hand. At this point we stopped prompting him to keep his hand beneath the table, and introduced a short period of time-out when he lapsed into lifting it. In 58 spoonfuls we used 19 prompts to hold his hand down and 17 periods of time-out, and Peter took 22 spoonfuls without attempting to lift his free hand or requiring a prompt to keep it down.

During the next mealtime Peter made no attempts to lift his free hand. In one mealtime we had successfully dealt with the first problem.

Step 2: Fading the prompt. At the beginning of the third mealtime Peter was being prompted to grasp the filled spoon and take it from the edge of the dish to his mouth. By the end of the meal we had succeeded in fading the prompt to the point where Peter required help only to grasp the spoon handle.

He lifted the spoon to his mouth on his own. To reach this end, in 60 spoonfuls we used 36 prompts and 5 time-out periods. (Time-out was used for dropping the spoon before it reached his mouth.) The remaining 19 spoonfuls were taken successfully without prompt.

No prompt was required for the first 10 spoonfuls of the following meal. At this point we decided we could move on to step 3.

Step 3: Grasping the spoon handle. Here we aimed to fade the prompt which helped Peter to grasp the spoon handle. There were two stages in this prompt. The first was guiding Peter's hand to the spoon, and the second was assisting him to grasp it. We faded the prompt to grasp first (backward chaining procedure). Being blind, Peter found this a difficult step. In order to help him we ensured that the dish was always in the same position on the table, and the spoon was always in the same position on the dish.

The first problem Peter encountered was that when attempting to grasp the handle unassisted, he often knocked the spoon into the dish, and so we had to hold the spoon firmly against the edge of the dish while he was attempting to grasp it. During the second mealtime in this stage his ability to grasp unassisted improved to the point where he was able to grasp the handle without us having to hold the spoon. However, his grip on the handle was often awkward. The spoon went to his mouth held at odd angles, with the result that the food sometimes fell off, or he had difficulty in finding his mouth. It took three mealtimes to overcome this problem. By this time we were in a position to begin fading the prompt of guiding his hand to the dish. It took nine mealtimes in all for Peter to find the spoon and grasp it successfully without need of a prompt.

Step 4: Returning the spoon. At the beginning of this stage Peter was able to find the filled spoon on the edge of the dish, grasp it and lift it to his mouth without need of a prompt. However, as soon as the food was taken from the spoon he dropped it. In this step we proposed to get Peter to take the empty spoon back to the dish. In the first two mealtimes he was prompted in a way that stopped him dropping the spoon. This prompt was faded by degrees, until, during the third meal, he began to take the empty spoon to the dish without prompt. He still occasionally dropped the spoon, and when this occurred time-out was used. It took seven mealtimes to teach him not to drop the spoon, but return it to the dish.

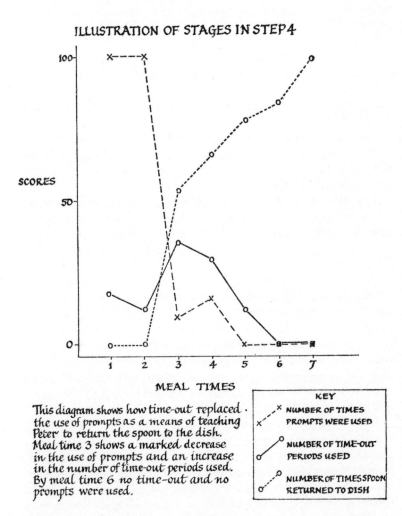

ILLUSTRATION OF STAGES IN STEP 4

MEAL TIMES

This diagram shows how time-out replaced the use of prompts as a means of teaching Peter to return the spoon to the dish. Meal time 3 shows a marked decrease in the use of prompts and an increase in the number of time-out periods used. By meal time 6 no time-out and no prompts were used.

KEY
x----x NUMBER OF TIMES PROMPTS WERE USED
o——o NUMBER OF TIME-OUT PERIODS USED
o·····o NUMBER OF TIMES SPOON RETURNED TO DISH

Figure 6. Illustration of changes in behaviour in a teaching programme

Step 5: Filling the spoon. We now come to the final step in the programme, teaching Peter to fill his spoon. This proved to be extremely difficult. Peter's blindness was probably the main reason for this. For the five years that Peter had been fed, he had been unable to see that the meal was always placed in front of him, and that spoonsful of food were always taken from the dish to his mouth. His experience of food was passive. He experienced it only when it entered his mouth. He therefore had to learn that at certain times of the day food was made available, and that he was able to help himself to it.

In addition to this, social contact was important for Peter, and mealtimes had always guaranteed at least half an hour of uninterrupted attention from his parents or teacher. As he became more skilled at feeding himself independently, the amount of contact was reduced. Peter fought against this and devised many ways of keeping our attention. At times he was certainly an uncooperative child, although his antics were never devoid of humour.

It took about a year and a half of hard work from Peter's teacher and parents to get him to the point where he did feed himself on his own without help. There were many stages in the process, too many to enumerate here. In summary, the school records show that it took about 40 mealtimes to get Peter to dig into the food without prompt, but his attempts to dig were usually poor. It took a further 50 mealtimes for Peter to improve the effectiveness of his digs, and then 120 before he reached a point where he could feed himself independently.

Initially his problem was in the control of his dig. He was unable to use sight to guide his actions. The spoon went into the food and then was withdrawn backwards. Hence most of the food fell off. He had to be prompted to push the spoon forward as he lifted it out. On other occasions he pushed his spoon down to the dish but missed the food altogether. In order to improve this we used a combination of prompting and allowing him to take empty spoons to his mouth. This was effectively a time-out procedure. Peter pushed the spoon across the top of the food, and then found he had no food on the spoon. Hence he was not rewarded for that type of digging action.

Slowly, through the aid of prompt and time-out, he learned

that when the spoon was pushed into the dish and resistance was felt (the spoon was embedded in the food), then food would come to his mouth on the spoon. When no resistance was felt and the spoon was light no food would come to his mouth. For a child like Peter, who was severely mentally handicapped, this very complicated piece of learning took a long time. If Peter had had sight his problem would have been far less complicated, and this final step in the teaching programme would probably have been completed more quickly.

Step 6: Independence. Overcoming these difficulties, however, does not account for the additional 120 mealtimes required before Peter began feeding himself independently. The final problem to overcome, once Peter had mastered the skill of digging the spoon, was phasing ourselves out of the feeding situation. He seemed to need continual assurance that we were there. During the time we were teaching Peter to make a digging action, we would praise him and clap after every successful spoonful. As the skill improved, and he became less reliant on prompts for good performance, we would occasionally remain silent after a successful spoonful. At first this would follow a run of five or six praised spoonfuls, and then slowly we would try to build up the number of silences. After a few mealtimes Peter reverted to making poor digs and dropping his spoon. This forced us to return to rewarding him with praise after every successful spoonful in order to re-establish good feeding behaviour. We would then go on once more to phase out the social reward. The process was rather like someone climbing a slippery slope, several steps upward and then a slide back. But eventually we made it to the top, with Peter reaching the stage where he would eat his meal with occasional words of praise and a helping hand if he lost his spoon.

FOOD FADS

This section will be of interest to teachers, care staff or parents who are worried about food fads in their children. Although this is not strictly a self-help question, it seems appropriate to include it in our discussion of other feeding problems.

A problem of degree

When we talk about a child being 'faddie' at mealtimes we usually mean that he is very selective in what he eats. The problem usually centres around persuading him to eat particular foods, greens being a classic example. However, there is probably a difference between the 'faddiness' which often occurs in young non-handicapped children and that sometimes shown by the handicapped child. With normal children, refusal to eat certain types of food is often short lived, and can be overcome relatively easily: parents may either ignore it or use such pressures as 'You can't go out to play until you have eaten all your dinner'. This may or may not work, but generally the situation calms down and after a few weeks or months the problem no longer exists (or the parents are no longer concerned by it).

With the handicapped child, particular food fads may be solved in this way, but they may become more serious as the child grows older. We remember for instance the case of a six-year-old girl whose diet consisted exclusively of milk taken from a particular bottle. She would not take any solid food, nor any liquids other than milk, although before the age of three she had eaten a normal diet. Another child with whom we worked would drink only milk and eat currant buns and biscuits. Attempts to get him to eat other things were met with blank refusals. Over a period of years the two children had developed very specific preferences. Their problem was not in what they had selected as their favourite food, but in their rejection of all else.

Food fads, of course, are not all serious, and parents are often worried by problems that are more irritating than serious. Most of the children who are called 'faddie' do eat a variety of foods, although their range may be limited compared with the family's diet.

The need for concern

It is not easy to say at what point a particular food fad becomes a problem. There are three questions which may help you to decide.

1. Does the food which your child eats provide him with a balanced diet?
This is probably the most important factor to consider, although

G*

it may also be the most difficult to answer. It is not within the scope of this book to attempt to do this, but we would suggest that if you are concerned you should discuss your child's diet with your GP or health visitor, or perhaps arrange an appointment with a hospital dietician. They may be able to suggest food supplements to be added to your child's diet while you are working towards a more permanent solution to the problem.

2. Does the range of food that your child is willing to eat cause inconvenience to you or your family at mealtimes?
This may be reflected in time taken to prepare food which is different from the rest of the family's diet; or in time spent in persuading your child to eat the food which is provided at family mealtimes. Either of these situations may lead you to decide that your child's food fads do present a significant problem, and that some form of feeding programme would be desirable.

3. Is there the possibility that your child may be rejected from a special school placement or a holiday placement because of his feeding difficulties?
This situation can occur, albeit infrequently, and would certainly warrant action to be taken at home.

The answers to these questions may help you to decide whether to consider your child's faddiness as a problem which needs fairly immediate action, or one which can be worked on over time.

Assessment
Before deciding on the first step in the teaching programme it is necessary to be clear about what your child does now. Tables 22 and 23, in the feeding assessment, outline some of the possible patterns. (Pages 188-189)

If your child takes only liquids, or eats only a very limited number of foods, his food fads are likely to represent a major problem. However, he may well eat most foods and dislike only a few specific things. In this case, if there is a problem at all it may be considered inconvenient rather than serious.

The next point to consider is whether your child feeds himself or needs to be fed. Obviously if he feeds himself he has much more control over what he eats than if you feed him, and if you feel that you want to tackle the problem directly and rapidly you may find it necessary to take over this control by feeding him yourself. Alternatively, if you feel the problem is less pressing, you may allow him to continue feeding himself, meanwhile trying to influence what he chooses to eat.

The aim of your programme

When a child tastes new food he may take an immediate like or dislike to it. However, these preferences may change in time. He may become bored with a food that he likes but has very often. He may learn to like things that he was reluctant to try at first. If a child eats a limited number of things, and persists in refusing everything else, he is not giving himself the opportunity to learn to like anything new. The aim of programmes in this section will be to enable you to persuade the child to try things that he generally refuses to eat. This will give him the opportunity to make the decision as to whether he finds them acceptable or not. It is not a matter of forcing him to like them—that is obviously neither possible nor desirable—but of giving him the necessary experience with which to make the judgement.

Nagging versus reward

If your child tends to be 'faddie' about eating, your success in introducing him to new food may depend on how you go about it. If he is physically forced to eat things that he is not used to, or if he is told that he cannot leave the table until he has eaten them, he *may* eventually come to accept the situation and eat what is presented. However, it is also possible that he will come to dislike all mealtimes because he comes to associate them with threats and punishments. Or he may come to see that by refusing to eat his food he is assured of being the centre of attention for long periods of time. Neither of these situations is likely to encourage him to eat well.

A better approach for all concerned would be to associate his eating of food with a rewarding situation. Remember to give him some of what he likes to eat, and a little of what he usually refuses. Do not let him fill himself with his preferred food, or he will never feel tempted to try what he does not like: in order to experiment we must feel a little hungry. If he does try a morsel of the new food, give him lots of praise. This is better than nagging him if he does not try it.

Your child may also respond to your own enthusiasm about his non-preferred foods. If, for instance, he will not attempt to eat green vegetables, you could make a point of saying 'Oh good we have peas today'. This may motivate him to give them a try. Watching how others respond to various situations can be an important method of learning.

Let us now look at these techniques in more detail.

Ways of encouraging your child to eat new foods

In this section we will offer a few suggestions that we have found helpful in the past. The methods we describe have been used with children who are able to feed themselves, and whose food fads are not severe. However, as in other sections, each approach is based on the interests of the individual child, and ideas which you may find useful will probably need to be adapted to suit the particular needs of your child. The only points which are likely to apply in most situations are:

(1) Start by getting your child to eat very small amounts of non-preferred food—as little as one spoonful—and increase the quantity slowly over time.

(2) Give him a plate with the food portion you expect him to eat that day, and try not to provide more than this. By seeing the amount, he is able to define the size of the task which faces him. If he sees a large portion he will not know exactly what is required of him, and may be deterred by the prospect of eating all of it. Once he is eating this small portion without too much difficulty, you can provide a little more each day.

When your child has eaten all the food that he usually eats, and is left with the small portion of non-preferred food, you need to find a way of persuading him to eat it.

Competition

Save an equivalent portion for yourself and say something like 'I have a spoonful of greens, and you have a spoonful of greens, let's see who can eat theirs first. The winner can eat this sweet' (or wear the winner's badge or whatever else you think he may enjoy). Unless he is being unusually slow or obstinate, let him win the prize at the end as his reward for eating the food.

Games

There are many variations on this theme, the most successful probably being those adapted from other games your child enjoys. Here are two possibilities. Feed your child's favourite doll with the same food as he is eating, and say how much the doll is enjoying the food. Tell him to eat it like his doll. Or close your eyes and ask him to make the food disappear. Open your eyes when you think it has been eaten and act surprised (as long as it has not been dropped on the floor!). Reward him with praise or a sweet or his favourite activity, when he has eaten the required amount.

This method may seem very trivial in the writing, but in practice it is extremely useful, provided your child understands the situation. If you feel he is not ready for this form of game, or the games may be too confusing for him, a more direct approach will be required. In a firm voice ask him to eat the remaining small portion of food and say that if he does so he can have his favourite reward (whatever activity or food he enjoys). If he will not cooperate, prompt him to eat the food, and as soon as he has swallowed it reward him. Provided the reward is something he really enjoys, it should not take him many mealtimes to recognise that it will follow if he makes an effort to eat the food. When he reaches this stage you can begin to increase the quantity by very small amounts. In any of these programmes it is important to remember not to increase the amount too quickly, because you run the risk of making the situation too unpleasant, from your child's point of view, to be balanced by the value of the reward.

FEEDING YOUR CHILD

If your child is unable to feed himself, or if he feeds himself but eats very small quantities or a very limited range of foods, you will probably need to use different techniques from those suggested above. The aim of the programme is also likely to be different. In the less extreme cases with the self-feeding child, you will be attempting to get him to choose to eat certain foods which he currently refuses to eat. With the child who does not feed himself, you will be trying to get him to accept certain types of food when they are fed to him. In this case the behaviours you are likely to be concerned with are crying, tantrums and spitting out.

Probably the most effective method of overcoming these behaviours is to use a combination of time-out and reward. These methods are both applicable to the child who is unable to feed himself. For the child who does feed himself, but chooses to eat a very limited range, you will probably find it necessary to feed him, because this will offer the quickest and most direct solution to his problem. This section, therefore, deals with problem behaviours which occur when you are feeding your child.

What to reward and what to time-out

Before you begin your feeding programme, you must first be clear on what behaviours are to be rewarded and what behaviours you wish to discourage by time-out. This will depend on what your child does now. The most frequent problem that we have encountered is crying, struggling and avoiding the spoon when the child is being fed particular foods. Once the food is in his mouth he may try to spit it out or he may be very slow in swallowing it.

If the disruptive behaviour is prolonged and severe, the use of time-out is unadvisable since the feeding session would become one long time-out period, with no food taken or reward given. In severe cases the most effective method is to persist in your attempts to give him a spoonful of food, in spite of his tantrum behaviour. Once the food is in his mouth, reward immediately. If he spits the food out, stop the reward. By using this method your child should come to understand that taking the food in his mouth produces a rewarding situation. This link between the reward and food is necessary before you can use time-out from reward effectively.

If, at the beginning of the programme, tantrum behaviour is mild it is possible to use a combination of time-out and reward from the start. In this case you would use time-out whenever your child struggles or cries during feeding, and give him attention and praise whenever he is cooperative.

This combination of time-out and reward would be effective in reducing tantrums, but it would not affect the way that your child eats the food once it is in his mouth. He may persist in spitting it out, or retaining it in his mouth for long periods. In many cases this is the final step in the programme. The procedure for this is to shift from rewarding passive behaviour (non-tantrum behaviour) to rewarding appropriate eating behaviour. Thus you reward when the spoonful of food has been swallowed.

Summary of the three possibilities
If your child is very resistant to taking any food, you must first establish an association between feeding and reward. Once he comes to realise that feeding involves more than an unpleasant experience, you are in a position to define the behaviours you wish to encourage, and those you wish to discourage. Step 2 (or step 1 if your child is not a severe problem) is to encourage cooperation in feeding. Anything which involves struggling, crying and resistance to the food is ignored (time-out). Passive or appropriate eating behaviours are rewarded. Once you have established cooperation, the next step is to reward your child when he has eaten a spoonful of food. Here you are defining appropriate behaviour not just as cooperation but as eating and swallowing. Where you begin on the above programme depends on what your child does now when feeding.

FOOD FADS WITH A CEREBRAL PALSIED CHILD

Example 2
Clive was an endearing three-year-old who suffered from cerebral palsy. His mother had used a very poor feeding technique ever since he had been taken off his bottle. She fed him with a filled table spoon, which was too big for his small mouth. Mealtimes were not enjoyable for him. He was forced to take very large quantities of food very rapidly and was given little room for protest in spite of his obvious discomfort. Consequently, when he came to school he was upset at meal-times. He cried at the approach of his plate and continued to cry and struggle through feeding.

Fortunately Clive was extremely keen on adult attention and, except for mealtimes, a happy cooperative child. His teacher therefore used attention as a reward for good eating behaviour.

The procedure. Clive was fed in a quiet corner of the classroom. In the early stages of the programme he sat on the lap of the person feeding him. He was given small spoonsful of food, and all the time that he was not crying or trying to avoid the spoon he was spoken to. As soon as he began to grimace and cry his teacher would stop speaking to him and turn her head away, so that he could not make eye contact with her. When he stopped crying she would begin talking again and give him cuddles.

At first Clive tried to bypass the time-out procedure by looking around the room for smiles and sympathy from other adults, so other people in the room were asked to cooperate by not looking at him or speaking to him during these time-out periods. The procedure was difficult to operate initially because it was so natural to feel sympathetic towards him. But to give in to his appeals would merely have prolonged his feeding problem.

Some problems with the procedure. Under these conditions mealtimes took up to an hour and a half to complete, although they seemed to last even longer. This, of course, would present significant problems to many parents trying to run a similar programme at home. But even so, we feel that such techniques should be attempted because the end result is worth the time invested in it. If the reward of attention is of real value to the child, and the time-out procedure is used correctly (which is to say by not giving in during any prolonged bouts of crying), then you should begin to see a significant reduction in the tantrums within a few days, if not sooner.

The procedure was successful with Clive. It took several mealtimes for him to realise that he could not earn sympathy by crying but he could get a great deal of attention by eating, albeit slowly. From then on he was fed in his chair next to another boy who was also a slow eater. Between them they progressed with their eating over a period of a year. Within this time Clive began to feed himself. At this stage his physical problems did not allow him to fill his spoon easily, but he was capable of taking the filled spoon to his mouth. At school at least he found eating an enjoyable experience, indicating that probably his early reluctance to take food was caused not by a basic dislike of food, but by the unpleasant experiences associated with feeding at home.

Example 3. A case of extreme food fad

Juliette's problems were more extreme than those of Clive. She came to the school at the age of five, and at that time presented two major difficulties. The first was that she actively avoided contact with adults. She spent her time in the classroom playing with the rocking horse, and had severe temper tantrums if this toy was used by another child. Attempts to get her to work with educational toys produced more tantrums. In addition to this, her diet consisted only of milk (although at one time, prior to a period in hospital, she had eaten solid foods). Her food fad was so extreme that she would take her milk only from a specific type of bottle, and would use only a particular form of teat.

Initial attempts at school to change the type of bottle were met with tantrums which often resulted in her refusing to take her daily quota of milk, even when we relented and returned her original bottle. This was extremely worrying because of the risk to her health, and so we decided not to interfere with her bottle feeding in any way. The alternative was to get her to take food other than milk from a spoon.

The problem of reward. Before any programme could be planned we needed to find an effective reward. This was an extremely difficult task because adult attention and food were not acceptable. After trying many things, we found that Juliette enjoyed playing with visually interesting objects—objects which sparkled, such as mirrors, blocks of uncooked jelly, torches and so on.

The problem of control. The second preliminary step in the programme was to establish an association between cooperating with the teacher and having access to the box of rewards that we had prepared for her. Over a period of a fortnight we took Juliette to a small room and worked with her on a series of simple teaching tasks such as removing balls from a rod and placing simple shapes into a board. At first she was extremely reluctant to work, and struggled to get away from the table to play with her rewards. We had to prompt her to do each part of the task, and allowed her to play with one or more of her objects for about a minute between each part. She quickly learned that she could play with the rewards when she had completed a component of the task, and that when the rewards were taken from her at the end of a minute they would be returned at the completion of the next step in the task. Within three or four 20-minute sessions, Juliette had been transformed from a difficult uncooperative child to one who was very eager to work under guidance with the teaching materials.

The key to this success was the large range of interesting rewards that we provided. She had access to these only in the small teaching room, and it did not take her long to realise this. Hence, when it was time for her special teaching period she was eager to come with us.

The feeding programme. Having established a good system of rewards and a level of cooperation between Juliette and her teacher, we were now in a position to plan the feeding programme. This was based on the simple idea that Juliette would be given a spoonful of food and then be allowed to play with her boxful of rewards for a period. Provided that she did not become bored with the rewards, we felt that she would soon learn to cooperate in feeding in the same way as she did in the teaching sessions.

We decided to use ice cream as the first food, since it was similar to milk, which she took readily from the bottle. From ice cream we planned to move on to custard and blancmange.

Step 1: Ice cream. In spite of being very eager to come to the room for the feeding sessions, and enjoying sitting on her teacher's lap, Juliette fought desperately whenever the spoon tipped with ice cream approached her mouth. At the beginning of the programme sessions lasted 45 minutes. A taste was defined as any quantity, however small, and in the first session we managed to give her 12 tastes of ice cream. In the second session we managed only five tastes. After each taste Juliette was allowed a few minutes' play with her toys. During the first four sessions, we struggled over each taste. On the fifth session we had a breakthrough. Juliette's first 10 tastes were accompanied by the usual struggle, but the remaining 15 tastes were taken willingly. Juliette had realised that by taking the ice cream quickly she was able to play more frequently with the rewards.

During the seventh session we began to increase the amount she had to take before she was rewarded. And thus in this session she was given 25 tastes, but was rewarded only 16 times.

In the eighth session Juliette took 35 tastes and was rewarded 15 times. She did not cry or avoid the spoon once in this session, and this was the first session to pass without a tantrum.

From then on we concentrated on getting her to take spoonsful rather than tastes. By session 13 she took the equivalent of 20 spoonsful of ice cream in 40 tastes, and was rewarded only five times. She tried to avoid the spoon twice in this session, but these were very brief incidents.

Step 2: Custard. During session 14 we decided that the time was right for introducing a food with a slightly different flavour and texture. The nearest approximation to ice cream we could find (we did not wish to make too large a change at this stage) was custard mixed with ice cream.

Juliette objected to the change. In the first three sessions we were able to give her an average of only 10 tastes in each, and at least half of these were preceded by avoidance behaviour (turning her head away at the approach of the spoon, or trying to push the teacher's hand away as the spoon came close to her mouth).

Over the next five sessions the number of tastes increased to between 45 and 60, but the avoidance behaviour accompanied over half of these. There was little generalisation between taking the ice cream and taking the custard ice cream mixture.

Step 3: Soup. The aim of the programme was to get Juliette to eat savoury foods. Considering the small progress we had made in step 2, it seemed that she would be equally rejecting of each new food, regardless of its similarity to the previous food. Hence we decided that in step 3 we should try Juliette with a savoury meal. We thought that chicken soup would be ideal, since its flavour was mild and it could be given in a liquid form.

The first 15 sessions in this step brought us up to the summer holiday, when the programme was discontinued. Little progress was made. The procedure we used was the same as for the ice cream. To begin with each taste was followed by a reward period. Each session averaged about eight tastes, each of which was preceded by avoidance behaviour. However, one positive gain was that at the end of each session Juliette was given a small ice cream which she ate willingly. She required only one reward period for doing this. This ensured that we were not losing ground with her feeding, even though her progress towards taking savoury foods was slow.

On her return to school after the holidays we had seven sessions similar to the previous 16, and then on the eighth session there was a sharp increase in the amount that she took, with an equally sharp decrease in avoiding behaviour. During this session she took 14 tastes, none of which was preceded by avoidance behaviour. By session 27 she was taking up to 60 tastes without problems.

At this point we began to introduce different flavoured soups (mushroom, oxtail and so on), and except for three 'off' days this improvement was maintained up to session 39.

Step 4: Mashed potatoes. Our next goal was to get her to eat solid food. We thought flavoured mashed potato would form a good transition between liquids and solids.

We ran 19 sessions, Juliette taking approximately 6 to 10 tastes each session, most of these being preceded by avoidance behaviour. From session 20 this behaviour stopped and over another eight sessions the amount she took increased to 35 teaspoonsful.

It was during this step that Juliette began feeding herself. This was not something we were working towards at this point in the programme. But one session she climbed on to her teacher's lap and, rather than wait to be fed, or hold the teacher's hand as the spoon approached her mouth, she took the spoon and began feeding herself. By now we felt that we were really on the way to seeing Juliette feeding herself and eating a normal diet.

Step 5: Spaghetti with minced meat. We moved from the smooth semi-solid texture of mashed potato to the introduction of lumpy food. In the first instance this consisted of finely chopped spaghetti and minced meat. Over 15 sessions with this, we recorded no instances of tantrum behaviour. The only problem in this stage was that Juliette found difficulty in learning to chew food. She would occasionally gag on pieces that were too coarsely chopped.

After 15 sessions, with the use of only one or two reward periods in each session, we began to give her the meals in the classroom with the other children. This did cause some minor problems, because up until then she had been fed in a quiet room and been given the full attention of at least one adult. She had been allowed to play with her favourite toys at each reward period, without interference from other children. And now she was expected to be just as cooperative in a crowded and noisy room with other children making demands on the teacher.

We attempted to make the transition between the two situations as easy as possible by ensuring that her teacher spent as much time as was feasible with her at mealtimes during the first few weeks in the classroom. We also continued to give her the same food that she had been given in the one-to-one sessions, and allowed her a reward period at the end of each meal. This change did cause some increase in her tantrum behaviour, but within six or eight months she was eating school dinners in the classroom on her own with no problem.

Feeding at home. At the beginning of the programmes Juliette's parents were extremely concerned about her reluctance to eat a normal diet, and they were very willing to cooperate with us. Before we began the programme it was decided that we should work only in the school with her feeding. We took this decision as an insurance against any problems for her health that might have arisen, if she had persisted in refusing to take any food at all.

As the programme progressed Juliette's mother began to give her at home the foods that she was taking readily at school. The first was ice cream, and then soup, and then mashed potato. By the end of the programme Juliette was making more progress at home than at school. This was possibly because feeding in the

classroom was a disrupted activity, whereas at home it continued to be a quiet one (Juliette had no brothers or sisters).

Problems with this type of programme. An extremely lengthy and
time consuming programme was required to get Juliette over
her feeding problems. Such a programme would not always be
possible to run either in the home or the school, because, to be
effective, it required very regular sessions involving the teacher
in nearly an hour's one-to-one session each school day. Few
schools could spare a staff member for this length of time.
Demands that a family make on parents' time also make the
running of such a programme at home extremely difficult.
Fortunately, however, it is not at all common to find children
who are as extreme in their food fads as Juliette, and hence most
programmes are likely to be less time consuming and less
demanding than the one we have just described.

One of the major problems with this form of programme is
the tendency to give up in the early stages, when one feels that
no progress is being made, and the only obvious result seems to
be the child's distress. With Juliette's programme we were able
to persist because we had confidence in the value of the rewards
we were using. Juliette was obviously very keen to come to the
room where the sessions were held, because she knew that she
would have the opportunity to play with the toys. In addition
we had seen how effective these rewards were in bringing her
behaviour under control in the preliminary teaching sessions.
Hence we continued with the programme through the difficult
early stages. Had we not had this confidence in the early
stages, we would have given up and considered the programme
a failure.

Example 4. Feeding problems of physically handi-capped children

The principles we have discussed so far in this section apply to
all children who have feeding problems of one type or another,
regardless of the form of their handicap. Special attention,
however, needs to be given to the problems of physically or
multiply handicapped children, particularly those who suffer
from cerebral palsy. If such children experience special
problems, they usually fall into two types: those associated with

chewing and swallowing, and those associated with the learning
of self-help skills.

Chewing and swallowing. Many young cerebral palsied children
have some problems with chewing and swallowing food. One
difficulty encountered fairly frequently with severely handicapped children is called tongue thrust. This can make feeding
a time consuming task. What usually happens is that as you put
food into the child's mouth, the tongue pushes out, bringing the
food with it. The extended tongue movement also prevents the
child from swallowing whatever food that remains in the mouth.

Physiotherapists say that this response is not specific to
mealtimes because it forms part of the child's 'general pattern
of extension'. However, at mealtimes it comes to the fore as a
problem. With a programme of treatment most children can
learn to bring this total pattern under some form of control.
With one severely mentally handicapped boy, we ran a
programme which aimed to reduce the tongue thrust response.

Example 5. Tongue thrust
David was a five-year-old athetoid child who was difficult to
feed at home and at school. He had a very limited understanding of language, but did enjoy his teacher singing one or
two particular nursery rhymes. We felt it would be worth
trying to use this to reduce the frequency and severity of his
tongue thrust, and also to increase the amount of food he could
take at one meal. We used a similar procedure to that described
in the food-fads section. A spoonful of food was given to David,
and at the time it entered his mouth we began to sing the
nursery rhyme. At the first sign of tongue thrust we stopped
singing and gave a short time-out period of about 15 seconds.

Over the first five sessions David took an average of 18
spoonsful without tongue thrust, and nine spoonsful when
tongue thrusts occurred. On the sixth session tongue thrust
occurred 28 times, but he took 40 spoonsful without tongue
thrust. The tongue thrust, therefore, was slightly more severe,
but his readiness to eat the food and the speed with which he
ate it improved immensely.

Over the next four sessions the amount of food he was taking
and the speed with which he ate it was maintained. However,

the incidence of tongue thrust decreased to around nine or ten occasions each mealtime. Thus the proportion of inappropriate to appropriate responses was very much reduced. There was a continued improvement over the next five sessions.

At this point we decided to reduce the amount of reward given. We began to reward David at the end of each successful spoonful, and to use the time-out procedure if the tongue thrust occurred. This initially had the effect of slightly reducing the amount of food he would take to between 30 and 40 successful spoonsful, but the tongue thrusts continued at a fairly low frequency. They averaged six times each session.

This simple and rapid programme demonstrates clearly that even a very handicapped child can learn to control these movements if sufficiently motivated. In the short space of time (23 sessions) he did not achieve complete control: additional programmes working on complementary skills would probably be needed to do so. However, David's case exemplifies an effective way of organising such programmes, and also demonstrates that specific problems can be reduced by working on individual target behaviours.

From soft to solid foods

Moving from a soft to a solid diet causes problems for some handicapped children, particularly those who suffer from cerebral palsy. Speech therapists recommend a variety of games or techniques that can be used to stimulate lip and tongue movements as preliminaries to learning to chew. Putting sticky foods on the lips and tongue is one such method. Foods the child likes, such as jam or peanut butter, are best.

Whatever preliminary methods are used, the important point to remember is that steps between the soft and solid diet should be gradual. If you move from a fine grade of minced foods to a more coarsely graded food too quickly, your child may begin to gag on the lumps. If this occurs, move back to a slightly finer food.

The feeding posture

Therapists attach great importance to a good posture in all activities for the cerebral palsied child. This, of course, applies to feeding, and Nancy Finnie in her book *Handling the Young*

Cerebral Palsied Child at Home argues the special importance of this, and provides illustrations of good and bad feeding positions. She recommends an erect position with support to the shoulders and back, and arms held forward. Any tendency to slump forward or backward should be discouraged. This applies to children who are fed on their mother's lap, or to children seated at a table.

SELF FEEDING

Self feeding is likely to present problems for children who have little control of their upper body movements, particularly if they lack control of the head and neck. This lack of control may take the form of involuntary movements, or of movements which have the opposite result from that intended. The degree to which children are affected varies enormously. Those who are mildly affected could be described as jerky or clumsy in their actions (ataxic), and such children are unlikely to present specific difficulties in learning the simple skills involved with self feeding. At worst, progress may be less rapid than that of a similar but non-physically handicapped child.

More severely involved children, however, are likely to have great difficulty in learning these skills.

Necessary preliminary skills

There are three skills which such a child needs to acquire before the beginning of a self-feeding programme: the ability to bring his hand to his mouth, some degree of head and neck control, and a balanced sitting posture.

In the early stages balance can be helped by the provision of a special chair and table, and various support aids. These may be designed by the physiotherapist who is based at the hospital clinic or school, if your child needs this form of aid. Hand control and control of head and neck will also vary considerably between children. In certain cases cerebral palsy mainly affects one side of the body (hemiplegic), or mainly the lower limbs (dipelgia). Neither of these conditions should present insuperable problems to your child learning self feeding skills. On the other hand athetoid children and quadriplegic children have their whole body affected by the condition. Both types are likely to find difficulty with arm function and head control. With practice and careful guidance, children can learn to overcome these problems to a greater or lesser extent.

Equipment

Having been professionally advised, and having satisfied yourself that your child has the necessary control and balance to begin, you may find that the usual implements are not entirely suitable for his needs. He may need spoons with long handles, built up handles or angled handles; and specially designed plates and non-slip mats. This equipment can be bought from The Disabled Living Foundation or supplied by your Local Authority or clinic. It is also possible to adapt ordinary cutlery and crockery. However, it would be worth discussing your child's particular difficulty with a physio-therapist before going ahead with this.

Teaching the skills

As with other programmes we have discussed, the most effective approach is for you to work on one component of the skill at a time. The first step would usually be to get your child to bring the filled spoon to his mouth. This might involve placing the spoon in his hand, only a few inches from his mouth. Any successful attempts should be praised. As he progresses you should require him to make larger movements.

Helping your child with prompts may be more difficult than helping the child who has no physical handicap. Prompting arm movements may result in an extension response. You need to take care to avoid increased muscle tension and rigidity. Slow smooth movements are essential.

Feeding problems, when they occur, can cause parents and teachers a great deal of anxiety. For this reason we have discussed ways of dealing with these problems at some length. Obviously we could not hope to cover every possible situation, but we feel that the examples given will help you understand some of the principles involved. This, in turn, will help you in developing an effective programme to deal with your particular problem.

12 : Dressing, Toileting and Washing

A child needs to learn a wide range of skills before he can dress himself completely. At the simplest level, he can help in the process by pulling up his pants, or pushing his arm into a jumper sleeve. He will need to learn how to pull things over his head, or to find the second sleeve of his jacket when one arm is in one sleeve and the second sleeve is dangling behind him. This will lead on to more difficult skills, such as how to tell the difference between the front and the back of a garment, and how to put it on so that the front actually appears on his front. At a more advanced level, he needs to develop enough skill with his finger movements to fasten buttons, and to learn the complex sequence of movements involved with tying shoe laces.

It takes a normal child several years to learn all these skills. At the age of two or three most children begin to help while they are being dressed. As they learn how to put on various clothes they contribute more help, until finally they are able to dress themselves, albeit untidily at first. Few parents feel the need to spend time teaching their children these skills, except perhaps for one or two of the more complex items such as shoe laces or neck ties. However, many handicapped children will need a structured teaching programme to ensure that they acquire as many of the skills as possible.

The time when most children practise dressing is first thing in the morning. For most parents this is the most inconvenient time in the day to consider working on a teaching programme, so it is probably better to set aside another time in the day or evening for working on the teaching of dressing. As your child learns to put on particular garments, you can then require him to use this skill in the morning or at other dressing times.

On those occasions when speed is not critical, parents can encourage their children to help while they are being dressed: by pushing an arm through a sleeve or pulling pants part way up. This sort of teaching is important because it demands participation in the activity rather than passive acceptance of being dressed (which some mentally handicapped children are very prone to). However, it does not constitute a teaching programme. A programme would involve the repetition of one aspect of the task until your child has learned that particular skill. You would then move on to teach the next part of the skill, again with as much repetition as necessary until that has been learned. This is the type of programme we will describe in this section.

To operate a dressing programme you need to set aside a certain amount of teaching time each day. Since in many families there is a limit to the amount of time to be spared for individual work with one child, the first question to ask yourself is whether this is the most productive way of spending this time. You might consider the following questions:

1. Has your child got the necessary skills to enable him to begin the programme?

To begin a dressing programme, he will obviously need to be able to reach and grasp objects. His grasp needs to be strong enough to pull at objects. He needs to be able to push with his arms and his legs. With these abilities he has enough to begin work on simple garments such as pants, vests and jumpers.

If you wish to progress on to more difficult garments such as jackets, additional skills will be required. For instance, the ability to persist in search for an object, and to recognise different parts of an object from touch alone, will be necessary to find the second sleeve of a jacket when one arm is in the first. The ability to make fine finger movements necessary for doing up zips, buckles and buttons will also be required.

If your child's ability to grasp is poor it would probably be better to spend your individual teaching time doing preliminary work on grasping. For instance, you could reward your child for holding on to a rod or thick piece of string and pulling it towards him. However, as we said in the introduction to the chapter on self-help skills, the skills that your child needs in order to participate in a teaching programme need not be developed to perfection before he begins. These basic skills, such as firm grasping or fine finger control, should improve as he practises pulling up trousers or fastening a zip. This is one bonus of such a programme.

2. What benefits will be gained from doing a dressing programme?

We have already mentioned that there can be beneficial side-effects from doing such a programme. However, the main benefit concerns your child's progress towards independence. The less dependent he is on your help in his daily living, the better his chances of reaching independence or semi-independence in adulthood. The earlier this teaching takes place the easier it will be to foster your child's feelings of independence as he grows older.

In addition there is the important point that although you may need to spend a great deal of time teaching your child to dress, your aim will be to have him dressing himself on his own. When you achieve this it will mean you are saving yourself time, which is an important consideration.

3. Will doing other types of individual teaching be of more value to your child?

The answer to this question will depend on what you feel are the aspects of your child's development which need most emphasis. For instance, parents of less severely handicapped children may think that teaching language or pre-reading skills are more important than teaching self-help skills, particularly if you can only afford the time for one regular teaching session. However, if you are a parent you must take into account what goes on at school. You may find that your child has regular language teaching sessions, but that little is done in the way of individual teaching of dressing skills. As a consequence teaching dressing at home could be seen as complementing the school curriculum.

GENERAL TEACHING PRINCIPLES

The aims of the programme

When you are planning a programme you should try to be clear as to the long- and short-term goals you wish to reach. If you are certain of what you wish to achieve, the steps you need to take should become fairly obvious. In this section we are talking about how to teach your child to dress himself. Consequently the long-term goal is that your child will be able to take off and put on his clothes with the minimum of supervision. A short-term goal may be to teach him to put on one garment. Start with something which will be within your child's present capabilities. Pulling up pants is usually simple enough to start with.

Pulling up pants would therefore be the first task in the programme. You will now need to think about the steps involved in teaching this task. These are the building blocks of the programme. Each one is taught separately. When your child has mastered the first, move on to the next step. In this way you should be able to build up your child's skill for dealing with an individual garment. When this has been achieved move on to the next item.

Ordering the steps and use of reward

In previous sections we have spoken of the use of backward chaining—teaching the last part of a sequence of movements first. Backward chaining is a useful technique to use with a dressing programme. According to this technique, the first step in putting on socks would be to prompt your child to pull them up from his ankles; or the first step in putting on a jumper would be to prompt him to pull it down from the chest to the waist. The reward will always come at this point. Whatever stage you have reached in teaching the particular task, he knows he must complete it to receive the reward. This is one clear advantage of using the backward chaining procedure.

Prompts

As with other teaching programmes, the use of prompts is likely to be essential. By using prompts you are showing your child what is required of him in order to complete the task. Rewarding at the end of a prompt is important, even if he has contributed little to the action at that stage in the teaching.

As with the prompts involved in the feeding programme, the size of the prompt and the number given throughout the teaching of each step will vary according to how capable your child is at each of the tasks. Assuming he is able to manage very little at the beginning, it is usual to start by guiding him right through the required movement. This is known as a full prompt. After several attempts you may feel that he is not relying totally on your guidance. At this point you can begin fading the prompt. Try fading the last part of the action first, so that he completes the action with minimum help. As you proceed with the session, or over a number of sessions, decrease the amount of prompt given until your child is doing it on his own.

Setbacks in progress

If problems begin to occur with your child's performance, there are three possible causes. It may be that you are not using a good enough reward. For instance, if you are using a sweet or piece of biscuit as a reward, and running the dressing programme shortly after tea time, he may not fancy the reward enough to persevere with the task. Alternatively, he may simply have become bored with the reward: you should be able to judge when this happens by his eagerness to have the reward. If there is a tendency to indifference, then one answer is to change the reward.

If, however, he remains keen to work for the reward but is still failing to do as well as expected, you may have faded the prompts too rapidly. It is easy to assume that because you have guided your child through the action a great many times he should now have a clear idea of what is required. Sometimes this is not the case, and very slow fading of the prompt is necessary. If this situation does arise, return to the previous stage in prompting and begin the fading process again.

A third possibility is that he is simply becoming naughty or uncooperative in the session. If you are using an effective reward, brief time-out periods can be used to eliminate this.

Putting on and taking off

When teaching dressing skills, problems frequently arise because people try to teach the putting on and taking off of a garment at the same time. Most children are able to pull off clothes before they learn to put them on, so it may be argued that, because a child is already able to take off his jumper, he should remove it himself during the programme to teach him to put it on.

If this is demanded of him, it may become difficult for the child to see the aim of the task. When he has successfully completed putting on the jumper he is given a reward. This should make clear the end of the task. However, if he is then asked to remove the jumper, and then required to put it back on, there is no clear division between the two activities. Although this confusion will not always arise, it is safer for the teacher to take the jumper off, and then to ask the child to put it on again. Thus the only activity the child need worry about is putting on.

INDIVIDUAL GARMENTS

Example 1. Pants

These are straightforward items to teach since they involve no buttons or clasps. The only difficulty likely to arise concerns putting feet into the correct hole. In your child's early attempts to do this he may often end up with both legs in one hole. There is no easy solution to this problem, other than prompting him to stretch the pants out before he begins to look for the holes.

If you use a backward chaining procedure, the first step to teach is pulling the pants up, from above the knees to the waist. If your child is not used to helping himself with dressing you may find prompting him to grasp the material difficult at first. This often happens when trying to prompt awkward manoeuvres. The first few attempts result in a tangle of fingers around the top of the garment, with you doing all the pulling. But once he realises that a reward comes at the end of the procedure he should begin to understand what is required of him. Your prompt should then develop, from holding his hand around the edge of the material while you pull the pants up, to guiding him to pull the pants up while he holds the material. When you get to this stage you are in a position to begin fading the prompt. Start by prompting him to pull the pants up, and as the pants are near the waist gradually fade the prompt.

As you become able to fade more and more of the prompt, begin to lower the starting position of the pants, and then increase the amount you require your child to do. The eventual aim of this part of the programme will be to reach the point where he is able to pull his pants up to his waist from his ankles. Once he has the idea of pulling up you should find that his progress is rapid.

The next step in the programme will be to teach him to pull the pants over his feet. Start by putting the pants over one foot, and prompt him to pull them over the other. Then allow him to pull them up to his waist for the reward. Prompt him to stretch the pants out so that he can clearly see which hole the leg goes into. If he places both legs in one hole, say 'no', remove the pants and start again. If this happens frequently, increase the amount of prompt, and also introduce a short time-out period when he gets it wrong.

Once he is getting his second leg into the pants without problem, move on one more step in the sequence. Position the pants so that they are stretched open and near both his feet. Prompt him to hold the pants in this position and then help him to place both legs correctly in the pants. Reward when they are pulled up to the waist. The prompts you need to use at this stage should be fairly minor, considering that by now your child should have a clear idea of what is expected. It is likely that by now the prompts are only serving the purpose of helping him differentiate between the correct and incorrect position of the feet in the pants.

For the final step in the sequence, you hand him the pants and prompt him to open them out and position them so that he is able to put them on without getting into a muddle. This final step is the icing on the cake. If you are able to get this far, teaching other garments should present few problems, because much of what he has learned will be generalised to these new clothes.

The skill that you are teaching in the final steps is more complex than just pulling up pants, because it involves learning to recognise a correct and incorrect position for placing his feet. Some children may have difficulty with this, while others will progress rapidly. The time taken will depend on how able your child is at learning to tell the difference between objects or between situations: how much ability he has to discriminate. If progress on this step is slow, you may feel that you have taught your child enough by getting him to pull his pants up from his ankles. This is a useful skill in itself, because it can be used not just at dressing time in the morning but also through-out the day at toilet times. However, if you decide to persist in spite of the difficulties, you will be teaching something which

H

should have wider benefits than merely learning how to put pants over feet. Once this discriminating skill has been mastered in one situation, it will make learning in other situations much easier. Learning to put arms into correct arm holes is one obvious example.

Example 2. Trousers

If you have taught your child to put on pants, teaching him to put on trousers should be simple. The only additional difficulties may involve doing up buttons or clips. At this stage in the teaching do not worry too much about this. Wait until he is able to put on most garments without help, and then teach a specific programme on buttons and zips. A simple solution is to use trousers with elastic tops. With these he will have no problem with buttons, nor with having to get the trousers the right way round before putting them on.

Example 3. Vests and T-shirts

When beginning to teach pull-over items, start with something simple like a vest. This does not contain a bulky material to get lost in, and the head and arm holes are easier to find than those of long-sleeved jumpers.

The sequence for teaching is similar to that of putting on pants. Begin by putting the vest over his head, with his arms through, and prompt him to pull it down. Reward him at this point.

The next step will be to place it over his head, with one arm through, and prompt him to find the second arm hole. Similar problems may arise at this stage as occurred with pants. There may be a tendency for him to try and push his arm into the wrong place. You may need to spend several sessions working just on this skill.

Once he is able to achieve this, move on to placing the vest over his head and prompting him to find both arm holes. Prompt him to try one at a time rather than allowing him to struggle with both arms at once. This will ensure that he is systematic in his attempts to solve the problem. This also applies to the final step in teaching: rather than prompting him to pick the vest up in a bundle and sort it out, teach him to lay it out flat on a surface, such as the bed or floor. This will make it easier to pick up and position correctly for pulling over his head. Also, once he gets into this habit, you will find it easier to teach him how to deal with clothes which have a difference between back and front.

Example 4. Other pull-over clothes

Having taught your child to put on simple pull-over clothes, teaching him to deal with long-sleeved garments such as jumpers should present few problems. A certain amount of time may need to be spent dealing with long sleeves and tighter necks, but by now your child should have all the basic skills needed to cope with this.

Example 5. Socks

Most children seem to find problems in putting on socks. Their difficulties generally lie with getting the heels in the right position, and knowing what part of the sock to hold when pulling them on. Pulling from the top alone often results in stretching the top end of the sock, without bringing the rest of the sock along the foot or around the heel.

A possible sequence for teaching would be to place the sock on the foot, leaving the leg of the sock rolled up above the heel. Reward your child for pulling the sock up his leg. When he is able to do this, move to leaving the sock rolled under the heel. Prompt him to unroll it under the heel, and then pull up. Work through a series of steps until he is able to place the rolled up sock over his toes, pull it along the foot, under the heel and up. Prompt him to change the position he is pulling from when appropriate.

By now your child should have learned one strategy for putting the sock on. However, difficulties may arise when you come to give him the sock without rolling it up first. There are two possibilities for this step.

(1) You could teach him to roll the sock before putting it on, but he may then find it difficult to get the heel in the correct position. The rolled sock gives no clue as to which way up it should be.

(2) The alternative is to allow him to place his foot in the unrolled sock, and then get him to bunch it up as he pulls it along the foot. This method means frequent

changes in the position of the hands when pulling it on: some of the sock is pulled over the toes and then along the foot to the heel, and then more is pulled over the toes, then pulled to the heel, and so on. Both methods have advantages and disadvantages, and it would be best to experiment with both in order to see which one your child manages most easily.

Example 6. Buttons

These are generally last to be taught in a dressing programme. They vary so much in size and difficulty that we have found it worth putting together a series of simple waistcoats, grading them for size of button hole and button, for children to practise on. You should find it fairly easy to prompt your child when working with large buttons, such as those used on an adult's raincoat. When he has mastered these, move on to smaller ones, working your way down in as many steps as you find necessary, until you reach shirt button size. If he can manage these he can manage any buttons.

The stages in teaching large buttons are straightforward. Push the button half way through the hole and prompt him to pull it all the way through. When he is doing this easily, prompt him to support the button with one hand from underneath when it is pushed half through. Now get him to pull it all the way through from the top with the other hand. The next step follows from this. He should be prompted to push from underneath until the button protrudes far enough for him to hold it with the other hand and pull it through. The final stage will be for him to position the hole and the button together, to enable him to make the pushing through and pulling movements.

Needless to say, this process is not easy with small buttons, hence the need for buttons of graded sizes. However, once your child has become competent with large buttons, moving downwards through the sizes should not be too difficult.

Other garments

We have covered the teaching of only four skills in the dressing programme. There are obviously others which may need to be taught. However, from the detail that we have tried to provide in the above section, it should be possible for you to work out the necessary steps for teaching. You may find many of the steps we have included in the above unnecessary, and there may be additional steps that you will find useful to teach. The guidelines we have given are really only to demonstrate that it is possible to break down very complex actions into a series of simple movements. Each movement can be taught separately and then linked to others to form a whole.

SELF-HELP SKILLS AND SESSION TEACHING

The mentally handicapped child learns more slowly than other children. He will usually need more repetition and practice than most if he is to learn basic skills, whether they are concerned with feeding, dressing or riding a bicycle. Consequently we have stressed the need to use special teaching sessions. This ensures that learning takes place more rapidly than it would do if you relied on your child picking up skills from his day-to-day living. Because of the need for repetition of very small steps over long periods, these sessions could become extremely boring, hence the stress on using rewards.

There is no doubt that this style of teaching is extremely effective. However, because these skills are taught under special circumstances, you may find that your child is reluctant to use them in his day-to-day living. You must ensure that he does.

You may find it necessary to continue rewarding your child when he dresses himself in the morning. It should be possible to phase him in due course on to natural rewards for doing these things: for instance, rather than giving him a biscuit or favourite game for putting on his trousers first thing in the morning, show him that breakfast is ready when he has finished his dressing. Likewise, going for a walk will follow when he has put on his coat and shoes. You may need to introduce this system carefully. Your aim, of course, is to get your child using the skills as a matter of routine, and it may be necessary to show him that there are rewards and benefits in this routine. This might be seen as the final step of every self-help programme.

TOILET TRAINING

This is a subject which some parents are concerned about early on in their child's career, while others seem not to worry about it until their child is nearly at school age. With normal children the beginnings of bladder and bowel control can appear as early as 12 months, but two years is nearer the normal time.

Most children go through various stages in toilet training. They usually start with habit training, when they are potted frequently throughout the day. On some occasions they will use the pot, whereas at other times they will fail to do so. At this point they are not controlling their functions, but are merely being caught by the frequency with which they are potted. This is the stage at which they begin to learn the reason for potting.

Once the association between the pot and its use is established, parents generally begin to pot their child less often, but keep him sitting on the pot until he has used it. Accidents may still occur between potting times.

If the child finds the experience of being wet or dirty particularly unpleasant, he will soon learn to ask for the pot, or at least begin to wriggle and squirm when he feels the need to use it. Usually it is not long after this that he learns to take himself to the toilet. Most children, by the age of four, have reached this final stage.

It is impossible to generalise on how much delay will occur with the mentally handicapped child. Obviously much will depend on how severe his condition is, whether there are mobility or communication problems involved, and how concerned his parents are to begin a training programme.

Each of these factors will influence the progress of the programme, and so it is difficult to give guidelines as to how long it will take and how much work will be involved in carrying through each stage.

A guide to the basic procedures

Explaining and rewarding. As with the training of the non-handicapped child, the first essential is for your child to understand the function of the pot. Explaining to your child what is required of him when he is sat on the pot is one method of doing this. However, for children who are slow in their understanding and use of language this may have little or no effect. In this case you will need to reward your child whenever he uses the pot appropriately. Praise, in some cases, may be adequate. But a special treat, such as a favourite game or a piece of chocolate, is likely to be more effective. This will serve two functions. It will be a clear demonstration to him of when he has used the pot appropriately and when he has failed to do so. It will also act as an incentive for performing appropriately the next time. Thus even for children who are able to understand an explanation of what the pot is for, the use of rewards is important as an incentive.

The importance of timing. When you are rewarding your child for using the pot, it is important to reward him as soon after the event as possible. This will help him to understand what he is being rewarded for. This is particularly important if your child has a limited understanding of what you say to him. Telling him he is good and giving him a sweet several minutes after he has finished is unlikely to be meaningful. If this happens frequently, it will cause some delay in his learning of the association between the reward and the pot.

Because of this your child needs to be checked frequently—if possible, once a minute. The use of a clear plastic pot may save you the trouble of constantly having to lift him in order to make your check, although if he produces only a small quantity this may not be visible unless the pot is transparent.

Between checks. In the very early stages your child may not feel happy about sitting on the pot. If this is the case, and he frequently tries to get up, or cries when you sit him on it, introduce him to the idea gradually. Sit him on the pot for a minute or two and give him a favourite toy to play with. Talk to him while he is sitting there, and prompt him to remain seated if he tries to get off.

During this preliminary stage you are rewarding him for being cooperative. However, when you move on to the next step, the beginning of the toileting programme, you need to reward your child only after he has used the pot. Hence it is advisable not to give him too much attention, nor allow him to play, while you are waiting for him to use the pot. This may sound unfair. However, the situation you need to avoid is one whereby your child sees sitting on the pot as a rewarding activity which comes to an end when he uses it appropriately. If this does occur, he is likely to learn not to perform in the pot as this terminates his play time.

The most effective method, therefore, is to say as little as possible to your child between and during checks. When he uses the pot give him a lot of attention and reward.

The toileting schedule

During the early stages of the programme you will find it useful if you can discover a pattern to your child's toileting needs. This pattern will enable you to judge when he is most likely to use the pot. If you can allow yourself the luxury of three or four days to concentrate on his toileting programme, a lot can be

A SUGGESTED FORM OF TOILET CHART SUITABLE
FOR USING ON AN INTENSIVE PROGRAMME

John's chart for Monday morning, June 3rd		
Time	*Wet or dry when checked*	*Uses pot*
8.30	Wet	Nothing
8.50	Dry	Nothing
9.10	Dry	Yes
Breakfast		
9.30	Dry	Nothing
9.50	Dry	Nothing
10.10	Wet	Nothing
Drink		
10.30	Dry	Yes
10.50	Dry	Nothing
11.10	Dry	Nothing
11.30	Dry	Nothing
11.50	Dry	Nothing
12.10	Wet	Nothing
Lunch		

achieved. In this time you can run a programme of frequent potting sessions and frequent checks. This will enable you to pinpoint accurately at what times your child's bladder and bowels function throughout the day. It will also give you a chance of catching him on the pot on a number of these occasions. The more frequently you can reward him for using the pot, the faster he will understand what is required of him.

A chart similar to this can be made out for the mornings and afternoons of the four-day intensive programme. Obviously it will need to be modified to suit the organisation of your day. Any events which interfere with the programme, such as lunch or going out shopping, should be noted.

During these first days, if possible, pot your child once every half-hour and leave him on the pot for about five minutes. Check his pants once every quarter of an hour to see if he is still dry, making a note of the times you find him wet and of the occasions he uses his pot.

You will probably find that using a chart similar to the one illustrated above is better than relying on memory. At every checking time and toileting time make a note of whether his pants are wet or dry, and then make a note of whether or not he uses the pot. You can compare the results over three or four days and this will give you a basis for estimating how often and when you should pot your child for best results in the future.

If your child learns quickly you may find that by the end of two or three days he has picked up the idea. You will then merely need to spend time helping him to consolidate this skill. You need to ensure that his key potting times (those times when he is almost certain to use the pot) are regularly adhered to.

Other children will learn more slowly. At the end of the three or four days intensive programme, your child may not be using the pot reliably. However, you may have found certain times in the day when he is likely to go. These times may be related to when he has his meal and when he has his drinks. A typical pattern might be that between 9.30 and 10.30 he is very rarely wet. He usually has a drink at 10.30 and by 10.45 he is usually wet.

If this type of pattern is found, then you will be fairly safe in

H*

not potting him before his drink. Allow a short period to elapse after his drink, and then pot him for ten minutes or a quarter of an hour. You will know that there is a good chance of catching him. This is the kind of routine you should be aiming for after the initial three to four days.

Owing to pressures of family and work, many parents will find that it is impossible to spend even a day working intensively on toileting. This should not make the task of toilet training impossible, but it is likely to take longer to establish an effective routine. In the early stages you will have to rely more on guesswork than information when working out your schedule. You may be lucky with this, or you may find you miss one or two key periods. However, in time you should be able to establish an effective routine.

How long to keep your child sitting on the pot. At the beginning of the programme we suggested five-minute periods at half-hour intervals. When you have a better idea of your child's key periods you will know when he is likely to want to use the pot. Then you are in a position to decrease the number of potting sessions but, if necessary, increase the time that you keep him on the pot. For instance if when you put him on the pot he is dry, and you know that he should use it about this time, you can keep him on the pot until he does use it. You may find that this could take anything up to 20 minutes.

As we have stressed earlier in this section, this should present no difficulties provided that you are able to check him at frequent intervals. Problems will arise if you leave your child on the pot for extensive periods of time without checking him. If this happens you run the risk of him sitting for long periods of time in a boring situation after he has used the pot appropriately. In effect he will be suffering a time-out period for a behaviour that he should be rewarded for.

Failure to use the pot. There are also bound to be occasions when your child fails to use the pot. On such occasions do not keep him sitting on the pot indefinitely. This is liable to make potting a punishing situation. Twenty minutes is probably long enough. If at the end of this time he fails to produce anything, remove him from the pot with as little fuss as possible. He must learn to distinguish between the occasions he is rewarded for appropriate use of the pot, and the times he fails to use it. Failure to use it after a maximum of 20 minutes should result in an equivalent time-out period. Lift him off the pot, and pull up his pants and put the pot away without comment. Criticism for not using it may be mistaken for the attention he would have got had he used it, and so a silent routine is recommended.

How long to continue rewarding. The reward will act as a way of telling your child he has done well, and also as an incentive for future performance. Consequently rewards should be used after each appropriate use of the pot, until your child reaches the stage when he begins to ask for the pot, or goes on his own. This should be a good indication that he clearly understands the use of the pot, and prefers using it to making himself wet or dirty. When he reaches this stage his use of the pot is rewarding in itself.

This stage of understanding is not reached suddenly. It develops slowly from the habit trained stage. When you become aware that your child is moving in this direction, you can begin to phase out rewards, first by cutting down on the occasions you give him a sweet or special treat, and then by reducing the amount of attention you give. You should reach a point where 'That's a good boy' is adequate reward.

The speed with which you phase out the use of reward will depend on how long the training programme took to complete. If it took only two weeks to accomplish, then you should consider a further two weeks as a suitable period for reducing the reward. However, if the programme took six to eight months a longer period should be taken.

If problems begin to occur during this phasing out period, it is a sure guide that you are phasing the rewards out too quickly. Return to rewarding the original way, and begin the process again, but more slowly.

A summary of the steps

(1) If your child is unhappy when first put on the pot, sit him on it for short periods of time and play with him. Reward him for being cooperative. Do not worry about whether he uses it or not (although if he should use it, reward him for doing so).

(2) If possible spend several days working with an intensive programme, checking him frequently throughout the day. Pot him frequently for short periods of time. Use a toileting chart similar to the one shown above as an aid to your memory. Pay him as little attention as possible while checking him on the pot. If he uses the pot, reward him.

(3) From the information gathered over three or four days, work out a schedule for toileting. Pot him at those times he is most likely to use it. Increase the time you keep him on the pot, and check him frequently while he is sitting there. If he fails to use it after 20 minutes, take him off but make as little comment as possible.

(4) When he is using the pot reliably, encourage him to make his own way to the toilet rather than be led there. If mobility is a problem, try to get him to ask for the pot, or make a particular sign to indicate his needs. Continue to reward him for appropriate use but begin to cut down the amount given.

From pot to toilet

Usually there are few problems when children make the transition from using a pot to using a toilet. Special clip-on seats can be provided for small children. These will make sitting on the toilet more comfortable, and decrease the risk of the child being frightened by the prospect of falling into the pan.

Certain children, however, may be reluctant to use the toilet even if they are reliably potty trained. Their reluctance to use the toilet is possibly a result of a strong habit of using only the pot, being discouraged from going anywhere else, and not understanding the use of the toilet.

We faced this situation in school with five-year-old twin boys. They were reliably potty trained, and took themselves to the pot whenever they felt the need to go. Accidents were very rare. However, they refused to use the toilet. Usually they would sit happily on the toilet, but they would get upset if they were desperate to go. They would cry and point to their pots. When this happened, the usual response was to give in to their request. Consequently their teacher had been trying for many weeks to get them to use the toilet, but without success.

We decided that an intensive and hard-hearted effort ought

to be made over three or four days. Usually they used the pot about three times a day. We felt that if we toileted them about once every quarter of an hour throughout the day they would eventually be forced to use the toilet. The high frequency of toileting would reduce the chances of an accident in the classroom.

Two problems intervened. On the first day the lunchtime assistant in the classroom relented and allowed them to use the pot. We had obviously not spent enough time explaining the programme. In addition, it was felt that they could not be allowed to go home in a desperate state for fear that they have an accident in the school coach. We therefore had to allow them to use the pot immediately before they left for the coach, if they had failed to use the toilet during the day.

On the first day there was no success because they used the pot midday. They held out to the last minute of the afternoon and were finally allowed to use the pot for the second time.

On the second day one had an accident in the playground and the other managed to last out until it was time to go home.

On Friday, the third day in the programme, one used the toilet during the early afternoon. He was rewarded heavily with sweets and praise, but was clearly so relieved to be out of the situation that this was reward enough. The other waited until the very last minute of the afternoon and was allowed to use the pot.

On Monday morning both used the toilet, and both used it at least once more that day. They were swamped with praise for this. By Tuesday they were taking themselves to the toilet quite happily, and the quarter of an hour schedule was dropped.

Unfortunately the gentle approach over many weeks had failed to bring results. But by applying concentrated effort over a short period of time a successful conclusion was reached.

Use of gadgets

There are many gadgets on the market which are designed to assist toilet training. These range from a simple battery operated buzzer box which is activated by moisture, to the very elaborate musical potties. The aim of the gadgets is to give warning to the adult that the child is doing something, and also to emphasise this fact to the child.

The buzzer box. This is worn by the child on a belt and connected to his nappy by studs. As soon as his nappy is made moist the buzzer is activated and he can be rushed to the toilet. Hopefully he will begin to associate the sound of the buzzer with going to the toilet, and then be able to predict when the buzzer is likely to go off by the physical sensation felt immediately before urination.

Used in this way the equipment is of limited value. It can, however, be useful as a means of determining when a child's key times for toilet use occur. It saves the necessity of constant checks during the initial stages of this programme, and could be found useful in classrooms when a teacher's time has to be shared between many children.

A better use for this form of equipment is to have it connected to material placed in the bottom of the pot. The child can then be left on the pot without the need for constant checking, because you have a guarantee that as soon as he performs you will be given warning. Again, this has particular value for teachers who may have several children on toileting programmes at the same time.

Musical potties. These are elaborate versions of the last idea. Not only do they give warning of the child's performance on the pot, but they also reward him automatically with music. The apparatus can be adapted to produce other effects, such as triggering off an automatic sweet dispenser or a model railway train.

This sort of apparatus can be particularly useful in schools or hospitals where several children can be efficiently toilet trained at the same time. However, it is expensive to buy, and no more effective than an adult willing to spend time working on the programme.

WASHING

The mechanical skills of washing are straightforward to teach. They amount to little more than prompting your child to rub his hands on the soap, rub his hands together and rinse off the soap. In addition you may want to teach him how to use a flannel and apply it to his face, then to rinse off the soap with clean water.

However, the full process of unsupervised washing involves much more. A step by step sequence of skills are listed in Table 24. Each of these skills can be broken down into steps and taught. The sequence can then be built up.

Table 24. Washing skills

(1) Is your child able to put the plug in the sink?
(2) Is he able to turn on the taps?
(3) Can he differentiate between the hot and cold tap?
(4) Is he able to judge a suitable temperature for the water?
(5) Does he know how to adjust the temperature of hot water by putting in the cold?
(6) Is he able to tell when enough water is in the bowl, and is he then able to turn off the tap?
(7) Can he apply soap to his hands?
(8) Will he rub his hands together?
(9) Will he rinse off the soap?
(10) Can he apply soap to a flannel?
(11) Will he wash his face with a flannel?
(12) Can he rinse his face?
(13) Can he pull out the plug?
(14) Can he dry his hands on a towel?
(15) Can he dry his face?
(16) When finished will he put the towel, soap and flannel back in their appropriate places?

One of the main problems, not considered in the assessment, is your child's awareness of the purpose of washing. As with toileting, he can be habit trained so that he knows he needs to wash his face and hands when he gets up and before he goes to bed. He may also be taught to wash his hands after he has used the toilet and before he has a meal.

Teaching your child to recognise that his hands are dirty and need to be washed is probably the most difficult part of the programme. It involves him learning to tell the difference between clean and dirty. This, in its turn, leads to knowing what part of his hands to concentrate on when rubbing them together, and how to judge when the task is complete. This should be seen as the goal of a washing programme.

The teaching

As with dressing, most parents of normal children find it unnecessary to teach the various skills involved in washing. With some exceptions, children begin by passively accepting being washed. It is a process which occurs every day, and because of the frequent repetition they learn how to participate in various parts of the process: they will begin to dabble their hands in the water in order to rinse off the soap without the need to be told. Or they may learn to pull out the plug. This is a simple action which produces an interesting effect. Slowly they learn the various skills until they reach the point when they can be trusted to go and wash their hands without need of supervision.

Handicapped children will probably need a more structured form of teaching if they are to learn how to do this. A washing programme is probably more easily organised than a dressing programme, because there are usually at least four or five opportunities a day in which to practise. The programme can thus be followed throughout the day, without the need to arrange special teaching times.

Backward chaining

This is a convenient procedure to use, not just in the teaching of the individual skills but for the whole sequence. You can begin by prompting your child along each step. Start by prompting him to fit the plug, then to fill the bowl, test the temperature of the water, rub his hands on the soap and so on. At the end of the sequence comes drying his hands. Teach this first.

Prompt your child to hold the towel with one hand and rub his second hand into the towel. Then prompt him to do the same with the second hand.

Reward him for this action. You can repeat this part of the

process several times on each occasion that he is washed during the day.

Your aim will be to fade this prompt. Do this in the way we have described in previous sections on fading prompts. Begin by holding his first hand firmly in the towel and prompting his second hand, perhaps by removing your hand from around his hand and moving his wrist. After several rubs prompt him to change hands and continue to fade the rubbing prompt. After several rubs put the towel down and reward him.

Teaching the rubbing action first is important for a number of reasons. It is the final step in the washing sequence, so the reward will always come at the completion of the task. It is also a skill similar to several others that the child will need to learn, for example rubbing hands on soap, rubbing hands together, rubbing flannel on face and so on. Thus there should be generalisation from teaching this step to teaching other steps in the sequence. This may well make the teaching of the steps more rapid.

Once your child is able to dry his hands, the next step to teach will be face drying. This should be fairly straightforward for the reasons we mentioned above. Again, prompt the action of holding the towel in both hands and rubbing the face, and then fade this prompt. Having completed this action require your child to finish the sequence by drying his own hands, and then give the reward.

Follow this procedure for each of the steps listed in Table 24. Probably the most difficult part of the sequence is teaching your child how to fill the bowl without overfilling it, and to adjust the water temperature. The difficulty lies in the fact that these are not simply mechanical skills, they require judgement and understanding.

There will be no difficulty in overcoming the problems of water temperature if your hot water supply is regulated to a moderate heat. In this case all your child needs to learn is which is the appropriate tap to turn on. However, most hot water supplies tend to run to high temperatures, in which case you could choose to teach him to use only the cold tap. This, in its turn, is likely to present problems. Once your child is able to turn on taps there will be nothing to stop him trying the hot tap when nobody is around, and scald himself. If you decide to teach your child how to turn on taps it would be best to teach him an awareness of the dangers, and ways to deal with them.

Learning how to deal with hot water could be combined with learning not to overfill the bowl, and could be taken as a programme on its own. Because it comes at the beginning of the steps in learning to wash, it will be the last part of the programme to be taught. Therefore it would be possible to leave this part of the programme until your child is more able to deal with it. This would not interfere with his learning of the other washing skills, although it would mean that he could not wash himself without assistance until he had learned this important step.

Hot and cold. If you take filling the bowl with water of the correct temperature as a separate programme, it would be advisable to use the reward at the end of the sequence. To begin with you might find it necessary to practise filling the bowl several times before you continue with washing. This will help your child learn the skill more rapidly.

There are six steps involved in this sequence:

(1) Prompt him to fit the plug.
(2) Prompt him to turn on the cold tap.
(3) Wait until there are several inches of water in the bowl and say 'Turn off the tap'. Prompt him to do this.
(4) Prompt him to put one hand in the cold water and prompt the other hand to turn the hot tap on.
(5) When the water becomes warm, say 'Turn off the tap'. Prompt him to do this.
(6) Reward him.

Having listed these steps, it is possible to see the difficulties involved in teaching this skill:

(1) It involves a long sequence of events to be followed in the correct order.
(2) It involves being able to judge either the appropriate length of time to leave the tap on or the right depth of water in the bowl before the tap is switched off.
(3) It involves learning on which side the cold and hot taps are placed on the bowl.

(4) It involves learning which way to turn the taps. It is easy to turn a tap on because it will turn in one direction only. Turning the tap off is more difficult because it is likely to turn in either direction.

(5) It involves learning to judge when the temperature is correct. The child will obviously know when to take his hand out of the water because it is too hot. But in practice he needs to learn to switch off the tap before the water reaches this temperature.

If your child is able to deal with the types of skills and judgements we have described above, there should be no problem in beginning this part of the programme. However, you may find it necessary to wait a while, and do some preliminary work with him. For instance, teaching him how to unscrew and screw with bottle caps, or with large plastic nuts and bolts, will give him some idea of directional turning. A variety of simple discriminations such as those described in the discrimination section in Chapter 8 may also be of use.

These last points clearly illustrate how the teaching of self-help skills is linked very closely to other forms of teaching. Your child can derive considerable benefit from self-help programmes by learning many useful skills which can be applied to other situations. Also, as your child learns these skills he is moving towards greater independence. This is important for your child's own self-respect, and it cannot fail to help you in your day-to-day living.

13 : Moving About

Problems with moving about or sitting up or developing head control are often the first signs that alert a parent or doctor that something is wrong with the child's development. Even where the child has a definite complaint that has been identified from an early age, it is often only when he is slow in reaching these important motor milestones that the implications of the handicap become apparent. Quite rightly, these steps are seen as vital for the child's future development and it is here that parents often feel the greatest need for help. After all, these are not things we normally expect to have to 'teach' our children, we expect to wait for them to 'happen'. But we can help even the most severely handicapped child improve his ability to control his own body if we know how to set about it.

A general book like this cannot go into too much detail on each physical problem, and if your child has any particular difficulties you will need the guidance of a physiotherapist who can show you the best way to handle your child. But not every child who is physically handicapped has access to a physiotherapist, and even where a physiotherapist is seen regularly it still rests with the parents or care staff to put the ideas into practice and to decide on the priorities for their child.

Unfortunately, as with most fields of expertise, there is no total agreement on the best methods to use. You may be told one thing by your particular physiotherapist and then be disturbed to meet or read about someone else's totally different approach. If your child is progressing slowly there may be a temptation to think that some other approach would be better, and of course that may be so; the problem is first knowing what to do, and then trying to get help in carrying it out.

What we hope to do here is to give you an outline of some of the methods that are currently in use in promoting the physical development of handicapped children, and by doing so to give you some information on which to base your decision. Following the initial discussion, we shall be outlining the major steps in physical development so that you can see where your child is now and thus what step you can be encouraging next.

Sometimes this will mean an actual teaching programme and we will indicate ways this might be done. Sometimes it will be best just to be aware of the next step and to use everyday handling and play situations to develop and strengthen this step. We will suggest some ideas for this as well.

Nancy Finnie's *Treating the Young Cerebral Palsied Child at Home* is an excellent guide to the treatment and handling of young cerebral palsied children, full of clear practical advice and diagrams. This book also gives some guidance on useful aids and toys—proper equipment can be a great help in maintaining your child in the correct position. Some of these aids are available on prescription or from your local social services department, but you will probably have to press for what you need as many social workers and doctors are not themselves aware of all the services to which you may be entitled. Guidance on what aids are available can usually be obtained from charities such as the Spastics Society, who run an exhibition of equipment and toys and will keep members in touch with their rights.

VARIOUS APPROACHES

Many physiotherapists will have developed their own approach out of their own experience with handicapped children. If you find a physiotherapist who works well with your child and is able to show you what to do, you would be unwise to turn your back on such practical expertise and guidance, whatever their approach. However, the decision is yours and hopefully the following information will at least help you put the practical advice in context.

Bobath
The treatment of children handicapped by cerebral palsy has been greatly advanced by the work of the Bobaths. They helped pioneer work on very young children and believe that by reinforcing 'correct' patterns of motor behaviour and preventing 'incorrect' or 'primitive' responses, the therapist can prevent many of the structural abnormalities that characterise

'untreated' severely cerebral palsied adults. More positively, they claim that by using 'correct' methods of handling and posture control the child is helped to control his own movements and is led more easily to chew, to handle objects and even to move about.

Physiotherapists following this approach will probably see their work as leading to the general development of the child (chewing leading to sound production, head control to being able to look at objects or people, grasping to being able to play, etc.), but their priority is the physical development of the child. The child is generally 'manipulated' by the therapist in ways that encourage the 'correct' movements, or hold the child in the correct position. The essence of this approach is that the 'correct' movements become automatic for the child and gradually supplant the 'incorrect' ones, so it is essential that the child is exercised regularly and is handled correctly throughout the day. The parents or care staff in most cases will be allowed to attend this therapy session so that they can be shown how to position the child correctly when he is sitting, lying or being carried, and how to continue with the exercises in his daily environment. If your child is seeing a therapist but you are not being taught how to carry on the therapist's work at home, or in the classroom, it would probably be a good idea to ask to be given such information. If guidance is not given, you would need to consider whether such infrequent exercise is of any use to the child.

The Bobath approach to physiotherapy is probably the most freely available in Britain, and it is often the first practical help that is offered to parents of a physically handicapped child. Increasingly therapists are involving parents in this treatment. But even when they are shown the treatment and its purpose is explained to them, some parents who find that their child is unhappy or even seemingly in pain during the sessions, wonder whether the benefits are worth all the effort. Not all children hate the sessions: others enjoy the social stimulus of working with the therapist and are pleased with her approval of their efforts. But the child is perforce being placed in positions that are uncomfortable, or at least require some effort to maintain, and being asked to make movements that do not come 'naturally'. The therapist needs a great deal of skill in reassuring and encouraging the child. You can help by making sure you reward him when you are doing the exercises at home. You may be able to show the therapist, if she does not already use rewards, how much better the child will work with them.

Peto

An alternative approach is not to try to reinforce exact patterns of motor behaviour, but to concentrate on the overall purpose of an action. The Peto method offers some guidance on motor patterns, but then leaves the child to find his own best or easiest way of performing a task. It is the tasks that are taught: grasping a rod, sitting, standing, rolling over, dressing.

The Peto system, as originally developed and used in Hungary, provides a complete framework for the education and care of physically handicapped children. Central to this system is the idea that one person is specially trained to be responsible for the entire care and education of the child, so the system really only works in special institutions with 24-hour-a-day control by three 'conductresses'. Considerable success has been claimed for it in Hungary. This total approach has not been adopted in Britain, although some schools, hospitals and training centres use some aspects of the Peto system.

The Peto training relies on repetition of actions, accompanied by chanting and singing to provide rhythm and smooth continuity between one action and the next. Thus the child might be required to roll over on his own (he may be helped initially by the instructor), but he is not required to do it in exactly the same 'correct' way each time. What he is required to do is to chant or sing the same thing each time. An example might be 'We roll over on to our tummy . . . 1 . . . 2 . . . 3 . . . 4 . . . 5'. There are two things to notice about this 'chant'. One is the use of 'we', which we will come to in a minute; the other is the use of counting. The counting continues while the action is performed, and this allows for both slow and quick actions. The evident purpose of the chanting and counting is to help the child 'pace' the activity, and to allow him to relate one situation to the next; but the primary function may be more profound. Cerebral palsied children have damage to the brain in the areas that control movement and so cannot control their movements in the smooth way necessary to build up skills such as dressing, feeding or walking. However, speech involves a different part of the brain, and it may be that by using speech to aid movement the child learns to use a different (undamaged) part of the brain to control the movements and thus to perfect the skill. Once the skill is established, the chanting can be phased out, or at least done silently. This is a plausible theory and a hopeful approach for many cerebral palsied children.

For very young or severely handicapped children who have not yet developed speech, the Peto method may be less suitable. Attempts have been made to apply it to these children by using volunteers, teachers or parents to chant for the child and put him through the movements. These classes are popular with parents and a lot is claimed for them but it is far from clear whether the benefits arise from the method itself, or from the simple fact of daily consistent working with the children.

The Peto approach is also characterised, in the institutions and schools that take it seriously, by particular wooden furniture in otherwise bare rooms. The rooms are intended to be distraction-free, so the child can concentrate, and the wooden furniture is designed to serve as equipment and apparatus for all the basic activities. There are wooden slatted plinths on which the child can grip to pull himself along, which also can serve as beds to roll over on and to sit up from, or as tables in conjunction with ladder-backed chairs. The chairs in turn serve as standing and walking frames and as supports for grasping or to encourage head control and balance for sitting. There are also rods, which the child learns to grasp and move around and large double-handled mugs which he learns to drink from. Much of the Peto system is independent of these props, but they do focus attention on the required movements and are generally versatile pieces of equipment. A parent would be expected to have only small pieces of equipment at home (the rod and the cup for instance). The rest are used in group work.

This brings us back to the 'we' in the child's chant, and to a further feature of the Peto system—the use of the group. Other physiotherapists are moving towards the idea of working with children in groups, but any method that depends on correct manipulation and exact maintenance of posture demands by definition a high ratio of therapists to children. The group treatment, however, is an essential part of the Peto system. Groups would ordinarily consist of several children and one 'conductress', although there will be one or two other adults around to assist. In the 'mother and baby' groups or 'nurse and patient' groups, the group principle is still essential. The idea behind the principle is thus not to cut down on the time-commitment of the physiotherapist (although this is a useful by-product), but to encourage the children to relate to one another; to praise each other's achievements and to spur each other on, though it is difficult to collect together a group of handicapped children all at the same level of development, it is obviously best if they at least need to practise the same activity, or some will become bored while others struggle.

Most therapists working with this method devise various games to alleviate the tedium, and the chanting can be developed into singing games to help the activity along.

Doman-Delacato

This approach has received a lot of publicity and is often known as 'Patterning', since this is its best known feature. In the past parents had to take the child for initial assessment to the Institute for Human Potential in Philadelphia, where they were given a programme of work for the first few months of treatment. They then had to go back for follow-up assessments and further programmes. But it has become possible to obtain the follow-up services in Britain.

Travelling and consultancy fees have made this a very expensive form of treatment, available only to those able to raise considerable sums themselves or by appeal. And even when the money has been raised, parents are faced with the tremendous problem of finding enough reliable friends to help them carry out the intricate daily programmes. Most of the programmes demand that the child be manipulated (or patterned) through a series of movements for very long periods each day. In addition to this 'patterning' the child's programme will involve work in other areas, and the parents cannot manage this alone. It is not uncommon for the whole programme to take as much as fifteen hours of the child's day.

Given this tremendous commitment in time, money and energy it may seem surprising that this approach has any following, but there are indications that it is becoming more popular. It is probable that the commitment itself may be a factor in the system's appeal. The basis of the approach is that children with brain damage can be 'patterned' so that the undamaged parts of the brain are stimulated into taking over the function of the damaged areas. This is an attractive notion without a proven scientific basis, although it does seem true that extensive or intensive and regular stimulation can excite responses that are not evoked by milder forms of stimulation. Glen Doman based his ideas for teaching young babies to 'read' on this theory, and elements of the same approach can be seen in many of the programmes for handicapped children.

Doman and Delacato make no claims to help children with any genetic or progressive disease; Down's Syndrome children for example would not be helped.

It is not possible to be specific about the kind of programme your child might undergo under Doman and Delacato. Each programme is based on the child's needs over many different areas of development. However, it would be fair to say that the basic approach assumes that every child should go through certain motor movements that attempt to follow the normal development of a baby. The child is made to creep and then to crawl even if he can already walk, if he has missed out creeping and crawling earlier on. The results that have been investigated do show considerable improvement in the children undergoing the treatment, but what is not clear is how much of this is due simply to the time and effort and attention which have been devoted to them.

The regime is clearly not to be undertaken lightly. It imposes a considerable burden on the parents and perhaps even more on other members of the family. The household must revolve around the handicapped child's needs every day, and this could not only be a problem for brothers and sisters, but also may not even be in the long-term interest of the child. If such a system is adopted then obviously much other experience must be missed out, and only the parents or care staff can really decide whether the benefits outweigh the losses.

The fact that, in spite of its obvious difficulties, so many parents are attracted to this system, at least initially, suggests that there is a real need for parents and care staff to be given a highly structured programme of work for their child in which they can be involved in a very practical way. If other systems were developed to offer this detailed practical advice, personal programme and follow-up service, it would become clearer how much value rests in the Doman-Delacato methods themselves, and how much depends on the enthusiasm of those carrying out the programme.

We welcome the structuring of the environment advocated by Doman-Delacato; but we would in principle like to see the child in a more active role in his treatment—learning to respond in a structured setting—than this particular treatment provides.

Down's Baby Society

This society aims also to develop the full potential of the child in all areas. Apart from some clumsiness as the child gets older—generally associated with overweight—most Down's Syndrome children do not have physical problems affecting their general mobility. Sometimes they are slow to sit up and to walk, but they are often within the range for normal babies. Rex Brinkworth has developed a programme of help for parents of Down's Syndrome babies covering all aspects of development, which in the early stages involves stimulation of movement. He also covers aspects of diet and health which may affect the mobility of the child. His work is based on his experiences and experiments with his own child, and then with a group of Down's Syndrome babies. The results seem encouraging—again, a factor may be that parents are given fairly precise ways to behave with their children from an early age, and there is support from the group.

Our approach

Unfortunately we cannot do a 'Which?' test on the various methods of promoting physical development for your child. What we can do is give a guide to the steps in the sorts of *behaviour* you want to see in this area. Then we can offer a guide to teaching methods. Specific physical problems, however, will need specific solutions: not all children need to pass through all the stages in each behaviour. Many children learn to walk without crawling first, for example, so it may be better to concentrate on teaching the former unless there is a particular reason for wanting a child to crawl. 'Tricks of the trade', such as getting the child to bear weight on his legs by pushing down from the hip or shoulder, are hard to describe in a book and better demonstrated by a physiotherapist. Similarly, it is very difficult to deal with the tenseness of a spastic limb and to move it appropriately for dressing or rolling over, unless the technique has been demonstrated. So this is not meant as a 'Teach Yourself Physiotherapy' kit, but simply to help you understand what is necessary, to judge the value of what you are told by other 'experts', and to help you cope when no better help is available.

Central to the approach we advocate in this book is the idea that obtaining appropriate responses from the child should be your main aim. If the aim is to get the child to walk, or to acquire head control, then that is the behaviour we work on—not a general behaviour that we hope will help in the long term. This is rather like the old argument that teaching the Classics in secondary schools helps the children to learn logic: if that is the only justification for teaching, then why not teach logic directly? We may not be able to start with the behaviour we want in the end, because the child is a long way from it: but everything we teach can be seen as a step towards that goal. If a step can be skipped, we skip it. Many normal children miss out a so-called 'normal' step in development, or develop some variation of their own. With learning time so precious, it makes sense to concentrate on proven or obviously essential steps.

CHECKLIST OF BEHAVIOURS

Although this chapter deals mainly with mobility, it encompasses all aspects of physical development, and thus includes posture and fine movements of the hand. A child does not need perfect posture to move about, but there are aspects of posture —such as balance and ability to bear weight on the limbs— which it may be necessary to acquire first. We will deal with posture, mobility and fine movements as three separate areas, and in most cases you will be able to help with all three areas of development at any one time. Where it is necessary to develop in one area first (such as standing balance before walking), this will be indicated.

Table 25. Posture

(1) Head control	(*a*) When prone (on his front), is the child able to lift up his head?
	(*b*) When supine (on his back), is he able to follow with his head when pulled by his hands to sitting position?
	(*c*) Is he able to maintain his head upright without support for indefinite period?
(2) Muscle tone	(*a*) In his neck, is there sufficient tone to allow for head control?
	(*b*) In his torso, is there appropriate tone to maintain posture?
	(*c*) In his limbs, is there appropriate tone to resist pressure?
(3) Control of 'Involuntary' movements	These are important for posture if they cause the child to lose muscle tone or to lose balance.
(4) Sitting balance	(*a*) Is the child able to sit supported by his feet and hands on a firm surface?
	(*b*) Is he able to maintain a sitting position unsupported?
(5) Weight bearing on legs	Is the child able to bear weight on his body in standing position?
(6) Standing balance	Is the child able to maintain balance unsupported when standing?
(7) Kneeling	(*a*) Can he do 'low' kneeling, with his bottom resting on his legs?
	(*b*) Can he do 'high' kneeling with his weight supported by his knees and calves?
(8) Balances on one foot	This is necessary for complicated skills such as hopping and skipping.

The stages in head control are likely to follow the pattern indicated, but there may be individual variations. A child who is blind, for example, is often very slow in attaining head control since he has little incentive to hold the head in any position. For the sighted child, head control is necessary to keep objects in focus, and he can be motivated by dangling brightly coloured objects so that he has to lift up his head to see them (see Chapter 7). The blind child can be encouraged to raise his head by stroking it with some soft object that also makes a noise. Then this can be moved away gradually, still shaking, so that the child lifts his head to follow it. As he lifts his head he can be rewarded for doing so. Alternatively, a child's head can be prompted—held in the correct position while he is simultaneously rewarded so he begins to understand what is required of him.

Lack of effective muscle tone and involuntary movements can both interfere with posture. These are not subject to direct physical guidance, but the child can be rewarded for maintaining a particular posture. In this way a child can learn to control even involuntary movements.

Similarly a child can be rewarded for sitting, standing or kneeling as required. The main point to remember is that simply putting a child in a particular position and leaving him there does not teach him anything about maintaining it. In fact, if he is uncomfortable and bored, he will be less likely to want to maintain the position of his own accord.

Many physiotherapists favour the use of splints to hold the child's limbs (especially the joints) in the correct position, say, for standing. Splints obviously work where bones have to be held in place as they grow, or mend when broken, but the principle applied to maintenance of joint position is more dubious. It has been tried on swimmers, expert at the crawl, who find it difficult to maintain the correct foot position for breast-stroke. These have had their feet taped into the right position, only to find that they spring back to their accustomed position as soon as they are released. If this happens where the individual is so highly motivated to maintain the position, the effect of splints on a handicapped child becomes very dubious. Whether or not this works for your child will be a matter of experiment, but a physiotherapist should at least be asked to justify what is often an uncomfortable procedure.

The problem of maintaining posture can be illustrated by considering sitting behaviour. When trying to teach a child to sit properly on his own, you will need at least two kinds of chair. One will be correctly designed to encourage sitting balance in the child: it will have no side support, but a firm back, and it will fit the child so that his feet are comfortably and firmly on the floor at right angles. He can be put on this chair, with the occasional gentle help if he threatens to lose balance, and rewarded and attended to constantly for maintaining this position. The length of time for which he can sit unsupported should gradually increase until, once it is a firmly established behaviour, it is safe to leave him unattended but with plenty of toys and still the occasional reward from you. But, while he is learning this skill, there will be times when you simply cannot give him your individual attention. What is needed then is a chair that supports him in the correct position safely. He may not learn how to maintain the position himself in this way, but his head and body will be in the correct position and he can continue to observe how the world functions from an upright position.

Table 26. Mobility

(1) Rolling and turning over	Is the child able to roll over on a firm surface from both a prone and supine position?
(2) Creeping	Is he able to pull himself across a firm surface—using his limbs?
(3) Crawling	Crawling can take many forms, but in its most correct form the body is supported on all fours and the child moves his limbs in a coordinated way to move across a surface.
(4) Bottom shuffling	This usually emerges as an alternative way of moving about to crawling. The child moves along on his bottom using two or more limbs to aid the process.
(5) Walking with support	Can the child shift balance from one foot to another, although he

	lacks either complete balance, or the confidence to walk unaided?
(6) Independent walking	(*a*) Can the child walk on his own? (*b*) Is he able to walk while pulling along a toy?
(7) Running	This may range from what is really a hurried walk to controlled running on tiptoe.
(8) Jumping	Has he learned to propel himself upwards, using both legs at once?
(9) Hopping	Has he, in addition to the skill of propulsion learnt in jumping, enough balance to jump on one foot?
(10) Skipping	Skipping requires an ability to pace movements and to balance momentarily on one foot, while giving a little hop; it may appear at the same time as hopping or after.
(11) Climbing	This skill usually develops soon after walking (before the more complicated skipping, hopping, etc.) and in fact the child who can only crawl can often climb, using all four limbs.
(12) Pedalling	This is a very complex skill. It requires strength in the leg muscles, but, more importantly, it involves maintaining a pushing rhythm between the two legs so that the pedalling is smooth. Pedalling a bicycle demands the additional skill of balance.
(13) Swimming	This may develop parallel to other mobility skills, depending on the experience of the child. Many children who are cerebral palsied, and have great difficulty moving around on land, can swim with ease.

We have mentioned a wide range of mobility skills, but we shall not be considering the more complicated ones in any further detail; the main goal of our training in mobility for the severely handicapped is to get them moving independently in some way if at all possible, and to aim for walking ability in the long run.

Obviously in order to learn to move a child must have the opportunity (that is, he must not be too tightly wrapped in blankets and constrained in a wheelchair or cot) and he must see the point of doing so. The fact that the child is enabled to come into contact with fresh experiences may be sufficient reward for movement, but it is never safe to rely on such rewards with the severely handicapped. Treat movement as you would any other skill, and encourage the child to move by offering some particularly attractive reward just out of reach. To begin with, the slightest movement will secure the reward, but gradually the child must move more and more to get it. This technique can be used to 'shape' the child's movements at each stage in his mobility: it can be used to encourage crawling or walking or even cycling. The advantage in using this method to encourage mobility is that the child develops first his own 'easiest' way of getting there, and so you do not have to consider whether or not to teach crawling to a child who already has standing balance. If he begins to walk without reverting to crawling, this can be accepted happily.

Of course, if you have a child who can crawl readily and you are trying to teach him to walk, then you do not allow him to choose his easiest method of movement. Instead, you can place him in a standing position between two chairs, placed in such a way that the child can loosen his grip on one and turn with one step to grip the other. When he has been rewarded several times for making this one step, the chairs can be moved further apart so that the number of steps needed is increased. Getting down and crawling is not of course rewarded—the child is brought back to the beginning to start again.

Similarly, if you want to train crawling and prevent a child from reverting to creeping—or simply subsiding on the floor—a towel or blanket can be placed around the child's middle while you hold its ends. But you cannot show him how to make the movements by this method, unless you have someone else to

I

help you. Ideally there should be three helpers, one to place her hands behind the feet of the child so that he has something to push against, one to keep him suspended in the correct position, and a third to offer him a suitable reward a short distance away.

When a child is blind or partially sighted, the world must seem a very frightening place, which the child is bound to feel reluctant about moving about in. Only one bad experience of tripping or bumping into an object may be sufficient to cause even greater withdrawal. So a blind or partially sighted child should move round and explore the environment first while being held securely by someone he trusts. Later he can be held away from the body for short periods, and swung gently if he enjoys this, to get used to being apart from complete contact with a safe object or person. Still later (if he has standing balance) he might find it fun to walk about by standing on your feet. In this way he can get the feel of 'walking' without having to launch himself into the unknown. He can also get to learn where things are in his environment. Eventually he can be left standing near some familiar place and encouraged by your voice to walk just a little way towards you. If the child has problems in hearing as well as sight, he may learn to feel his way along a loose ribbon that will not actually support him but will show him the direction to follow. Obviously such children will take a long time to gain the confidence to do this, and each step should be taken slowly (see Example 6, Chapter 5, page 86).

Any sight problem, such as a bad squint, can cause difficulties with mobility, and these are not always explained to parents or care staff. If the squint is severe enough the child may have monocular vision, that is, he sees only through the dominant eye. He can see clearly, but will get no understanding of depth of field—that is, distance of objects from him. In time, a person with monocular vision learns to recognise other signs that indicate differences in depth of field, but a young child crawling around may fall down the same step over and over again because he literally cannot 'see' it. Knowing this can help a parent plan to guard likely areas of danger, or mark each step in a certain way so that the child can learn that this is the point where the level changes.

Table 27. Fine motor movements

(1) Retaining palmar grasp	If something is placed in the child's hand, do his fingers close round it, and can he retain his hold?
(2) Chance grasping	(*a*) When the child's hand comes into contact with an object, will the hand open and grasp it? (*b*) Once an object is grasped in this way, does the child bring it near his face so he can examine it visually? (See Chapter 7.)
(3) Involuntary or extensor movements	Such movements inhibit the child from examining visually what he has grasped, for, as the hands move in towards the midline of the body, the head automatically shoots to one side. The child has to learn to control these movements so that he can eventually look at objects while he holds them in front of him.
(4) Reaching and grasping	Unless the child is blind, reaching and grasping is usually controlled by what the child sees. Is the child able to direct his movements towards an object he is looking at?
(5) Finger/thumb apposition	Does his thumb come to stand in opposition to each of the fingers of the hand, enabling fine finger grasping and manipulation?
(6) The pincer grasp	This develops from finger/thumb apposition, and governs the precise grasp between the index finger and thumb which greatly assists fine manipulations, including holding a pencil or cutlery correctly.
(7) Controlled release	A child can learn to grasp an object long before he learns to let it go. He may drop the object, but does he have the skill to let it go when and where you want him to?

| (8) Two-handed coordination | This starts with learning to bring the two hands together to clap, but develops into smoothly coordinated skills such as threading (where one hand feeds the thread to the other to pull), mixing, where one hand steadies the bowl as the other mixes, and even to knitting. |

If your child does not retain his grasp on objects, he can be taught to do this by rewarding him when he does so, and stopping the reward when he drops them. Once he has retained his grasp for 30 seconds or so reliably, it is probably best to go on to teach him something else to do with the object as you do not really want to train passive holding (see Chapter 7).

It is far more difficult to train finer and more controlled grasping and releasing, since it is difficult to prompt the child to show what is required. What can be done is to select carefully graded tasks that can be done only by use of the required skill, and then to reward the child for doing them.

EXAMPLES OF TEACHING PROGRAMMES

We now turn to some examples of methods of teaching.

One general point needs to be made about motor training. There is strong evidence that if the physically handicapped child is left without physiotherapy and without movement of any sort, he will develop further complications to his condition such as twisting of the spine and limbs. To this we can add the fact that the child will be massively educationally deprived. Whatever else is done for the severely handicapped child, parents, teachers, care staff and nurses must get guidance on simple exercises that can be done to prevent the worsening of physical handicap.

Example 1. A programme for encouraging standing balance

Richard was a child of five when we first knew him, attending a day centre for multiply handicapped children. He had a genetic abnormality which had led to mental handicap, and may also have been responsible for his generally poor muscle tone. Richard had had good head control and sitting balance for at least two years, but attempts to make him stand always failed as he simply buckled at the knees. The physiotherapist had tried splints, but as soon as they were taken off he would buckle once more! She then decided to place him in a standing frame. But Richard was miserable in the frame, and would still manage to bend his knees slightly by suspending himself from his arms. We decided to play with Richard while he was in the frame so that he would not be able to rest on his arms. He would have to straighten his knees in order to play and yet would enjoy the experience. If he did slouch then we would turn away at once. Richard had not learned to stand unaided at the end of eight weeks, but he didn't buckle at the knees so readily even when he was taken out of the frame and encouraged to walk up and down with help.

Example 2. From bottom shuffling to walking

Sheila was a severely handicapped five-year-old attending the same day centre as Richard. She had been bottom shuffling and crawling effectively for some time, and although she had standing balance and could walk with support she preferred to get around in the easiest way possible. At school she would only manage one or two steps before sinking to the ground. The teachers at school were using a book to reward and to encourage her (she liked to flick through books), but they were also giving her a lot of attention every time she fell or sat down; they would run to pick her up and fuss over her before setting her back on her feet to try once more. At the same time Sheila was walking very well at home for her mother, who had developed a much more effective technique. She was using a stronger reward (a crisp) and was giving her no attention other than a brisk putting of her back on her feet when she sat down. The school adopted the methods used at home and found Sheila able to walk adequately across a room after only one session.

Example 3. Going down stairs

Agnes was able to walk well but was afraid to walk down stairs. Her mother also felt that she was not safe on stairs, and feared that she would have an accident if the gate at the top of the stairs were left open. She had already hurt herself several times by tripping down the single step into the garden. It was decided to teach Agnes to negotiate the steps on her bottom, as this would give her better control and lessen the chance of her slipping. She was taught to sit down at the top of the stairs and to wriggle forward until she could get one foot on to the next step but one. Then she could follow with the other foot and finally swing down her bottom. To begin with her feet were moved forward for her, but she eventually came to do this for herself and after ten sessions was very confident at coming down stairs by herself.

Example 4. Retaining grasp

Fred was a very severely handicapped blind boy with no head control. He was taught to retain his grasp on a wooden rod so that he could eventually learn to shake bells and have some way of amusing himself and interacting with his environment. The rod was placed in his hand, and he was sung to and his cheek was stroked as long as he retained his grasp. The singing and caressing stopped when he let go. To begin with he was also given a spoonful of food if he managed to keep his hold for one second. This time was lengthened gradually, so that he would have to hold for ten seconds before getting the food. At that point he was rewarded with another spoonful if he kept hold for 20 seconds. Once he could hold the rod reliably for 30 seconds most times, he was no longer rewarded for simply holding but was given a rod with bells attached and was rewarded for any movement that made them ring.

Example 5. Developing a pincer grip

Agnes, the child who had been taught to bump down stairs, was also taught to develop her pincer grasp. We got her to pick up progressively smaller items, beginning with one-inch cubes. She could manage to pick up small pegs and put them in a peg board at the end of 14 weeks. She was rewarded for all attempts at first.

Example 6. Controlled release

Nigel was a severely handicapped child who suffered from involuntary extensor movements and had great problems in learning to release objects with precision. He was taught initially to drop large blocks into a biscuit tin, then rods into a smaller box. Eventually he could place one-inch diameter rods into their holes, or give them to the teacher by placing them in her hand. Dropping objects which made a noise when they landed proved rewarding in itself.

CONCLUSION

In this chapter we have discussed various types of physiotherapy, and given a framework for assessment and teaching. This area is one which causes a great deal of concern to parents and teachers alike, often because of the difficulty in getting treatment. What is clear is that the child must not be allowed simply to lie for hours unattended. This will frustrate all educational efforts and could have serious consequences in terms of the development of further physical problems.

14 : Behaviour Problems

WHAT IS A BEHAVIOUR PROBLEM?

When a child is very young or severely handicapped, it may seem inappropriate to talk of 'behaviour problems'—you wish the child could be 'naughty' like other children! But the term 'behaviour problem' does not refer only to behaviour we would normally describe as 'naughty', but to any behaviour which makes life difficult for the child or for those who care for him.

This makes defining a behaviour problem a very subjective matter. But there are some criteria that could be helpful in deciding whether a problem is serious enough to warrant your intervention.

1. Does it disturb you sufficiently to interfere with your peace of mind or your relationship with the child?

This would almost certainly seem good reason for defining a habit as a behaviour problem: unless it is you who are being abnormally disturbed by the behaviour. You might consider that you were abnormally disturbed, for example, if the behaviour upsets only *you*, and the same behaviour by other children is accepted by their parents or care staff. In this case you may seek help yourself. You might also consider you were being abnormally disturbed if it was an abnormal environment that made the behaviour disturbing. If, for example, a child had learnt to call for attention in a large ward of a hospital, this might be very annoying to a harassed nurse trying to cope with 20 other children in the ward; but here it is not the behaviour of the child that is the problem so much as the unsatisfactory conditions in which the child and nurse are placed.

On the other hand a child who spits continually, or who keeps you continually awake at night because he doesn't sleep, would try almost anyone's patience. These practices may not be immediately harmful to the child himself, but by making those who care for him less able to cope he is having an indirect effect on his own welfare, and in the long term he is making himself less socially acceptable. All this would suggest sufficient reason for trying to change the behaviour.

2. Is it a dangerous behaviour? Is it causing actual direct harm to himself or to others?

This is the most obvious and clear kind of behaviour problem. Usually there will be no difficulty in recognising the child who physically damages himself or others as having a problem. But even here there may be confusion, especially if there are overtones of 'blame' attached to the label 'behaviour problem'. Hence, if the child is seen to attack himself when unhappy or to attack others when frustrated by his handicap, parents or care staff may feel, because the behaviour 'is not his *fault*', that it is not really problem behaviour. This is to confuse the possible *causes* of behaviour with the behaviour itself, and for the moment we are concerned only with defining the actual behaviour.

3. Is the behaviour a barrier to development? Is it blocking the child's development of more constructive skills?

This covers behaviour which might once have been perfectly acceptable, but which has somehow become 'stuck' so that the child produces it as a stereotyped response to certain situations. An example might be the child who sucks and chews everything. To begin with, this was an encouraging sign of 'normal' development—the child managed to bring objects to his mouth and explore them by taste. But when the child's only response to objects, months (or even years) later, is the same, we can safely assume that the educational benefit of such behaviour has been exhausted and that the child should learn to differentiate between situations where tasting and eating are appropriate, and those where they are not.

4. Does the behaviour help to isolate the child from the community?

The behaviour may be such that it does not actually hurt

I*

anyone, or even annoy or embarrass those in direct contact with the child. But it does directly isolate the child, or cause the child himself to withdraw, or simply make him stand out as different—frantic arm waving when excited, or unusual guttural noises or squeaks, for instance. These may not be 'bad' behaviours in themselves, but if they prevent other people from approaching him, it may be worth trying to modify them or teaching the child alternative, more socially acceptable behaviours.

DEFINING THE BEHAVIOUR

Having decided, therefore, that there is a behaviour problem, we need to be more precise about what it is before we can attempt to deal with it. As we argued in Chapters 2 and 3, we must know exactly what the child *does* before we can decide how to change it. It is not sufficient simply to say the child is 'messy' with his food if we do not say what *actual* behaviours we are going to classify as 'messy' and attempt to alter. Do we count the number of times food drops off the spoon on the way to the mouth—whether this is accidental or deliberately thrown by the child—or do we try to judge intention in the act? If we decide we must go for deliberate acts, is there an objective way of deciding on intention: does the child pause before turning the spoon over, for example?

Whether or not we conclude that the action is deliberate will help decide our methods of working. Intention implies that the child has control over his actions that will make it easier for us to alter the behaviour. All we have to do is find a way of making it more worthwhile for the child to do what we want him to, than to continue with his behaviour. If on the other hand the child 'cannot help' what he is doing, for lack of control or skill, perhaps, the behaviour will have to be worked on in a different way.

What is essential is that you describe what the child is actually *doing* that is aggressive, for instance. Try to work out what it is you are really concerned about—pulling his sister's hair, biting other people? Sometimes all such behaviours can be worked on at once if they form part of a definite behaviour

pattern, such as a temper tantrum. But they may be independent behaviours—caused by different situations and thus
needing different methods to control them. We have also to be
careful that we do not *interpret* the behaviour—assume the child
is jealous or frustrated or aggressive. What the child thinks or
feels of course is important, but we should get better clues about
that when we examine the situation in which the behaviour
occurs.

A description of the behaviour may include some measurement of the degree of the behaviour (the intensity of the
response), its duration, and its frequency. Information about
these three aspects of the behaviour will in the first place help
us to decide whether there is a behaviour problem, or we are
abnormally worried over something minor. For example, a
child may seem to scream a lot, but measurement may show
that he screams only when in pain—say, with wind—and so
what seemed an inexplicable frustrating behaviour becomes
understandable and therefore bearable. Just the step of sitting
down to observe the behaviour may help put the problem in
proportion. It will also define its severity. We shall need to know
about this if we are to measure the effectiveness of our work
later.

OBSERVING THE BEHAVIOUR

We have discussed observation in other chapters, but the style
of observation needed for behaviour problems is a particular
one. As we have said we may need to know about the intensity,
duration and frequency of a behaviour, but the relative
importance of each of these three measures depends on the
behaviour we are considering. Sleeplessness or restlessness at
night will need measuring in terms of frequency (how often the
child wakes up) and duration (how long each bout of wakefulness lasts)—intensity will not mean anything in this context
unless it is the child's *crying* when he wakes that you really want
to alter, not the wakefulness itself. Screaming will require all
three measures, whereas spitting only requires a measurement
of how often (frequency).

A chart for measuring a behaviour along all dimensions
might look like this:

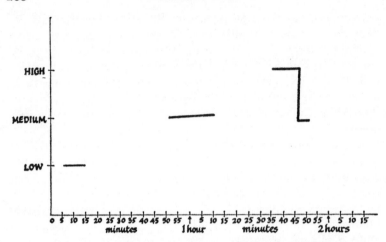

Figure 7. A graph for plotting behaviour problems

The intensity scale is in three parts, High, Medium or Low. Time is along the bottom axis and is marked off according to the type of behaviour and its likely occurrence. If, for example, we want to measure temper tantrums that last for half an hour on average and occur throughout the day, we might have a chart for each day marked off in five-minute intervals. The line would be drawn each time a tantrum started at the appropriate five-minute mark and would continue until the tantrum stopped—giving the duration of the tantrum to the nearest five minutes. This would provide a great deal of information about tantrums, but such detailed recording could not be continued for long so recording in this detail might be limited to an hour or so each day. So the hours observed should be varied from day to day in order eventually to get a detailed picture of the child's tantrum behaviour over a complete day.

Recording can be simplified if the behaviour does not vary in intensity (i.e. he either screams loudly or doesn't scream at all, he either bites himself or he doesn't). It can be further simplified if the duration is not crucial, for then we can simply note each time the behaviour occurs (say, in a day) and get a total of its frequency.

To measure intensity, you must first develop a scale which will not, of course, be objective but which will give some basis for comparing one event with another. It will probably be enough to just have three points on the scale, e.g. 'soft', 'medium', 'loud', but you may want to distinguish further: 'very soft', 'soft', 'medium', 'loud', 'very loud'.

Once you are actually working on changing the behaviour, it may become more difficult to record. But records and observations are important because they give real information about what is happening, rather than guesses or impressions. Observing before we attempt to change the behaviour, and then perhaps at weekly or monthly intervals to check progress, will usually be sufficient, unless we feel we are not clear ourselves about what is happening. Behaviour may change slowly (and frequently get worse before it gets better), so it is often only the reassurance of regular observations that keeps us from giving up when in fact we are winning.

Once we have defined the behaviour (B) we want to record, we can add to our records notes on the Antecedents (A) and Consequences (C) of the behaviour. As we saw in Chapter 2, it is these which we may well want to change in modifying the behaviour. So we need clear notes on what they are. These notes should be brief, and say what was happening before (A) and what happened after (C) the response.

We will now talk about changing the consequences as a way of changing behaviour in the context of behaviour problems. This extends our discussion in Chapter 2.

PUNISHMENT

'Punishment' is a loaded word, so it is important that we recall the definition of the term. Punishment is what we do *after* a particular behaviour that either stops that behaviour happening again, or at least makes it less likely that it will happen again. It may also show its effect by altering the intensity of the behaviour (making it less intense) and/or its duration (making it shorter). Thus punishment acts in a negative way on behaviour, in the same way that reward acts in a positive way. If it does not do this, then it simply isn't punishment as we use the term.

This point is worth emphasising. Paradoxically, some 'punishments' may in fact be rewarding for the child. This may be because any attention (even if meant to be unpleasant) is better than being ignored; or because the child enjoys seeing you angry and upset because it is exciting; or because your reaction demonstrates his power to control you. Thus, an attempt on your part to control the child can be turned by the child into a way of controlling you.

It is common to hear people say—'I've tried punishing him and it just doesn't work!' What they mean is that they have tried things which they thought *ought* to act as punishments, and found that they weren't punishments after all. If, after a consistent trial over a period, when a punishment has been used immediately following the behaviour each time the behaviour has occurred, it has not altered the behaviour or it has made it worse, then we must conclude this is not punishment for that child. The definition of a punishment therefore concerns the effect it actually *has*—not what you expect or *want* it to have.

So, why doesn't it work?

If, then, you shout at or even smack a child when he does something you do not like, and he still goes on doing it, we must assume the child is not being punished effectively. There may be various reasons for this and we should ask ourselves two pertinent questions:

(1) Did you administer the punishment *immediately* after the behaviour you wanted to stop? If you give the child the chance to do something else in between, it will be the last behaviour that is being punished. If your child shouts with delight after he has torn a large rent in the curtains, you will become alerted and may rush over and 'punish' him. This may work, but, especially if it takes some time to reach him, what may be being punished is the shout, so he will just learn to rip the curtains quietly! So often it is behaviour that leads to a child getting 'caught' that is punished, rather than the naughty behaviour itself. It is difficult to avoid this happening, for we cannot after all punish a behaviour until we have noticed it. But it should make us think carefully on the value of punishing a handicapped child in this way unless actually 'caught in the act'. Normal children (past the

toddler stage, at any rate) can more easily be punished in this way because you can use language to point out which behaviour it is that you want to discourage, but even then most children learn that the real crime is to be found out!

(2) Did you *always* punish that behaviour? If the child normally gets away with the behaviour, it will take a long time (unless the punishment is unusually severe) for the punishment to have any effect. This is the same situation as when we reward a behaviour. We must be consistent in our approach for the child to learn to associate a particular action on his part with a consequence produced by you—whether it is a reward or a punishment.

If the answers to both questions are 'yes' and the child does not alter his behaviour, then we must conclude that we are not punishing the child. We may of course be hurting him, which might make him upset or angry, but if he finds a lot of satisfaction in the forbidden behaviour (which he probably does if it has been established for some time) it will take a very harsh punishment to make him stop. For aggressiveness, hurting a child is liable to trigger off more aggressiveness and so is obviously self-defeating.

It seems strange to many parents, teachers or care staff that a child can actually enjoy making adults angry—even if it results in being smacked or shouted at. Obviously you do not usually ignore your child deliberately, but parents and care staff are often tempted to take the opportunity to get on with their own jobs when he is being good or at least quiet; while you cannot help but notice and pay attention when he does something that annoys or worries you. After a while the child learns that the quickest and most effective way of getting your attention is to do something naughty.

TIME-OUT

You will remember that time-out means 'time away from reward'. Sometimes it has been misunderstood to mean simply ignoring the child or taking something from him. But although these are crucial elements, the point of this deprivation is that there must first be something rewarding for the child to be deprived of. After all, we are concerned with using punishment to stop a behaviour—but with time-out the only punishment is that there is no reward for a set period of time. If the child does not notice he is being punished in this way—because he is frequently ignored, or he has not been interested in the dinner you have just removed, or finds the small quiet room you take him to better than the noisy confusion he has left—then obviously this method will not work. So first you must establish that the child is in a generally rewarding situation—that there are many opportunities for him to get rewards for appropriate behaviour—before you can consider giving him time-out from that situation to punish a particular behaviour.

Provided this is true, time-out can be a very effective way of controlling behaviour. You decide first what acts as a reward for the child (does he want your attention, does he like listening to music, does he enjoy the food he is being fed?), and then deprive him of it for a set period following a naughty action. Very often the child is deprived simultaneously of many rewards. He may be taken to a quiet, bare room for a minute or so or (in the case of a tantrum) until he has quietened down. This is one end of the spectrum—most homes and schools would have to make do with sitting him 'in a corner' or taking him into the hall or corridor. At a simpler level, time-out may mean removing a dish of food for ten seconds each time a child puts his fingers in the food—perhaps coupled with turning one's head away and even deliberately paying attention to someone else. The child is simply brought back into the room without comment, or his dinner is returned to him without comment, at the end of the time-out period. If the behaviour re-occurs, then the time-out is repeated. If the child is smacked on the way to the time-out room, or his hand is slapped as it goes into his dinner, this may work but it is subject to the same reservations about straightforward punishment as we gave above. Time-out, if used consistently, should work without these additional punishments.

There are some possible hazards, however, in the use of time-out. It can only be used in situations where you are sure you can 'win'. If a child, for example, is used to banging his head to get your immediate attention and suddenly you start ignoring the head banging the child is not likely to stop immediately. It is far more likely that he will persist with the behaviour that has worked in the past, and he may even try harder—so you get greater head banging, for a longer period. If you can hold out he may eventually learn that head banging no longer works, and, if you are also showing him better ways of getting your attention or getting what he wants, he will learn the more appropriate behaviour and head banging will gradually die out. But if he has been banging his head for years to get your attention, it is going to take some time for him to learn new ways and he may bang his head so severely in the meantime that you cannot ignore it and have to give in. Then, of course, all that he has learnt is that ordinary head banging doesn't work and he must really go to town to get what he wants! Giving in just once will also make it much harder for the technique to be effective in the future. So if the behaviour is something you know you will not be able to ignore or prevent, it is probably best not to try it at all.

COMBINING THE CARROT AND THE STICK

We mentioned in Chapter 2 and in the section on time-out that the child is more likely to stop behaving in an undesirable way if he is being taught an alternative way of behaving at the same time. This applies whether we have decided to use punishment as such, or time-out to stop the undesirable behaviour. What it means is that it is really pointless to try to get rid of one behaviour if the child is not given an alternative to put in its place. We don't have this problem with non-handicapped children because their naughtiness is largely a matter of choice —we just have to make it worth their while to choose a more acceptable behaviour. When the child is severely handicapped, we have to go one step further and actually teach the child to do something else. This is often forgotten when we are dealing with a severe problem, and then we are surprised when the child reverts quickly to his old ways.

An exceptionally effective technique is to teach the child to do something that actually prevents him from doing the thing you don't want him to do. Thus the new behaviour you are rewarding will compete directly with the bad behaviour you are ignoring or punishing, and greatly increase your chances of success. For example, if he twirls everything in front of his eyes you could teach him to build towers of blocks and knock them over; or, if that is too difficult, to hold objects and transfer them from one hand to another. These new behaviours would probably need to be rewarded strongly, and for some time, before you could expect them to compete successfully with the undesirable behaviour, which may well have some intrinsic reward on its own. Also, many behaviours that are not necessarily altogether undesirable but have become excessive, can be limited by this technique.

CONTROLLING OR PREVENTING BAD BEHAVIOUR

As we have seen, there are some behaviours that are difficult to control by use of direct punishment or time-out, and it is often these behaviours (aggressive or self-mutilating behaviours in particular) that are the ones we are most concerned about. In such cases it is obviously best if the behaviour can be prevented in the first place, or at least stopped in the early stages before it has become well established. This means noticing the first signs that the behaviour is starting, or better still, noting the situations or events that 'trigger off' the behaviour. In describing the A of our observation, a pattern may emerge. It may be as simple and broad as a statement to the effect that 'every time Timothy is ignored he starts to spit and play with his spittle'. This gives us a clear idea of what we can do to prevent the behaviour. We can train Timothy to do other things, so he can amuse himself in other, more acceptable, ways; and we can prevent him playing with his spittle by physically making him do something else with his hands instead, and rewarding this. If we attempt simply to ignore the bad behaviour we are unlikely to be successful in stopping it. Even if we combine time-out with training the alternative behaviours, since in this case it is known that being ignored is itself a signal for the undesirable behaviour to start, the chances that the child will give up an evidently intrinsically rewarding behaviour are slight. There is a better chance that interfering, and preventing the major part of the behaviour, will gradually make the initial spitting unrewarding, and that the child will learn to use the new behaviours you are teaching simultaneously. The idea is that by preventing the behaviour from developing in its normal way you in fact break the habit and gradually establish more acceptable behaviour.

OVERCORRECTION

When a child's bad behaviour results in someone else being hurt or upset, or in articles being destroyed or damaged, it is very natural for us to want to include in our treatment of the behaviour some attempt to show the child the effect of his actions and where possible to help him make amends. Sometimes the act of making amends can be extended so that it contains elements of both punishment and training an alternative behaviour. Thus, if a child throws objects, he is made not only to pick up the items he has thrown but to pick up or tidy other items in the room. If he attacks another child, he must not only comfort that child but help and be of service to that child for some time. This may be a useful technique, especially where the child shows some awareness of the more distant consequences of forms of punishment. It must be judged on its results, but all too easily it too may become the child's best method of getting an adult's undivided attention.

THE ETHICS OF PUNISHMENT

This chapter has tried to show that punishment, when used correctly, is just another teaching tool—helping to communicate to the child what is required of him. Seen in this light it is not 'cruel' to punish a handicapped child. Indeed, it may be cruel not to! Remember that punishment does not necessarily mean inflicting pain, and that this should always be avoided—if only for our own peace of mind. On the other hand you should not feel guilty about smacking a handicapped child if the smack is used as a direct and immediate communication—signalling your disapproval. Most severely handicapped children may be unaware of the more subtle signals of disapproval, such as facial expression or scolding. What we hope we have done is shown you some other ways of dealing with undesirable behaviour, so that you do not need to hit out in frustration and rage because you cannot see how to control the situation.

Even when this function of punishment is conceded, parents and care staff are often worried by the implications of the control over the child's behaviour such techniques imply. Where the undesirable behaviour distresses the child himself, the justification for control is obvious; but control of simply 'annoying' habits poses serious problems. It is worth repeating that the criterion on which a behaviour is selected as needing change must be the long-term interest of the child. No child should be made to fit into an inhuman or restrictive environment simply because he is less trouble that way or makes less work. The more effective our methods of control, the more we have to examine our own motives, and our aim should not be to produce nice, controlled children for all occasions, but to eliminate those of the child's methods of control that will ultimately damage him, and to substitute more acceptable ways for him to control you. Control systems are two-way, and by teaching the child to use behaviour that is appropriate, you are teaching him how to obtain reward from you, and thus how to control *your* behaviour.

TOKEN SYSTEMS

In discussing reward and punishment, we have dealt mainly with attention or food as the prime reward, and removal of these rewards as the most effective punishments. Sometimes, however, a child is not responsive either to food or attention, or there are reasons why it is not possible to withdraw such rewards. If the undesirable behaviour occurs at mealtimes for example, you may be unwilling to deny the child food for periods long enough to correct the behaviour. Similarly you may be unwilling to withdraw your attention from a child who has little else positive in his life. Yet the behaviour problem needs to be tackled. You may resolve these situations by use of physical punishment, but there is an alternative open to children who are capable of grasping the idea of a token—an object that 'stands for' a future reward.

Under this system the child is given tokens in place of direct rewards when he performs appropriately, and these are saved up and then exchanged for goodies or whatever the child wants at some fixed time, or after so many have been collected. This system has obvious advantages, since tokens are easy to give: they can be stars, or ticks on a chart as well as actual 'tokens'; they can be given for small pieces of behaviour yet saved up to 'purchase' something worthwhile; they keep the same value whoever gives them; and they give the child the opportunity of choice and variety in his reward. They also reward the child in a way similar to that in which the adult world is rewarded, because of their resemblance to money and the payment of wages.

The most important advantage as far as punishment is concerned, however, is that they provide a method of punishment: removal of the token. This method is free of many of the difficulties involved in physical punishment or time-out. No pain is inflicted, but there is an immediate reaction to the undesirable behaviour. Another advantage is that the token can be earned back by appropriate behaviour. If the behaviour persists, more tokens can be removed, but the system's success depends on the tokens being so valuable that their loss outweighs the reward from the undesirable behaviour. It also depends on the child never being allowed to 'spend' all his tokens, but to retain a few as insurance against bad behaviour before he has had a chance to earn some more.

Severely handicapped children would obviously need considerable teaching to get a token system established. The 'exchange value' of a token would need to be established by giving him ample opportunities to exchange a token for an array of goods like sweets, drink, fruit, toys, or any idiosyncratic objects liked by the child; or for a particular activity like a ride on a swing, opportunity to play the piano, or being tickled. Initially also, it should require only a little effort to earn a token. It will gradually become harder to earn a token and, at the same time, the child will be learning to save tokens and exchange more than one at once. In this way children can learn to save for special treats, and they can learn the consequences of their inappropriate behaviour by seeing tokens removed. The disadvantage of the system is that the effort required to teach it to the most severely handicapped children would probably be better spent teaching them more directly relevant skills. The system is thus only really suitable for children with a fair range of behaviour. Also, being by its nature a system of long-term reward, it cannot always compete adequately with the immediate rewards to be obtained from the unwanted behaviour.

THE BALANCE OF REWARD AND PUNISHMENT

One temptation in setting up programmes is to try to get rid of a whole batch of problem behaviours early on. If we then look at the child's programme we find that it is a series of 'stop doings'. If we stick to the principle that for every piece of behaviour we punish or time-out, we must teach the child an alternative one, through reward training, then we have gone some way to preserving balance. But nonetheless it is important to bear in mind that the ratio of reward to punishment or non-reward which the child experiences should remain high. We have suggested before that at least 80 per cent of experiences should be positive. In the case of problem behaviours it may be better to try to get rid of one problem at a time rather than try to deal with several at once. This will also be easier for you.

TWO PROBLEM BEHAVIOURS: HYPERACTIVITY AND SELF-MUTILATION

The term hyperactive is a very commonly used one, and tends to be used in several different ways. Sometimes a child will be called hyperactive as if this were a diagnosis, like Down's Syndrome. At other times the child is talked of as showing hyperactivity. Whichever way the child is described he is usually a child who rests little, who is difficult to teach because he is always on the move, and who may be noisy. Some medical authorities give the child stimulants in the belief that this will reduce hyperactivity, others will try to sedate the child.

There seems no doubt that some children, by reason of brain damage, are difficult to control. What is worth emphasising, however, is that this 'hyperactivity' is not some kind of disease or permanent affliction. There can be several reasons for it and several ways to control it. We have mentioned these in earlier chapters and will bring them together here.

The child may race around because this is the only activity

he has learned for which he is rewarded and which he enjoys. The child who has not learned to play with small toys may well only have high activity games. Similarly, he may be difficult to teach because he has never been rewarded for sitting down and doing a task. We saw early in this book how it was possible to teach a child to sit and work at a rewarded task. Many of the children who have responded very successfully to that kind of programme would be called hyperactive. One child, Jeanette, was taken from a situation where she would sit for a maximum of 30 seconds to one where she sat for 27 consecutive minutes within eight sessions. She was rewarded with small sweets for looking at a picture book.

Another possible factor in producing hyperactive behaviour is that the child has not learned to choose and stay with his choice until he has finished with one piece of equipment. A sure sign of a pseudo-hyperactive child, if we can invent some jargon too, is the fact that he will settle and play with something for an extended period if his choice is restricted.

Once again, we are not saying that children are not over-active or that drugs might not help some children. What we are saying is that there are good explanations why some children may be over-active, and that there are ways of dealing with this behaviour which can bring the child under teaching control. These techniques are needed even if drugs are used. Drugs can only damp down behaviour, they do not teach the child anything. If drugs are used, the thing to watch for is that the child is not so drugged that he can't learn anything!

Self-destructive behaviour is any behaviour which leads or could lead to the child injuring himself by his own actions. So the child who hits himself, or sticks his fingers in his eyes, would be seen as showing self-destructive behaviour. There are several possible causes for this. Sometimes it clearly serves the function of providing extra stimulation: a blind child pressing his eye will produce sensations of 'light' through mechanical action on the optic nerve.

Sometimes, the child finds that self-mutilation gets attention. Hitting your head on the wall usually evokes horrified gasps from adults. It is a very powerful way of controlling others.

Other explanations would call on more complex ideas such as self-punishment. From watching some children, it is clear that they are 'playing out' being physically punished. Again this may be a means of attention getting, and persist as a behaviour because of the effect it has on adults.

Or self-destructive behaviour may result from extreme frustration. We worked with one child, Hazel, who would get very agitated if her meals were delayed. She would rock and scream and then as the tension built up, suddenly get up, crouch and bang her head on the floor. The effect was quite magical, she got her lunch very quickly.

Clearly how we deal with these behaviours will depend on their causes. If we suspect that the child is deprived of stimulation, this can be provided by other means. But getting rid of self-destructive behaviour sustained by attention needs a two-pronged attack. The child must be prevented from being rewarded for self-destruction—for instance his hand can be held for self-hitting, or in extreme cases a protective helmet used; but at the same time we must develop other means of eliminating the behaviour through rewarding alternative responses. So the pure attention-getter needs to be taught other ways of getting attention, the frustrated child other ways of dealing with frustration. Hazel was rewarded for sitting quietly looking round whilst waiting for lunch. This was a successful tactic with her, but more active solutions may be necessary with other children (see also Chapter 5).

If the child is self-punishing, this behaviour itself needs to be stopped directly, again possibly by restraint and developing competing behaviours. In addition, the adults should avoid modelling punishment.

EXAMPLES OF TEACHING PROGRAMMES

We now turn to a selection of examples of programmes for eliminating problem behaviours. These may suggest ideas or act as models for your own teaching efforts.

Example 1. Time-out for spitting food

Joan was a little blind severely handicapped child. When we first knew her she was two years old and attending a day centre for multiply handicapped children. Joan had very little behaviour. In fact she spent most of her time curled up like a little rag doll, so it was obviously high priority to teach her ways of interacting and playing. But there was also a behaviour problem that needed to be dealt with—Joan had begun to spit out all her food. It was not that she disliked the food, for she had always been a 'little gannet', but she was now spitting out *all* her food at home and at school.

Observing the behaviour, it was noted that the spitting seemed to start whenever the adult (mother at home, teacher at the centre) turned to talk to another child. Once Joan had spat out a spoonful the adult would immediately switch attention back to her—scolding her and scooping the food from around her chin. It seemed therefore that Joan's behaviour problem was a response to being ignored, or at least a response to someone else getting the attention. The response was being rewarded by the immediate switch of attention back to her.

It was decided to use time-out in this situation because it would simply mean the adult reversing her behaviour so that she rewarded Joan for eating and turned away from her to pay attention to another child each time she spat. This, in turn, was only possible because the other children at school, and Joan's sister at home, were young and docile enough not to demand attention from the adult while Joan was being fed. Time-out could be used, although it was the signal for the bad behaviour, because the bad behaviour could be prevented from occurring during the time-out period simply by not giving Joan any more food to spit out.

So Joan was fed. Whilst she kept food in her mouth, chewed and swallowed it she was praised continually. As soon as she spat out a spoonful the adult would remove the dish, noisily, so that it was an obvious act, and immediately started talking and playing with the other children. After only ten days of this treatment, Joan had stopped spitting out her food. She was later to learn other disruptive ways of controlling the adults around her, but they too had learnt an effective way of controlling Joan's behaviour; and at least the spitting problem had disappeared.

Example 2. Punishment for vomiting
Noel was another child at the same centre, but he was five when we first knew him and was severely physically and mentally

handicapped. His problem was also concerned with feeding, but it was far more acute and serious than Joan's. Noel would eat only a few foods from a few people in very rigid circumstances. He lived with his mother, a single parent, and his grandmother. If there was any change of routine, for instance if mother tried to feed him breakfast because she didn't have to go to work that day, or if grandmother tried to give him his tea because mother had to work late, he would refuse to take the food and vomit violently. Even if the 'right' person was feeding him at the 'right' time he would take only a very limited range of food and was difficult to feed because of constant choking or phlegm. The main problem was at school, where he would take nothing all day and the sight of his bowl and bib alone was sufficient to start him gagging and vomiting.

It was necessary to prevent this gagging and vomiting in order to produce some eating behaviour that could be rewarded. We had to bear in mind that the very attempt to start feeding him was the trigger for the response, and the behaviour seemed to be self-rewarding in that he avoided having to eat. He also was getting additional attention by being cleaned up after he had vomited. However, Noel loved music and being sung to and played with, so that could be used as a reward. He could be given time-out from music and play for vomiting. But in order to start the reward, Noel had to produce an appropriate response and the only way to break into the behaviour pattern was to punish Noel for vomiting, and to try to get this punishment in as soon as Noel began the process of gagging. The aim was to prevent the vomiting.

The punishment chosen was a loud shouted 'NO', plus angry glare. This was given as soon as Noel began to gag on sight of the bib and bowl. Each time he started to gag he was shouted at angrily, and then as the first minute speck of food had touched his mouth and he had not gagged he was sung to and played with enthusiastically. This process continued until he had 'eaten' a spoonful of food, then the food was taken away for that session. The first session took half an hour—Noel had taken one teaspoon of food, had gagged 30 times but had not vomited. So the process built up gradually. Each day a very little more food was taken and the number of times Noel gagged dropped steadily. Occasionally there would be a reversal and he would vomit, but by the end of ten weeks the vomiting had all but disappeared and Noel was eating approximately 15–20 spoonsful of food a day. He was still needing to be sung to and played with as he ate, but not so frantically as at first. When he did begin to gag he was shouted at still, to prevent the action developing, and the singing and playing would stop abruptly.

Example 3. Developing competing behaviour for dominating activities

The third example also concerns a child from the same day centre. This time the problem behaviour did not concern eating. Alex was six when we knew her and was a deaf and severely retarded child, but she could walk and was more active than Noel or Joan. Alex had developed some behaviours which obviously mimicked her mother, and she used these behaviours obsessively to the exclusion of all others. The most important of these were 'dusting' and 'backcombing her hair'. It was fascinating to watch the detail in these behaviours: Alex would use any object as if it were an aerosol can of spray polish, while a sock or a coat would be grabbed to serve as a duster. Her 'backcombing' needed even less in the way of 'realistic' props. Anything that was given to her to play with would be used as if it were a comb, as she stretched and teased her hair with it.

The behaviour showed that Alex was capable of finely observed mimicry, which might be useful later in her training. But it had become so all pervasive that it was preventing her from learning anything new. It was decided to train Alex to do other things with objects. By rewarding constructive uses, it was hoped that new behaviours would begin to compete with the dusting and backcombing. Alex was a difficult child to reward since she didn't like food, drink or cuddles very much, and she could not hear music or praise. In the end the only effective reward found was for the teacher to let Alex watch the teacher brush her own hair or put on lipstick. Obviously there is a limit to the number of times the adult could put on lipstick in one session, so Alex was rewarded only after between five and 12 correct responses. This was sufficient to maintain her behaviour. If she tried to dust or backcomb her hair with the equipment during these training sessions she was prevented from doing so, and the apparatus was taken away from her for a few moments.

In this way Alex learnt a variety of new skills, including stacking, colour matching, and threading. During the training sessions she made no attempt to use the apparatus in her formerly obsessive way. Her mother began to work with her at home, and she also was able to get her to use toys constructively for the first time. But Alex did not stop her 'dusting' and 'backcombing'. Whenever she was allowed 'free play' they would return. They were obviously still rewarding for her. But once an adult intervened and was prepared to reward her for new behaviours, Alex would now cooperate well. The behaviour problem had not disappeared but it was no longer really a problem since it was not blocking all other learning.

Example 4. A token system

Dan was an autistic epileptic boy attending a special school for autistic children. He was a reasonably bright child of eleven, but suffered from an incapacitating behaviour problem which not only interfered with his own learning but interfered with the learning of all the other children in the class, since it monopolised the teacher's time. Dan had severe and violent temper tantrums in which he would hurl furniture and equipment round the room and kick and lash out at teachers and other children. The teacher was coping with this by physically restraining Dan during these periods, but not only was this exhausting and time consuming, since Dan would spend several hours in the day being restrained in this way, but it was not making the behaviour any better. In fact Dan seemed to be getting worse.

A system of direct rewards would have disrupted the class, and there would still have remained the decision about how to deal with the tantrums—they obviously were too destructive to be ignored safely. So it was decided to use a token system. Dan was sat down on the first day and given a cowboy belt with a pouch to hold the tokens. He accepted this readily. Then he was asked to do a very small piece of work—well within his capacity. As soon as he had completed it, in a matter of seconds only, he was handed a token and told to put it in his pouch. Then he was asked if he would like to 'exchange' his token, and rather bemused he was led out of the room to another room where a selection of his favourite foods, drinks and toys were on display. He was told he could buy something with his token. He could buy a small piece of food, say a spoonful of banana and cream, or drop of drink or a minute's time to play with a toy, or a short tickle. When he had chosen something he was asked for this token and given his choice. Then he was asked again what he would like but when asked for his token was told 'Oh look—they've all gone—let's go back and earn some more'. The process was repeated with numerous tokens, and as yet he had had no tantrum behaviour to punish. Then Dan started having to 'earn' two tokens before they could be exchanged, until after three days he had to earn 10 tokens. He had to work reasonably hard for each token and he could exchange them only at set periods of the day—at break time at the end of the morning and at the end of the afternoon.

During all this time Dan had had no tantrums, so he had to be punished for a minor offence so he would learn that naughty behaviour was punished by token removal. The behaviour was running off or going into the wrong classroom. After a week he did have a tantrum. Taking away the first token did not stop it, but when the second was removed he was asked if he wanted a tickle and he stopped immediately to look for a token. Finding he did not have any he went back to work willingly to earn a token. After that, removing the tokens became more effective in controlling the tantrums. The main effect of the token system was that Dan's tantrum behaviour all but disappeared and he became a hard working member of the class.

He did try to compensate for the loss of all the teacher's attention he had been getting during the tantrums by finding other ways of seeking her attention. He chose whining, which the teacher found particularly irritating, but when token removal was initiated for this and the teacher gave him more attention by starting him on a reading scheme, this behaviour also lessened to tolerable limits.

Obviously the speed with which the system worked for Dan would not be typical for all situations. It reflects the fact that Dan did know other ways of behaving, so that the remedy was simply a matter of making it worthwhile for him to behave in a more acceptable way, and having a penalty for his tantrum behaviour.

Example 5. Increasing the amount of equipment

Because the mentally handicapped child often lacks play skills, he will often resort to stereotyped or self-directed behaviour. This is very commonly seen in bare subnormality hospital wards. David was a child in a hospital in which there were very few toys for the 20 children in the ward. David would walk around the room, occasionally looking out of the window and occasionally scratching at the faces of children he passed. This 'aggressive' behaviour worried the staff greatly and made David very unpopular with them.

David's behaviour was observed for several days. His peak period of aggressiveness occurred between 4.00 and 4.30 in the afternoon. There seemed two possible explanations for his scratching. The first was that he was simply bored, the second that he was bored but was also being rewarded for the aggression by attention from the staff. This was the telling off which he got when he attacked other children.

A set of observations was made while David was given a toy for the half hour on some days and not on others. In addition, on some days a staff member was present and ready to tell David off if he was aggressive. On the other days there was no one in obvious attendance. This way we were able to tell whether David was being aggressive when he was without anything else to do, or whether his aggressive behaviour was being maintained by the attention of staff.

The results were quite clear. The presence of staff made no difference. But David's aggressive behaviour disappeared completely when he had something to play with. Nor did the toy have to be novel. Giving him a car to play with which he had seen many times before successfully competed out aggressive behaviour.

The effect shown with David does not always occur in as clearcut a fashion. Often it is the case that aggressive behaviour is an attempt both to stir things up a bit and to get adult attention. In these cases we have to ask whether the child is getting enough attention. In one study in a subnormality hospital we found that, with three to four nurses and 20 children in a ward, the average amount of individual attention any child could be given in a week was less than two hours! The only solutions possible here were to decrease the number of children or increase the number of adults, in order to create a more humane environment.

Example 6. 'Mummy, she's pulling my hair'

Our next two examples illustrate fairly common problems which brothers and sisters experience with their handicapped siblings.

Jenny was a two-year-old highly active child. She could not understand or use speech and had little constructive play. She had a sister, Leslie, who was six at the time. Leslie had long blonde hair which Jenny liked to pull. Leslie would be sitting watching television when Jenny would rush up and pull her hair as hard as she could. Leslie would scream, call her mother and occasionally cry, pull herself free and then chase Jenny away. Jenny, who seemed to enjoy this, would then drift off only to come back a few minutes later and do it again. She got smacked by her mother, shown that she had made Leslie cry and told it was naughty, and occasionally had her own hair pulled by Leslie 'to see how she liked it then'. Smacking and having her hair pulled made her cry, but had no effect on her pulling her sister's hair.

Leslie said she hated Jenny. Possibilities like cutting Leslie's hair off were discussed. Then we put to Leslie the likely reason why Jenny was pulling her hair.

We suggested that Jenny was rewarded by Leslie screaming and then rushing after her. The idea of a reward was carefully explained and Leslie clearly understood. We then suggested that the problem would go if Leslie could try not to react.

We arranged things carefully so that Leslie's mother was in the room next time Leslie was watching television. Sure enough Jenny pulled Leslie's hair. Her mother immediately prompted Leslie 'OK, love, now hang on, don't cry'. Leslie managed to bite her lip and get Jenny off and not to chase her.

Their mother then went and gave Leslie a cuddle and told her she had done very well.

Over the next two days Leslie went through a bad time. Once she sat there with tears rolling down her cheeks, biting her lip and 'not reacting'. During this time her mother and father gave her a lot of extra love and support. But it paid off. Jenny's attacks got fewer and petered out after two weeks. Leslie was not troubled again.

Once the hair pulling was solved, Leslie was helped to play with Jenny, which she did very effectively. Her fear and dislike diminished as well.

In technical terms this was a very simple programme. All Leslie did was to remove the reward that her sister got for hair pulling.

Example 7. 'John's a girl'

This example is different from the previous one, in that here we made a consistent effort to reward new behaviour between two brothers in order to solve a behaviour problem.

John was eight. His handicapped brother Dennis was six. Dennis was a fairly capable but difficult child. They played together a bit, but mainly rough play. John liked television, Dennis was clearly bored by it. Whilst they were watching Dennis would chant 'John's a girl . . . John's a girl . . . John's a girl . . .'. Their mother would tell Dennis to shut up, but that had no effect. Eventually this would be too much for John who would thump Dennis. Then John's mum would smack him for hitting his brother.

The boys' mother thought the whole thing was very unfair all round, but she also felt that John should not hit Dennis. We said we felt John was being backed up into a corner. He could not stand being called a girl, but if he reacted he got smacked. He just couldn't win.

A two-pronged attack was agreed. The boys' mother would explain to John that Dennis was probably taunting him because he wanted attention and enjoyed the rough-house which happened when John reacted. So instead of hitting him, John should ask him some question or other, like, 'What did you have for breakfast?'

The second prong of the attack was to set up a number of games which both could play, like Ludo, Bingo or Snakes and Ladders. Here we discussed setting up the joint games with their mother, emphasising the need to reward both equally and to reward especially for cooperation.

The first part of the programme was very successful. John's mother explained the plan very carefully to him. She then prompted him when Dennis started 'John's a girl' and rewarded him when Dennis subsided without an incident.

She also used the second part of the attack, the attempt to build up cooperation between them and non-rough play. This was not as successful, partly because it required rather a big shift in the way their lives were run at the time. People need energy to change what they are doing, and one change, the programme to get rid of 'John's a girl', was enough to cope with.

However, that bit of the programme was successful.

Example 8. Jealousy

This is not really an example, but an attempt to describe how jealousy may come about and what to do about it. Clearly mentally handicapped children can and do become jealous.

We can say that 'jealousy' arises in a situation in which one child sees that, while another child holds the attention of an adult, he, the first child, does not get rewarded. The other child therefore becomes a signal for time-out from reward. The jealous child may respond by pushing the other child away, screaming or by being 'extra good' or cute.

Jealousy is not necessarily a bad thing, especially if it leads to some good behaviour. But if we want to avoid it, it is necessary to prevent another child becoming a signal that reward will not come. This can be done by arranging either separate or cooperative activities. Or, better, you can make sure that one child continues to be rewarded at a high level while the other child is being attended to.

Example 9. 'She won't go to sleep!'

Sleep problems are quite common with mentally handicapped children. Sometimes they can be helped by drugs—our next example covers this—but sometimes this is not necessary.

Lovella was a six-year-old, very active and charming and very wakeful. She would go up to bed, then come down repeatedly. When she was finally 'put upstairs' by being shut in her room, she would cry until allowed down again. Sometimes she slept in the early evening because she was so tired after school.

The approach taken involved ensuring that she did not sleep

K

early on, by taking her out if possible or having her brother play with her. Second, a collection of her most interesting toys were made and 'reserved' for her bedroom. It was agreed that if she came down after eight she would be taken upstairs with no fuss and shut in her room, with her light on. If she cried she would be checked to see if she was in trouble, and if not, left.

Both parents felt very bad about leaving her in her room. It was pointed out that she had plenty to amuse her. The first evening she cried for about 90 minutes, the second for 50, the third for five.

After that they did allow a little leeway. She was allowed one trip down after going up to bed. The problem tended to build up again periodically, but with one 'firm evening' was essentially broken.

Example 10. Changing the pattern of sleep

The careful use of drugs can have good effects on certain types of sleep problem. In the following example we discussed this issue with the mother and teacher of a 12-year-old girl. At school Janet was extremely quiet and often unwilling to play or take part in many activities. The reason for this became clear when we spoke to her mother. She described Janet as being an appalling problem at home, particularly at night after the family had gone to bed.

She would begin to liven up during the early evening, and at the family's bedtime she refused to go to sleep. She was extremely noisy and would move around the house sometimes until 4.00 or 5.00 in the morning. This was very disturbing for the family, and Janet's mother was also worried about the effect of her disturbance on neighbours. However, she was not keen on using drugs as a way of controlling Janet's behaviour because she was concerned about dependence and other side-effects of the drugs.

We discussed the problem extensively, but were unable to come up with any solution other than one involving the limited use of drugs. The aim was to try to reverse Janet's sleep pattern. By giving the drugs so that they took effect by about 11.00 in the evening, we hoped that Janet could be persuaded to bed about the same time as the rest of the family. At the same time Janet was to be given as much exercise as possible at school. It was hoped that she would be made tired enough to appreciate her sleep at night.

The drugs were used for a three-week period. Towards the end of this period the dose was gradually reduced. The programme was effective in altering Janet's sleep pattern, even after the drugs had been phased out. She became far more active at school and began to use the climbing frame and other apparatus in the classroom. Her sleeping was much improved at home. Although she still seemed to require a lot less sleep than most children of her age, she became more ready to go to bed and sleep for longer periods than she had previously been.

CONCLUSION

We can summarise the steps which you might take in analysing and planning an approach to behaviour problems:

(1) Check back to the questions at the start of the chapter to make sure there really *is* a problem.

(2) Define the problem in terms of what the child actually *does*.

(3) Decide what measures are appropriate for observing the behaviour.

(4) Observe the behaviour, including a description of what preceded the behaviour, the Antecedents (A), the general situation, the Behaviour (B), and what happened afterwards, the Consequence (C).

(5) From the observation, decide on intervention. Aim for prevention if possible and remember to reward alternative behaviour. Change the Consequences but don't forget to consider whether the child's general environment can be altered so that the behaviour will be less likely (changing the A).

(6) Observe again after 'treatment' to see how effective it has been. Does it need more work? Remember, if you stop rewarding alternative behaviour, the problem may reappear.

15 : Getting More Help

Parents, care staff and teachers working with handicapped children will vary enormously according to the amount of help they need, and their need for help will be different at different times. So perhaps what is first wanted is information about what sources of help are available so that they can call on them when the need arises.

The Handbook for Parents with a Handicapped Child, by Judith Stone and Felicity Taylor, published by the Home and School Council, is a source of the names and addresses of all the main agencies you might need to contact for advice, help, or information.

What we propose to do here is offer a very selective detailed guide to the sort of help available, and ways of obtaining it. We shall also point to some of the shortcomings of the services offered.

MEDICAL SERVICES

The role of the General Practitioner in relation to a handicapped child is not very different from his role with non-handicapped patients. He may or may not know very much about your child's particular handicap, but he will be kept informed by hospital doctors of diagnosis and treatment, and in most cases he will still be the child's first line of medical advice in case of illness. If the illness is severe or related to his general treatment under the hospital doctor, or if the doctor is not sure of the child's likely reaction to the usual treatment for an illness, he (or you) will probably refer the child straight to the hospital. Monitoring of the child's general medical condition and developmental progress will most commonly also be done by the hospital doctor, whether a paediatrician (a child specialist) or a psychiatrist (a specialist in mental handicap).

The specialist doctor will not usually be concerned with the child's coughs and colds unless they are particularly severe; but he will generally be responsible for drug treatments, for overall assessment of the child, for giving genetic counselling (or putting you in touch with a further specialist who can give this advice), and for offering general guidance on treatment and handling. He may be part of a team of other specialists— physiotherapists, psychologists, speech therapists, each of whom may test your child. Sometimes the parents will have direct contact with this multidisciplinary team for advice and help; sometimes the specialist only will see the parents and give his interpretation of the advice to them.

It is usually the doctor who first 'breaks the news' to the parents about the child's handicap, or who first confirms their own suspicions. This is obviously a traumatic time for the parents, and, if the doctor is sensible, he will answer any questions parents have then, but he will also make another appointment to deal with the questions the parents meant to ask but couldn't think of at the time. If this doesn't happen it is worth ringing the specialist for an early second appointment to deal with current worries. The doctor should also be providing practical advice, and putting parents in touch with more specialised agencies. Unfortunately, it is often up to the parents to ask for such information.

It is worth remembering that if parents want the specialist to be frank with them they must convince him that they are able to handle his frankness. Keep asking questions and don't be afraid to question treatment. Sometimes for example doctors will offer drugs without considering other ways of dealing with the problem. Theirs is inevitably a medical bias, so parents need to be aware of this bias and of alternative treatment. Thus a hyperactive child may be put on a drug by the doctor to give the parents some much needed rest. There is nothing wrong with that if it also benefits the child, but if the drug has nasty side-effects the child may get worse and the parents will be even less able to cope. So it might be better to put the parents in touch with someone (a psychologist or teacher) who can offer practical help by showing the parents how they might handle and control the child's hyperactivity without the use of drugs.

Doctors are placed in a very difficult position if they try to answer questions about a child's future. Even if the handicap is a common one, so that it is familiar to the specialist, no two children are similarly affected and certainly no two children are alike. A child is an individual, and how he develops depends on his personality, his environment and on what treatment he receives at least as much as it does on the handicap. Doctors often respond to this uncertainty by simply avoiding the issue, or by making extreme statements in an effort to be definite. Some, because they want to foster hope, reassure the parent in an unrealistic way instead of giving concrete advice on how development can be aided by effective teaching. Few parents of a severely handicapped child are totally deceived by such reassurance, but to have one's dearest wishes confirmed with some authority can make the truth much more devastating when it is eventually faced. At the other extreme, parents may be told that it is pointless to try to help their child as 'he will always be a vegetable'. If this were true it would be cruel to put it this way, but the fact that it is virtually never true makes such a statement criminally irresponsible.

What parents should try to get from the specialist is some indication of the difficulties their child is going to face in learning and developing, and how they can help him overcome or by-pass some of these problems. A profoundly handicapped child may have a whole range of physical and sensory disorders which add to the main handicap of slow learning. If the parents are told what the disorders imply in terms of the child's development—will he ever be able to bear weight on his legs? will he ever be able to hear normal speech sounds? will he be able to learn to chew?—and are shown how to teach him in the ways outlined in this book, they will have some idea of the difficulties in store, but also some hope for the future. It is then up to them to decide how much additional help they require and up to the social and educational services to see that it is available.

Health visitors should be in contact with all children under five, and their parents. They may take a special interest in a family with a handicapped child. A health visitor can reasonably be expected to offer advice on the young developing child in a general way, but would not usually be able to deal with specific queries on a particular handicap.

THE SOCIAL SERVICES AND THE SOCIAL SECURITY

People often confuse the responsibilities of Social Services and the Department of Health and Social Security. The Social Services have wide and major responsibilities for provisions for the handicapped. They are the main agency in the community through whom you can get help and access to services. You can contact your Social Services Department by looking them up under the name of the Local Authority in the telephone directory. This will give you the address of your local area office. You can then ring them and ask for them to come and see you, or you can call to find out what they can do in the way of advice, support or practical help. Please note—they will not contact you, it is up to you to contact them.

There are some branches of Social Services Departments in hospitals. If your child is in hospital or has been in hospital, you may already have a Social Worker from there. These Social Workers have access to the same facilities as Area Social Workers since they are part of the Social Services structure.

The Social Security is a different department. This deals entirely with allowances and money matters. You can find the local Social Security office number by looking it up under Department of Health and Social Security in the telephone directory. You usually have to go and see them, although they will send someone to see you if you ask.

What can these agencies do?

Social services

Social workers are trained in a variety of skills. They can provide emotional support and counselling if you feel you need it, and they represent *the* major source of advice on facilities and resources. These facilities and resources should not be seen as 'charity', but as a means of helping the child to develop his potential within a satisfying family setting. Social Workers can advise on benefits (although these are the responsibility of Social Security), and they can arrange for special services, such as free disposable nappies which are available in some areas, and on adaptations to your home and special equipment. These last might include ramps, rails and grips or remodelling doors and toilets to accommodate wheelchairs, and the provision of free telephones or expensive pieces of equipment like possum typewriters. In order to claim these benefits the child should be registered under the Chronically Sick and Disabled Persons Act. The Social Worker will help you to apply.

Through the Social Worker you may also get a free place in a Local Authority Day Nursery for your child, if the education authority is unable to make suitable provision for him. The Social Worker will also give access to Local Authority residential accommodation, whether for a few days with a foster family, a short stay in a children's home or a longer term arrangement. If there is no Local Authority residential provision in your area, the Social Worker will try to make arrangements with other authorities or agencies. More is said about this under question G. Social workers may also be able to arrange for holidays for your child.

Social workers are hard pressed and many visit only infrequently unless they receive a cry for help. Looking too competent may be a disadvantage! Another point is that social workers nowadays do not specialise, so you may find that your social worker has little specific experience of handicap.

Social Security

Your Social Security office should be able to tell you what benefits you are entitled to. In particular you should ask for details about the Attendance Allowance and the Mobility Allowance. The Attendance Allowance is paid officially to the child, and it is paid only for children over two. Up to the age of two it is apparently held that the parents would be in constant attendance in any case, which assumption provides a clue to the qualifications for receiving it. Great stress seems to be placed on whether the child is a problem at night. Does he wake up and need regular attention, for instance? Other benefits are available, including the Invalid Care Allowance, which is payable if you are already getting the Attendance Allowance. It is paid to the mother or father, mainly if the person has had to give up work to look after the child.

If the parents draw the Supplementary Benefit, they can apply for extra diet and heating allowances if these are necessary for the child or handicapped adult.

Some parents are reluctant to take up benefits, either because they are not desperate financially or because they see them as 'charity'. But they are really a means of helping the child and the family to live a fuller life. It might be remembered that even with the full total of benefits, a child staying at home is likely to cost the state less than taking him into care.

THE ROWNTREE FAMILY FUND

Not exactly a benefit, but worth mentioning in this context, is the Rowntree Family Fund. This was set up by the government to fill some of the gaps in the services provided by the state or the local authorities. The fund will give grants for a variety of purposes, but will not duplicate the services of an authority. If you are having difficulty getting an aid from the local authority which it is their responsibility to supply, you cannot avoid the problem by getting the Family Fund to supply it. But they have a liberal brief to provide help and relieve stress in families where there is a severely handicapped child under 16 years of age. They have helped for instance towards the purchase of cars and caravans, have paid for family holidays, have paid 'extra' babysitting expenses, have bought innumerable washing machines and dryers, paid for telephone rentals and travelling expenses to visit a handicapped child.

CITIZENS' ADVICE BUREAUX

If you are not clear about your rights, the Citizens' Advice Bureau in your area should be able to help.

EDUCATIONAL SERVICES

In 1971 the responsibility for the education of severely mentally handicapped children was transferred from the Health Authorities to the Department of Education. Since then there has been a virtual revolution in the education of the handicapped child. New schools have been built, schools starved of equipment have been well stocked, and staffing ratios have been substantially improved, allowing existing staff to do their jobs more adequately and bringing in a large number of enthusiastic and well trained young staff. The whole atmosphere has

K*

changed from that of a cinderella service provided on the cheap, to a relatively well staffed service with positive goals.

You may not come into contact with the educational services until your child is assessed for school placement at the statutory school age of five, although in fact the 1944 Education Act provides for education of handicapped children from the age of two. Sometimes educational authorities will help with some form of education at this earlier age, but the extent of help varies. It is often left to parents to request help for their children, so if you are told that early education is not provided by your authority it would be worth discussing the problem with the Head of the local special school, the Education Officer in charge of Special Education or your local parent organisation.

It is only for children whose primary handicap is sensory (hearing or vision impairment) that there is a national system of educational help at a very early age. And this is changing. Where in the past these children were taken into special schools as early as possible for the specialised help they needed, hearing-impaired children or children who would otherwise need boarding placement are more often being sent to an ordinary playgroup. The parents are given extra help and advice, and the child extra education, by a peripatetic teacher. Later on the child may be sent to a special school or unit.

This principle of providing peripatetic teachers to help both the young handicapped child and his parents has been extended in some areas to include young mentally handicapped children. Thus a special advisory teacher may visit the home once a week or so, to bring suitable toys and show the parents how they can use them to extend development. This excellent scheme is, however, often under-staffed so some parents get no help and others get help too infrequently to be of very much use.

Educational authorities are also sometimes prepared to pay the fees of young children with other than sensory handicaps to attend ordinary playgroups or nursery classes. Where the handicap is severe, they may provide an extra welfare assistant or nursery assistant to make the attendance possible. Where they provide no such service, they may pay fees for children to attend treatment centres—specialising in a particular handicap —run by voluntary bodies.

As we shall see in the section on Voluntary organisations, there are Opportunity Groups in many areas that cater for very young handicapped children. These are usually run by voluntary organisations, although some are run by local authorities or by social services departments. The education authorities may pay for the services of a teacher or nursery nurse, or both, to run the group.

Once the child comes up to the age of assessment for school, he will be in contact with an Educational Psychologist. Some of these psychologists work in the community, taking an interest in the playgroup or opportunity group attended by the handicapped child, and available for advice to the teachers or to the parents. They may even run 'Parent workshops' where parents can learn practical techniques of handling and training.

Parents may be dissatisfied with the assessment given to their child before school, feeling that the child has not performed at his best in strange surroundings. Some psychologists accordingly are assessing informally in the home or playgroup, especially when the child is severely handicapped and there would be little point in formal tests. Parents who recognise that their child is likely to be best educated in a special school, with its special resources, may still want their child to come out as well as he can in any 'test': partly because this is recognition of their own hard work, and partly because they fear that a poor assessment will mean poor expectation of him at school, so he will perform accordingly. Parents of children with particular handicaps, like Down's Syndrome, also complain that the type of school best suited to their child is often decided on the basis of the label rather than on what the child can do.

Parents may also come into conflict with the educational authority over the choice of school. Obviously no authority can provide perfectly for each child, and every choice is a compromise. But parents of severely handicapped children are often offered no choice at all. They may find the local school unsatisfactory either in its approach to education or its treatment of the children, but if the local school has room the authority will resist pressure for a child to attend a school further away. The parents may get their way if the school of their choice is under the same education authority, although free transport is not usually provided for schools other than the nearest; but they are less likely to be successful if the school is under a different authority or is run by a private or voluntary body.

Once the child is placed in school parents will not necessarily meet the educational psychologist again, although he or she should see the child for reassessment from time to time. But if parents have particular problems they may ask for an appointment to see the educational psychologist. Through the school, he or she may help to work out an educational or management programme that can be carried out both at home and school. Where the educational psychologist is not available, a knowledgeable and sympathetic headmistress or teacher might also be able to help parents to work with their child. Some schools have 'liaison' teachers who work both in the school and in the homes with the parents to deal with problems as they arise, and help to see that the child has a consistent approach to his education. Parents and teachers can give each other much valuable information and can develop a united programme to help him progress more quickly. If parents feel that the teacher is not sympathetic to their way of working, or that she is not herself aware of the best ways to help the child, it is best to look for ways to show her how the child responds to a different approach, without implying that you 'know better than she does' or making her feel inadequate. Some staff are not trained in modern teaching techniques and they see their role primarily as a caring, mothering one. They may not even realise that you cannot wait for a child to be 'ready' to sit up, or walk, or talk. But even in these circumstances conflict should be avoided if possible, for an unhappy threatened teacher is not likely to work well with a child.

VOLUNTARY BODIES

Almost every handicapping condition has a national society that promotes the welfare of its members. They are listed in the *Handbook for Parents of a Handicapped Child* and in *Voluntary Social Services* published by the Bedford Square Press. For parents of severely handicapped children, the two most useful societies are probably:

The National Society for Mentally Handicapped Children
(NSMHC or MenCap),
86 Newman Street, London W1P 4AR.
The Spastics Society,
12 Park Crescent, London W1N 4EQ.

Both societies will put you in touch with your local branch.

The range of societies is vast and the help they are able to
give is correspondingly varied. Some societies run their own
schools—including the Spastics Society and the Autistic Society.
Some offer residential care. Nearly all offer some advice and
information, publicise needs and promote research. We cannot
hope to do justice to all these societies so we will concentrate
on a brief description of the services of the few most obviously
relevant.

The National Society for Mentally Handicapped Children

This society and all its many branches cater for all the mentally
handicapped—no matter how severe the handicap, nor whether
the child has other handicaps as well. They provide some
residential facilities in order to offer relief for parents in
emergencies, opportunities for training or holidays for the
children, and specialised courses and advice on problems of
education and welfare, speech therapy and physiotherapy.
Local branches support parents, often provide transport for
their members to other facilities, and run other services
themselves such as babysitting.

The Spastics Society

The society provides a vast range of training and educational
establishments, including a college for training staff. Running
costs of local centres are usually met by the local branch of the
society, but the main society runs its network of special
residential schools. In London they have a family service
offering advice to parents and a display of toys and equipment.
They also have an assessment service and a flat for parents to
stay in while their child is assessed. The Spastics Society does
much to promote research on handicap, and understanding and
tolerance for the handicapped. They have been in the forefront

of providing housing in which the handicapped can be self-supporting.

Opportunity groups

Opportunity Nursery Classes vary in format but are based on the ideas developed in the first group in Stevenage. Parents can be referred to the group by a health visitor, social worker, peripatetic teacher or doctor, or they can make the initial contact themselves. Entry is usually free and freely available to all handicapped children from birth— no matter how severe the handicap. The child does not need to be officially diagnosed or assessed—it is sufficient that the parent is worried over some delay in development and the person running the group thinks that worry is justified. The mixed group of handicapped children form approximately half of the group, and the other half are ordinary children who are usually brothers and sisters of the handicapped children or children of the voluntary helpers.

There is usually at least one paid member of staff but a high staff/child ratio (one to one or one to two) is maintained by using volunteers. The other feature of the group is that space and time are nearly always provided for the mothers to meet together while the children attend the group, to offer help and advice to one another or simply to have tea and chat.

Toy Libraries Association

Sunley House, 10 Cunthorpe Street, London E17RW. This is the address of the National Association who will be able to send a list of libraries on request, and to tell you where your nearest toy library is. Toy libraries are funded in different ways—some are voluntary, some run by different authorities. Most of them restrict their membership to families where there is a handicapped child (regardless of handicap), but there are some catering for the needs of the socially deprived, for child minders and some even attached to ordinary nursery schools and classes.

As the name implies, their aim is to lend appropriate toys to handicapped children and to their brothers and sisters. They offer advice on play and the development of play skills as far as is wanted, and as far as the organiser (who may or may not be professionally qualified) is able. Most libraries go beyond that to offer play sessions for the children, talks for the parents and outings and social events for all the family.

FINDING OUT MORE ABOUT VISUAL COMMUNICATION SYSTEMS

More can be found out about British Sign Language and Makaton from:

Royal Association of the Deaf and Dumb,
7–11 Armstrong Road, Acton, London W3.

About Paget-Gorman from:

Miss Elma Craig,
City Literary Institute,
Keeley House, Keeley Street,
Kingsway, London WC2.

About Bliss from:

Blissymbolics Communication Resource Centre (UK)
South Glamorgan Institue of Higher Education,
Western Avenue,
Llandaff,
Cardiff, CF5 2YB.

WHICH SERVICE?

This final section has been written first and foremost for parents. However, teachers and other professionals may find it of value as well.

Perhaps the clearest way of indicating which service is appropriate to which problem, is to make a list of questions which parents of the severely handicapped child might want to ask, or problems they might need help with, and suggest which agencies might reasonably be expected to offer help in that area.

QUESTION/PROBLEM	SOURCE OF HELP

A. I'm worried about my child's development. I think he may be handicapped.

(1) *Health visitor*
(2) *Social worker*
(3) *General Practitioner*—who may refer you to a
(4) *Medical specialist*
(5) *Educational psychologist*—if child is school age—or Community or Clinical psychologist if available.

B. I want to know more about my child's particular handicap.

(1) *Voluntary society*—specialising in that handicap.
(2) *Specialist*
(3) *Library*—it may not keep books on that subject but should be able to get them for you. The more interest the public shows, the more likely it is that such books will be made available.

C. I need advice on handling my child and how I can best help him develop.

(1) *Books*
Such as this one, or other texts produced by research and welfare organisations. Most voluntary societies have booklists relating to their own interests. The Nottingham Toy Library has a leaflet with a suggested reading list for parents.
(2) *Toy library*
Help should be available, from the first stages of development when you need toys to get the child to develop head control or to learn basic tracking, reaching and grasping skills.
(3) *Opportunity groups*
These are also available (in areas where they exist) from as soon as you suspect your child is handicapped. You should be able to ask for help and advice from the organiser of the

group, and you can learn from the experiences of other parents.

(4) *Educational/Community/Child psychologist*

These may be available to offer help from a local research centre, or from some community project such as a parent workshop. Your local sub-normality hospital may offer a service along these lines.

(5) *Medical specialist*

The specialist may himself be equipped to offer such practical help, or he may refer you to others (psychologists or therapists) who can give it.

(6) *Teacher*

There may be a peripatetic teacher you can ask to visit you, or there may be a liaison teacher attached to a special school. Failing that, teachers of opportunity groups or in special schools are often more than willing to meet and discuss methods with the parents.

(7) *Therapist*

Speech therapists and physiotherapists may be available for help in specific areas concerned with their own expertise.

(8) *Kith and Kids*

This is a voluntary organisation run by parents for parents, but very active in areas of parental self help and showing parents how they can help the development of their child. Your Social Services Area Office should be able to tell you if there is a branch near you. If there is no branch there may well be another parent organisation which can serve the same ends.

D. Where can I get aids or equipment to help me cope at home?

(1) *Medical specialist*
He will be able to prescribe medical aids such as wheelchairs, baby buggies and walking aids.

(2) *Social Services*
Your Area Social Worker will put you in touch with the section of Social Services concerned with aids and arrange for you to see someone there.

(3) *Rowntree Family Fund*
They can help you purchase aids or pieces of equipment that are not available from the authorities. Your Social Worker or Social Services should be able to help you with application.

(4) *Toy library*
Many toy libraries stock basic pieces of equipment to help the development of the child, as well as toys.

(5) *Disabled Living Foundation*
This has a permanent exhibition of aids, and provides an information service with practical suggestions on aids and clothing.

(6) *Voluntary societies*
Some societies (such as the Spastics Society) keep a permanent display of aids and most societies will be able to put you in touch with suitable sources. Many aids can be made (or basic household equipment adapted) by local mechanics or students of art or technology, and some colleges offer such a service to schools or voluntary bodies.

E. Where do I go for the right kind of toy? How can I teach my child to play?

(1) *Toy library*
This is the most obvious source of help here, since this is the main purpose of toy libraries.

(2) *Peripatetic teachers*
They will be concerned with teaching the child to play themselves, and with showing you how to continue. They may also leave toys or equipment for you to use.

(3) *Schools or opportunity groups*
These may offer general advice on play and may even be able to lend toys or equipment over holiday periods, say.

F. I need someone to talk to. Someone I can discuss my worries and problems with.

(1) *Voluntary societies*
Where there is a local branch there will usually be a parents' meeting with opportunities for discussion. The society may have its own welfare visitors or social workers.

(2) *Social worker*
You can ask to be visited. Or you can call at your local Area Office (in the phone book).

(3) *Toy library*
The organiser will usually lend a sympathetic ear and there will be opportunity to meet other families.

(4) *Opportunity groups*
A group for mothers is a feature of most opportunity groups, and some have professional social workers visiting the group.

(5) *Kith and Kids*
Their approach is very much one of mutual support.

G. What about short- or long-term residential care?

(1) *Social worker*
The social worker should help you to discuss your problem: to see if it is one that is best solved by residential care for the child, or whether with other sorts of help (a holiday, more money,

better aids, more practical guidance on handling and management) you would prefer to keep your child at home. If you decide on residential care, the social worker should know what is available and can begin the process of referral. Three types of residential care are available. Local Authority Social Services Departments often provide a range of services from short-term foster care to full-time residential care. If they do not provide this now, they can be encouraged to do so. The Social Services Department can also try to arrange for a child to get a place in a home run by a voluntary organisation. They may then pay some or all of the costs. But this accommodation may be a long way away. Finally, there may be a place in a subnormality hospital, but again this may be a long journey from the child's home. Enquiries about such places should be made through the GP in the first instance, since the Social Services cannot help you with this kind of placement.

Always ask to visit a place. Residential places for the severely handicapped are so scarce that people are often frightened to question, and your social worker may not have visited the place she recommends. You have a right to see the kind of care your child might receive before making up your mind.

(2) *Educational psychologist*

If you think of a residential school as best for your child or your family as a whole, then the referral must go through the Educational Psychologist.

(3) *Medical specialist*

Some will have the time (or make the time) to discuss your problems with you. Like the social worker, they may be able to arrange other sorts of help that will make residential care unnecessary, or they may be able to arrange admittance to a local hostel or subnormality hospital.

H. I am anxious about having other children. I am worried in case my other children are 'carriers' of the condition.

(1) *General Practitioner*

Your local doctor should have the address of the nearest genetic counselling service and will put you in touch with them.

I. He seems to be getting worse; has he got a progressive disease?

(1) *The specialist*

If you are open and frank about your fears and show that you want to hear 'the truth', most specialists will be honest with you. Often they do not know themselves and may need more tests. They may also be able to reassure you that it is a temporary setback because he has been ill, is suffering side-effects of drug dosage, or is just not receiving the right kind of treatment or education.

(2) *Teacher*

If your child attends a school or group, it is worth seeing if the teacher has noticed the deterioration and can offer an explanation. Perhaps there has been a change of staff or classroom routine which has set him back temporarily. Do not be too ready to accept explanations of a drop-off in performance; he may just not be receiving the attention he needs.

J. I want to choose a school for my child.

(1) *Head teachers*
Visit all the schools around: this will give you an idea of what to look for. You must also find out whether the head will accept your child if the educational psychologist recommends it.

(2) *Educational psychologist*
Your child must be assessed as fit for a certain type of education by the educational psychologist. He or she may also recommend a particular school, or simply assume you want the nearest.

K. We need more time to ourselves. Where can I get reliable babysitters or time off in the day?

(1) *Make Children Happy*
This organisation arranges outings for handicapped children, and also has a babysitting service in some places. Your Social Services Area Office should be able to tell you the address of this organisation or similar organisations, if there is one in your area.

(2) *Voluntary societies*
These often run 'minding groups' during the holidays and shopping crèches at weekends. They may also run a mutual babysitting service.

(3) *Social worker*
She may be able to arrange weekends away at holiday 'clubs', or camps run by special agencies, or weekends in hostels. Failing all else she may be able to offer some part-time placement in a Local Authority hostel or a voluntary hostel. Local Authority Social Services may be able to arrange a place in a day nursery or with a registered and experienced child minder to give you a break during the day.

(4) *Volunteers*

Volunteer groups of students or community workers will often arrange playgroups, or offer babysitting services or help in the home. Contact your Social Services Area Office or local Council for Voluntary Service.

(5) *Gateway Clubs*

Junior Gateway clubs cater for mentally handicapped children and provide a few hours of 'fun' while the parents are free to do other things.

L. I need help with transport.

(1) *Education*

The Education Department arranges free transport for the children to day and boarding schools.

(2) *Social workers*

There are several sources of money to help with transport for parents and children. Although those may not be the responsibility of Social Services, your social worker should be able to find out where you can get assistance.

(3) *Rowntree Family Fund*

They will often assist with the cost of a car, or pay the taxi fare for a special journey, or help with transport costs of visiting a handicapped child in hospital. The social worker should be able to help you with details of the application.

M. I am worried about my other children. I need support that will involve all the family.

(1) *Social worker*

She will be able to discuss your worries about your other children with you, and help you decide whether you are worrying unnecessarily.

(2) *Educational psychologist*

If the worries about the other children are justified, it may be necessary for them to have specialist help by visiting the local psychiatric clinic to see the educational psychologist or the psychiatric social worker.

(3) *Voluntary societies*

Most of these offer support of a general kind for all the family (e.g. friendship, outings) and this is especially true of the Toy Libraries and of Kith and Kids.

(4) *Opportunity groups*

Young brothers and sisters get a chance to mix with both normal and handicapped children, and to see other youngsters in a similar position to themselves.

N. I am worried about my child's physical development.

(1) *General Practitioner*

This is likely to be the first source of help, and he can put you in touch with more specialist help.

(2) *Physiotherapists*

If you have not been able to see a physiotherapist through your doctor or hospital or school, you may be able to contact one yourself. NOT all physiotherapists know about handicapped children, however.

O. I am particularly worried about my child's speech or lack of it.

(1) *Teacher*

'Speech' problems in mentally handicapped children are usually more problems of language, or general development. In this case the teacher is the person with whom parents should discuss general problems of speech and communication.

(2) *Speech therapist*

You may be referred to one by your doctor or school, or contact one directly through local authority clinics or privately. Speech therapists interested in speech and language problems in the handicapped usually work closely with schools. Work with the mentally handicapped tends to be a specialised field. Most speech therapists should be able to advise on problems of speech production.

P. I want him to have a social life of his own.

(1) *Opportunity groups*
These usually represent the first chance a child has to learn to manage without his parents for a short period.

(2) *Gateway Clubs*
These cater for mentally handicapped children and offer games and outings.

(3) *Adventure playgrounds*
These are a few specially designed adventure playgrounds catering for handicapped children. The most severely handicapped may need a helper, but there are qualified staff at hand to help the children play. Your local Social Services area office should know about these.

(4) *Make Children Happy*
Local branches may arrange several outings a year for handicapped children and put on special shows for them.

(5) *Guides/Scouts/Woodcraft Folk/Red Cross*
All these organisations are prepared to accept handicapped members, and the Red Cross in particular arranges particular events such as camping for handicapped children.

Q. How about holidays?

(1) *Voluntary societies*
Many societies have their own facilities for family holidays or for holidays for the handicapped child.

(2) *Social worker*

The social worker should be able to arrange a holiday for your child, and possibly for the parents also if you give enough warning. Parents may be asked to contribute to the costs of these holidays.

(3) *Rowntree Family Fund*
They are prepared to pay for short holidays for the families of handicapped children.

(4) *Camping Club*
This club has one site catering specially for handicapped members.

R. Can my child take part in any sport?

(1) *Riding for the disabled*
Even the most handicapped child can manage this as long as he can sit on a horse. Helpers lead the ponies around.

(2) *Swimming clubs*
Many mentally handicapped children enjoy the swimming pool. All over the country there are special swimming clubs catering for all degrees of handicap. They usually have special arrangements with a local pool to warm the water more and to clear the pool for their sessions. They also usually provide helpers for the children.

S. My child has to go away to a hospital. How can I get help with visiting?

(1) *The National Society for the Welfare of Children in Hospital*
They will help you gain the right to visit, if necessary, and in some circumstances can help by arranging for other children to be looked after, or help with transport.

(2) *Medical social worker*
If you have financial difficulties connected with visiting, or worries about your other children, the medical

social worker at the hospital should be able to help.

T. I am worried financially. I need more money.

(1) *Social worker*

She can help to ensure you are claiming all the benefits, and may know extra sources of aid. She can also help you make better use of your money if you need planning advice.

(2) *Rowntree Family Fund*

If you are short of money for a particular purpose they may be able to help.

(3) *Round Table*

Organisations like these are often willing to give money to buy particular things for your child. Again, ask the Social Worker or someone from the local parents' organisation.

U. I am worried about my child's future. What happens if I die?

(1) *Home Farm Trusts*

This and similar organisations help to set up permanent homes for the handicapped. See if you can help to get one going.

(2) *NSMHC*

They run a trustee scheme which helps secure the future for your child.

(3) *Social worker*

Start getting your child used to a particular hostel, if you can find one he might be able to enter should anything happen to you. It is better to plan for this, and it may be even better to allow him to go into such a place before you become too old or ill to manage, and while you can still visit him and 'bridge the gap'. Remember, however, that the handicapped child is like any other child. He needs to find independence. Try to work with the hostel staff in giving

V. What do I tell my child about sex? How can I help him cope with sexual feelings?

him independence rather than trying to keep him dependent.

(1) *Social worker*
The social worker should be able to put you in touch with specialist agencies who can give you advice on this.

(2) *Voluntary societies*
These are becoming of very aware these problems, and many run special courses or information services on the subject.

(3) *Teachers*
The problem is still not dealt with in many schools, but if you ask for advice an experienced teacher may be able to help you with any difficulties.

(4) *General Practitioner*
He will be able to prescribe contraceptives where necessary, or put you in touch with specialist agencies.

(5) *The Family Planning Association*
They run a special advice service to help handicapped people with their sex problems.

W. What about drugs?

(1) *General Practitioner*
Your General Practitioner will prescribe the 'ordinary' drugs, like antibiotics if the child is ill with a normal complaint.

(2) *Medical specialist*
Normally a medical specialist will prescribe extra drugs if necessary. There are a wide range of drugs available for different purposes. Many are given to control fits, others to control depression or activity.

'Fashions' in giving drugs vary widely amongst medical specialists. Some use a lot, some very little. If your child is put on drugs it is sensible to ask exactly what effects the drug should have and what side-effects you should watch for. The effects of a drug depend on the weight of the person but also on their individual make-up. So there will be individual differences in effects. In particular some people pass drugs through their body more rapidly than others. This makes it necessary to check the blood level of any drug taken over a long period of time. Otherwise there could be a build up. Blood levels should also be checked whenever dosage is changed. If your child is on a drug for a long time without the blood level being checked it is wise to ask for this to be investigated.

(3) *Teachers*

Teachers will often notice the good or bad effects of drugs. Try to tell teachers when drugs are being changed and ask them to look out for effects.

We hope to have given you at least some idea of where to go for help. Don't be afraid to ask for help and don't be too humble. You are almost certainly an expert on your child and it is ultimately up to you to decide what help you need and how you want to organise your life.

Bibliography

NANCIE R. FINNIE. *Handling the Young Cerebral Palsied Child at Home* (Second Edition) 1974. London: William Heinemann Medical Books Ltd.

DOROTHY M. JEFFREE and ROY McCONKEY. *Let Me Speak.* 1976. London: Souvenir Press.

JUDITH STONE and FELICITY TAYLOR. *Handbook for Parents with a Handicapped Child.* 1973. London: Home and School Council.

Index

Note: ex. after a page number denotes a teaching example.

Attention, Chapter 3, 47–51

Blind, feeding teaching, 195–200 ex.

Chaining, 42, 125, 222–3, 224–9, 240–3
Choosing—assessment, 91–3
    teaching, 93–4 ex.
Citizen's Advice Bureaux, 297
Colour discrimination teaching, 119–20 ex.
Communication, 28, Chapters 8 and 9
    American Sign Language, 140, 145
    Assessment, 159–72, 174–5
    basis of, 134–6
    Blissymbols, 151–3, 155, 156
    British Sign Language, 140–3, 145–6
    communication boards, 149–50
    Coramese, 156–7
    flash cards, teaching, 182–3 ex.
    idea of, teaching, 174 ex.
    Imitation—assessment, 165–7, 170–2
    imitation teaching, 179–82 ex.
    naming—teaching, 175–6 ex.
    non-verbal, 136–8, 303
    Paget Gorman Sign System, 143–5, 146
    Premackese, 153–4, 155, 156
    Rebus, 150–1
    signing, 140–6
    Sign languages, 17
    signing, teaching, 175 ex.
    signing and speech, teaching, 146–8 ex., 183–5 ex.
    social words, teaching, 177–8 ex.
    Symbolic thought, 155
    verbal development, 138–9
Competing out, 27, 273–4, 283–4 ex., 286–7 ex.., 287–8 ex., 288–9 ex.
Concentration, 48
Coping, 27, 274–5

Discrimination, 118–25
Dressing, 219–21
    teaching, 221–4, 224–9 ex.
    generalisation, 229
Drugs, 279, 290–1, 316

Early detection, 20
Education, 15, 297–300, 314
Exploratory play, 29, 125–32
    assessment, 126–7
    teaching squeezing, 127–30 ex.
    teaching, turning, 130–2

Feeding, 53; Chapter 11, 186
    assessment, 188–9
    aversion to food, 209–14 ex.
    food fads, 200–5
    food fads, teaching, 207–9 ex.
    physical handicap, teaching, 214–18 ex.
Fine motor assessment, 259–60
Forgetting, 55, 56

Generalisation, 54, 89, 229
Goals of education, 16
Grasping, teaching, 108–9 ex., 262 ex., 262–3 ex.

Head control, 254
Hyperactivity, 47–8, 93–4 ex., 278–9
Home teaching, 61–4

Imitation assessment, 165–7, 283–4
Interests, development of, 80–2, 82–4 ex.

Jealousy, 289

Looking, 48
    assessment, 101–2
    teaching, 103–4 ex.

Match to sample, teaching, 123–5 ex.
Medical services, 292–5, 304

Mobility—assessment, 255-7
    crawling, 257
    partial sight, 258
    stairs, 261-2
    standing, 260-1 ex.
    walking, 261

Nagging, 39-40, 203-4
Normal development, 19

Object permanence, 115-17
    assessment, 116
    teaching, 116-17 ex.
Observation, 24, 158, 159

Physical handicap, 57-8, 59, 244-5
Physiotherapy—Bobath, 245-7
    Doman Delecato, 249-51
    Peto, 247-9
Play-environment, 18, 56-7, 63
Posture—assessment, 253
Priorities—setting for teaching, 26,
    31, 32, 60-1, 264-6
Problem behaviour, 26; Chapter 14,
    264
    aggression, 87-9, 287-8
    assessment, 27-8, 266-9
    attention-getting, 37
    defining, 266-7
    feeding, 191-3, 272-3
    head banging, 273
    overcorrection, 275
    screaming, 87-9
    self-destructive behaviour, 276-
        8
    self-hitting, 87-9
    'silly' behaviour, 86-7
    sleep, 289-290 ex., 291-2 ex.
    spitting out food, 195-6 ex., 280-1
        ex.
    tantrums, 284-5 ex.
    throwing, 85
    vomiting, 39 ex., 281-3 ex.
    wandering, 27
Prompt and fade, 42-3, 50, 193-4
Punishment, 25, 27, 38-40, 269-71,
    278
    ethics, 275-6
    social, 69-70, 84-6 ex.
Puzzles, 125

Reach and grasp, 29, 57-8 ex.
    assessment, 107-8
    teaching, 109-110 ex.
Recording, 44-5
Rewards, 25, 28, 55; Chapter 5, 68,
    206-7, 278
    assessment, 72-6
    delay, 82 ex.
    development of, 78-82
    edible, 71
    physical contact, 77
    self-reward, 94-5 ex.
    sensory, 71
    social, 69-70, 82-4 ex.
Reward teaching, 32-6
Rowntree Family Fund, 297

Search—assessment, 117
    teaching, 117-18 ex.
Self-control—assessment, 91-3
    teaching, 95-7 ex.
Sensori-motor play, 100-1
Shape discrimination, teaching, 119-
    20 ex.
Sitting down, 47-8 ex., 49-51
Size discrimination teaching, 119-
    20 ex.
Social Security, 296-7
Social Services, 295-6
Sound, response to—assessment, 111
    teaching, 111-13 ex.
Structured teaching, 20, 52

Teaching-environment, 65-7, 173-4,
    286-7
Thinking, Chapter 7, 78
Time out from reward, 35-8, 271-3
    for attention getting, 37
Toilet training, 219-21
    teaching, 230-8
Token systems, 276-8, 284-5 ex.
Touch discrimination, teaching, 120-
    3 ex.

Visual exploration—assessment, 10?
    teaching, 103-4 ex.
Visual following—assessment, 105
    teaching, 106-7 ex.
Voluntary societies, 301-2, 304

Washing, 219-21
    assessment, 239
    teaching, 238-43